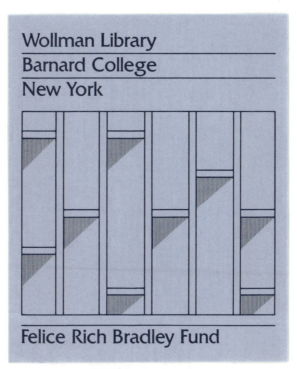

Hate Crime

Crime and Society Series

Series editor: Hazel Croall

Published titles

Hate Crime

Nathan Hall

WILLAN
PUBLISHING

Published by

Willan Publishing
Culmcott House
Mill Street, Uffculme
Cullompton, Devon
EX15 3AT, UK
Tel: +44(0)1884 840337
Fax: +44(0)1884 840251
e-mail: info@willanpublishing.co.uk
website: www.willanpublishing.co.uk

Published simultaneously in the USA and Canada by

Willan Publishing
c/o ISBS, 920 NE 58th Ave, Suite 300,
Portland, Oregon 97213-3786, USA
Tel: +001(0)503 287 3093
Fax: +001(0)503 280 8832
e-mail: info@isbs.com
website: www.isbs.com

First published 2005

ISBN 1-84392-130-8 paperback
ISBN 1-84392-131-6 hardback

British Library Cataloguing-in-Publication Data

A catalogue record for this book is available from the British Library

Project managed by Deer Park Productions, Tavistock, Devon
Typeset by GCS, Leighton Buzzard, Bedfordshire, LU7 1AR
Printed and bound by T.J. International Ltd, Trecerus Industrial Estate, Padstow, Cornwall

For my parents and my grandparents

Contents

Appendix:

Acknowledgements

While researching for this book I remember reading a comment by James Waller, whose work I have referred to, that two of the great joys of finishing a book are firstly getting one's life back and secondly having the opportunity to thank everyone who has contributed in whatever way, be it professionally or personally, to the completion of the project.

Professionally, there are many people I would like to thank. In this country I am grateful to the police services that have allowed me in to conduct my research, and whose officers have allowed me to shadow them and have taken the time to speak with me. In particular I would like to thank John Grieve, without whom the research would not have taken place, and Mike Thompson of the Metropolitan Police Service for his help and support from the start. I would also especially like to thank the many victims of hate crime who shared their experiences with me.

In the United States I am grateful to Dennis Blackman, Michael Osgood, Vanessa Ferro and the team at the NYPD's Hate Crime Task Force for allowing me to spend so much time with them and for allowing me to go about my research without hindrance or restriction. I am grateful for your openness and especially for your patience for an Englishman with too many questions. A special thank you also to Tammy, the NYPD's own 'International Boo', for looking out for my welfare while I was far away from home! In Philadelphia I am grateful to Commissioner Johnson and Deputy Commissioner Giorgio-Fox for allowing me to spend time with the department, and to Gordon Wasserman and Sgt Ed Zongolowicz for their help in arranging my visit. I am particularly grateful to the officers at the Conflict Prevention Resolution Unit for allowing me to follow them as they went about their work.

Closer to home I am grateful to colleagues and students at the Institute of Criminal Justice Studies at the University of Portsmouth. Particular thanks to Steve Savage, Mike Nash, Les Johnston, David Carson, Francis Pakes and Andy Williams for their advice and support, and for commenting on draft chapters and draft ideas. I am grateful also to the students who studied my hate crime course at the university, whose persistent complaining about a lack of British textbooks on this subject ultimately provided the catalyst for this project. Thanks also to Brian and Jim at Willan Publishing for their patience and support throughout.

On a personal level I am as ever deeply grateful to my parents and my grandparents for their continuing and unwavering support in everything I do. I am also grateful to all my friends for their encouragement and for regular reality checks, in particular Sharon Cicco for invaluable advice on how to write a 'pamphlet'! A special thank you also to Frank Dwyer for all that you have done. I can never thank you enough.

And finally to Natasha. Thank you for your love, support and patience throughout – as ever you are all the light I need.

The above have contributed to this book in many ways, but as always any errors are solely my contribution.

NH

Foreword

John G.D. Grieve

This is an important and timely book for three reasons. Firstly it addresses a terrible and corrosive crime; secondly, it contributes to our understanding of intelligence-led policing as a strategic level of analysis; thirdly it helps push further the agenda set in motion in the aftermath of the death of Stephen Lawrence. Nathan has picked up an important torch for us all. Some years ago, in the teeth of some ill-informed opposition, I introduced postgraduate students into the heart of the police intelligence system in the role of criminal intelligence analysts. This book epitomises what we were trying to achieve.

Hate crimes are complex events to investigate. The impacts they have on communities are far reaching. The way the investigation is handled and, in particular, how the family of the victim of a hate crime is supported, can be crucial to ways in which policing is viewed by the community. We now know more about the skills that the investigation of hate crimes requires. These include: fairness; proactivity; the effective use of knowledge; a focus on outcomes; regular contact with community leaders; sound communication; cunning; integrity; resilience; cooperation with communities (and not just keeping in touch with them); an understanding of families and their community context; and a detailed knowledge of law, especially about evidence and exhibits. These are all essential investigative policing skills that need to be intelligence-led. There is also an increasing need to be an 'intelligent customer' of intelligence services. This book educates customer and practitioner alike.

To deal with potential critical incidents that are also hate crimes we need educated teams and individuals. Lord Laming (2003) in his recent study of 'policing failure', useful in a wider sense because he studied and criticised other disciplines as well as policing, offers a model of the informed and effective practitioner:

> ... a healthy scepticism, an open mind and, where necessary, an investigative approach ... If the unquestioning acceptance of information given by a carer is undesirable in a social worker, it is unacceptable in a police officer. (para. 14.78, p. 322)

We could cluster under 'healthy scepticism', leadership, vigilance, resilience, cunning, proactive, intelligent and well founded interpretation of salient features. An 'open mind' would include flexibility, integrity and fairness. An 'investigative outlook' would include the use of classification, structured logic, decision and choice, investigative interviewing, communication and cooperation with communities and families and sound file-management.

Nathan, in my view, contributes to the development of these skills and competencies in a number of ways. First, the strategic analysis of hate crimes that he provides is operationally and tactically informed. A full understanding of the role of policing strategies must grasp the process connecting top-level decision-making and the click of the handcuffs. Nathan has been there and heard that click.

Secondly, as part of a process of enhancing community engagement, 'intelligence' needs to be reclaimed from the secret world of practitioners and made less threatening. Intelligence should no longer be about the insidious 'penetration of communities' but should rather be used as a service for communities, as with the growing use of community impact assessments. Nathan's work furthers that process.

Thirdly, at certain crucial moments in the development of criminal intelligence, investigating officers need to work closely with academics to provide changes in strategic direction which investigation often requires. Nathan's work offers such access.

Fourthly, contrary to some accounts or interpretations, intelligence-led policing is not derived from a negative, as a response to the ineffectiveness or failure of policing in the past, but from a positive evolution of street tactics and analysis of them. Nathan's book offers us an insight into this evolution. The book offers us not just a valuable overview of hate crime – in many ways it stands as a vital investigative tool.

John G.D. Grieve
Deputy Assistant Commissioner (retired)
Former head of the Racial and Violent Crime Task Force
Metropolitan Police Service

Preface

Hate crime is a complex phenomenon. As an object of academic study it is a relatively new and under-explored issue, particularly in Britain. Despite a long history of what we now label as 'hate crimes', it was the murder of Stephen Lawrence in London in 1993 and the subsequent public inquiry that followed in 1999 that has served as a catalyst for raising the profile of hate crime as a social and political problem deserving of serious attention in its own right. While the Stephen Lawrence Inquiry focused on the issues of race and racism, the debate that followed served to draw attention to the experiences of other targets of hate-motivated offending. This in turn has sparked significant interest among policy-makers, academics and criminal justice practitioners in all forms of hate crime and in particular how the problem might best be responded to.

This situation is more advanced in both academic and criminal justice terms in the United States. Although the term 'hate crime' was only coined in the mid-1980s, interest in this behaviour as a distinct motivation for crime has a somewhat longer legacy and has been the subject of more detailed academic investigation and lengthier practitioner interest. Perhaps inevitably much of the existing literature on hate crime is of American origin and is drawn from the American experience of the problem. By focusing on both Britain and America it is hoped that this book will go some way to redressing this balance.

Many of the issues surrounding hatred as a criminal motivation are generic and remain pertinent regardless of context or country. But where differences between countries do occur, for example in terms of defining the problem and the criminal justice response to it, then these will inevitably hold both positive and negative lessons that can be learned. This is particularly important because I believe that as a society we are trying to respond to an issue that we do not yet fully understand.

The underlying purpose of this book is therefore to highlight the complexities of hate crime, the extent of our understanding of these, and the implications for effectively responding to the hate crime 'problem' that we currently face. By exploring seven basic questions (what is hate crime? how much of it is there? who is involved or affected? where is it occurring? when is it occurring? why is it occurring? and, crucially, what, if anything, can we do to make the situation better?) this book aims to provide the reader with a more holistic understanding of the phenomenon of hate crime, but also with an appreciation that in truth we know relatively little about it.

Structure of the book

Before we can begin to examine any of the issues relating to hate crime it is, of course, crucial that we have a clear understanding of what it is we are talking about. The question 'what is hate crime?' may seem straightforward, but providing an accurate answer is fraught with difficulties. Like any other crime, hate crime is a social construct, but there is no consensus among academics, policy-makers or practitioners about what hate crime actually is. Chapter 1 therefore examines the social construction of hate crime through a consideration of the various attempts that have been made to define it. The chapter also examines the inherent difficulties associated with defining hate crime and discusses the considerable implications of the various attempts to do so.

What is clear, however, is that this tiny, four-letter word 'hate' masks a number of complexities. This is in part because when we talk about *hate* in the context of hate crime, we often find that what we really mean is *prejudice*. But prejudice is a far more expansive concept than hate, covering a far wider range of human emotions, and this rather complicates our understanding of hate crimes. Chapter 2 therefore examines the origins of prejudice and hatred, and asks where they come from, how they develop and how they lead to expressions of violent behaviour. The chapter also dispels the common myth that hatred is an abnormal trait that 'bad people' have by arguing that the very foundations for hateful expression are entirely normal to the human condition.

Societal concern with hate crimes is a relatively recent development. But given that hate is a normal and natural part of being human, it seems reasonable to suggest that violent and discriminatory acts motivated by prejudicial attitudes will have a lengthy history. This is indeed what we find in Chapter 4, where it is argued that while societal interest may only be contemporary, in fact examples of behaviours that now constitute hate crimes are littered throughout history. Because of this, in addition to examining the history of hate crime, this chapter also charts the rise to prominence of hate crime as a contemporary social issue both in the US and in Britain.

Many of the reasons for focusing on, and responding to, hate crime as a distinct form of criminal behaviour are derived from an understanding of victimisation. Treating hate crimes more punitively is often justified by claims that these offences have a disproportionate impact on both the victim and the community to which they belong, that they are socially divisive, and that they are increasing in both incidence and violence, and therefore should be responded to more severely. Chapter 4 examines the evidence that underpins many of these claims by considering the extent, nature and impact of hate crime victimisation, and suggests that such claims are not always as clear-cut as they may at first appear.

Having considered victimisation, Chapter 5 will consider the perpetrators of hate crime. As a consequence of a predominantly victim-oriented approach to criminology over the past twenty years or so we find that information about offenders is actually relatively scarce. Nevertheless, this is an area in which research activity is beginning to make up for lost time, and this chapter examines what is currently known about those who commit hate crimes, both through theoretical developments and through emerging empirical research. This chapter also challenges the common misconception that hate offenders are predominantly members of organised hate groups, and argues that in reality hate offenders are for the most part 'ordinary'.

Chapter 6 focuses on what I have termed 'extreme' hatred. I use this term to distinguish the content of the chapter from the comparative ordinariness of the last. Here I consider organised hate groups in the US and the Far Right in Britain. In particular the chapter examines the apparent rise in organised hate groups and offers explanations for this. The chapter also considers the darkest side of human hatred, namely genocide and mass killing, and offers insights into the factors that lead to the perpetration of acts of such extreme violence. It is suggested that such acts are not the work of 'monsters' or 'madmen' but are predominantly perpetrated by 'ordinary' people. In this sense, the acts are extraordinary, but those committing them are not, and it is argued that even extreme forms of hatred have their roots in the ordinary prejudices that are found in us all.

In Chapter 7 we turn our attention to the regulation of hate crimes, in this instance through the use of legislation. Over the past 25 years or so there have been significant legal developments in this area in the US, and latterly in Britain, and this chapter outlines the key legislative measures currently in use in both countries. Having considered the law as it currently stands, the chapter then examines the particular difficulties associated with prosecuting hate crimes under these laws, and assesses the effectiveness of the laws in practice.

The very existence of these laws is, however, the subject of a considerable theoretical and moral debate. Their creation has been the subject of much controversy, particularly in the US, but also to a lesser extent here in Britain with the most notable example arguably that currently surrounding the proposals for a new crime of *incitement to religious hatred* contained within the Serious Organised Crime and Police Bill currently before Parliament. Chapter 8 considers both sides of the legislative debate, and concludes with an examination of the various legal challenges brought against the various hate-based legislative provisions that have shaped and delineated their boundaries.

Chapter 9 begins our consideration of the policing of hate crime. This chapter focuses on the policing of hate crime in New York and Philadelphia, and is based upon my own research conducted in the two cities throughout 2003. Here I outline the policies, procedures and overall police approach to hate crime and discuss some of the key issues associated with these.

In Chapter 10 I similarly examine the policing of hate crime in London. Again, this is based predominantly on my own ongoing research in this area. The chapter begins with a consideration of the murder of Stephen Lawrence and discusses the subsequent public inquiry and its findings. The changes to the policing of hate crime in London that followed the publication of the inquiry are then described. Many of these represent significant developments in the way hate crimes are policed and, in theory if not always in practice, represent models of good practice for improving the police response to these crimes.

Having considered how hate crime is policed in New York, Philadelphia and London, Chapter 11 examines many of the key problems and challenges that the police service as a whole faces when policing hate crimes. Inevitably there are often significant gaps between what proscriptive policy says should happen, and what actually happens 'in the real world'. Some of these key issues are examined and the reasons for the existence of such gaps are speculated upon. Finally, suggestions for improving the police response to hate crimes are made.

Of course an effective response to hatred in general, and hate crimes in particular, is not and cannot be the sole responsibility of the police. The problem is far greater than the police organisation; it is deeply rooted in society. With this in mind, Chapter 12 examines both the role and the limitations of the wider criminal justice system in responding to hate. It is argued that the best hope of 'success' lies in a holistic approach and considers alternative ways of dealing with hate and hate crime.

In concluding, in Chapter 13 I consider what we have learned and question both the nature of hatred and our response to it. Specifically, I ask whether our apparently unquestioning efforts to combat hatred are in fact based on questionable foundations. Many of the assumptions that underpin responses to hate crime are challenged, as is the assumption that hate can be, or even should be, somehow prevented. By addressing questions that at present have uncertain answers, my overriding hope is that this book, and the issues raised here, will serve as a starting point for debate and discussion about how we can best respond to hate crime.

Limitations and scope of the book

Because hate crime is an expansive concept, so the same is true for a book that addresses the subject. In other words, because of the vast range of issues that potentially (depending on how we construct the problem) relate to hate crime, at the outset this book also had the potential to vastness. It has been necessary therefore to impose various limitations on what has been included in this volume.

My overriding intention is to provide the reader with a detailed account of the views of the key writers within this field. Because hate crime is a relatively new social problem (at least in academic and political spheres), few texts deal specifically and comprehensively with the issue, particularly those of British origin. I have therefore focused particularly on the work of a relatively small number of writers that in recent times have contributed much to our understanding of hate crimes, and I have attempted to redress the US–UK balance where possible.

It is also my intention to present the opposing viewpoints that exist in the key debates that serve to reflect the complexity of the hate crime 'problem' and the difficulties we face in determining our responses to it. Many of the debates concerning hate crime are ongoing, particularly concerning how we should define and conceptualise hate crime, and whether or not we should use legislation to combat it. In many instances these debates raise more questions than they have thus far answered. In my consideration of these I have in some cases been deliberately inconclusive so as to allow the reader to make up their own mind.

To provide a comparison to the 'United States' I also frequently refer to the 'United Kingdom' or 'Britain'. While many of the issues that are discussed are equally applicable to England and Wales, Scotland and Northern Ireland, it should be remembered that these are separate jurisdictions, often with distinct 'hate' problems. Religious sectarianism is perhaps the most obvious, but there are also subtle (and not so subtle) differences in other spheres such as law and policing, although the underlying principles are often the same. For the most part when I refer to the British Isles I am referring particularly to England and Wales primarily because that is where I live and work and because it is the jurisdiction with which I am most familiar and in which much of my research has taken place. Issues specific to Scotland and Northern Ireland are referred to separately where necessary, although issues specific to these jurisdictions, as crucial as they are, have not been my primary focus. My focus is predominantly 'hate crime' per se.

Finally, it should be remembered that while there are relatively few books that address 'hate crime' specifically, there are many that deal with the issues that collectively constitute 'hate crime'. In particular there are, for example, a number of key texts that examine race and racism, in particular in relation to policing, and those that examine the psychology of prejudice. This book should be viewed as complementary to these rather than as a comprehensive alternative. No single volume on hate crime can ever cover everything.

Chapter 1

Defining and conceptualising hate crime

Offences that we now recognise as hate crimes have a long history, as we shall see in Chapter 3, but until relatively recently they were not officially labelled as such. Today politicians, criminal justice agencies, the media, and the public use the term fairly liberally. Society's concern with this 'new' type of crime is therefore a relatively recent development. But what is it exactly that we mean when we talk about 'hate crime'? Before we can explore any of the issues associated with the concept it is crucial that we have an understanding of exactly what it is that we are talking about. As we shall see, much depends upon the strength and depth of this understanding. As such, this opening chapter will seek to define and conceptualise hate crime, and will examine the inherent difficulties and complexities associated with doing so. The wide implications associated with the use of various definitions will also be explored.

Defining hate crime

Barbara Perry (2001) suggests that, as is the case with crime in general, it is very difficult to construct an exhaustive definition of 'hate crime' that is able to take account of all of its facets. Crime is of course socially constructed and means different things to different people and different things at different times, and what constitutes a crime in one place may not in another. As Perry suggests, crime is therefore relative and historically and culturally contingent, and as we shall see this is particularly true of hate crime. Indeed, as will become clear, 'hate crime' is a notoriously difficult concept to define accurately and effectively. Given this inescapable complexity it should not come as any surprise that numerous academic and professional definitions exist around the world. Boeckmann and Turpin-Petrosino (2002: 208) set the scene by stating that:

> There is no consensus among social scientists or lawmakers on definitional elements that would constitute a global description of hate crime. Part of the reason for this lies in the fact that cultural differences, social norms, and political interests play a large role in defining crime in general, and hate crime in particular.

In attempting to explain the phenomenon of 'hate crime' a number of definitions have been put forward by academics. In addition to simply defining hate crime, a consideration of these various definitions is important because it will allow us to deconstruct this phenomenon of 'hate crime' and present a deeper understanding of the complexities of the concept.

At the most simplistic level hate crimes are criminal offences that are motivated by hate, but this simplicity masks a number of important issues that are central to a true understanding of hate crime. Gerstenfeld (2004: 9) suggests that:

> The simplest definition of a hate crime is this: a criminal act which is motivated, at least in part, by the group affiliation of the victim.

Similarly, Craig (2002: 86) defines hate crime as:

> an illegal act involving intentional selection of a victim based on a perpetrator's bias or prejudice against the actual or perceived status of the victim.

Gerstenfeld acknowledges that her simple definition is not as precise as we might want and hides a number of important complexities. The same might also be said for Craig's definition. Some of these complexities are noted by Wolfe and Copeland (1994: 201), who define the phenomenon of hate crime as:

> violence directed towards groups of people who generally are not valued by the majority society, who suffer discrimination in other arenas, and who do not have full access to remedy social, political and economic injustice.

Clearly, for Craig a hate crime involves an illegal act motivated by the offender's prejudice towards an individual victim, while for Wolfe and Copeland the act committed is specifically one that is violent in nature, aimed at a specific group, and based upon the prejudices evident in wider society to which the offender presumably also subscribes. The latter definition also assumes that victims of hate crime are already marginalised in a number of other ways, implying that hate crime is somehow simply an extension of the existing oppression experienced by minority groups in society (Perry, 2001).

This oppressive view of hate crime is shared by Sheffield (1995: 438), who states that:

> Hate violence is motivated by social and political factors and is bolstered by belief systems which (attempt to) legitimate such violence … It reveals that the personal is political; that such violence is not a series of isolated incidents but rather the consequence of a political culture which allocates rights, privileges and prestige according to biological or social characteristics.

Perry (2001) suggests that Sheffield's definition is useful not only because it highlights the political and social context in which hate crime develops but also because it notes the significance of existing and deep rooted social hierarchies of identity that underpin hate crime. Thus Sheffield is suggesting that society is organised hierarchically along notions of 'difference' where people are afforded a position based on identifiable characteristics such as race, gender, sexuality and so on. Simply, society is organised on perceptions of power, and hate crime is simply one way to express that power.

Perry suggests, however, that the definition is somewhat incomplete because it fails to take full account of the effect of hate crime on those involved. Instead, Perry argues that an adequate definition of hate crime essentially needs to consist of certain elements of the definitions put forward by Wolfe and Copeland and Sheffield. In doing this Perry (2001: 10) argues that:

> Hate crime involves acts of violence and intimidation, usually directed toward already stigmatised and marginalised groups. As such, it is a mechanism of power and oppression, intended to reaffirm the precarious hierarchies that characterise a given social order. It attempts to re-create simultaneously the threatened (real or imagined) hegemony of the perpetrator's group and the 'appropriate' subordinate identity of the victim's group.

Deconstructing 'hate crime'

So what then do academic definitions tell us about hate crime? The first point to note is that there is nothing new about the crime element of hate crime. The actual offences themselves already exist and are outlawed by other existing criminal legislation. In this sense then it is society's interest in the motivation that lies behind the commission of the crime that is new. That motivation is, of course, an offender's hatred of, or more accurately prejudice against, a particular identifiable group or member of a particular identifiable group, usually already marginalised within society, whom the offender intentionally selects on the basis of that prejudice.

In addition the implications of Barbara Perry's definition are of particular interest. Under her definition, she suggests:

> ... hate crime is a crime like no other. Its dynamics both constitute and are constitutive of actors beyond the immediate victims and offenders. It is implicated not merely in the relationship between the direct 'participants', but also in the relationship between the different communities to which they belong. The damage involved goes far beyond physical or financial damages. It reaches into the community to create fear, hostility and suspicion. (Perry, 2001: 10)

For Perry, the intent of hate crime is to subordinate and intimidate not only the victim but also the entire community to which they belong. Hate crime is therefore symbolic in that it sends a message to the entire group to which the victim belongs that they are 'different' and that they 'don't belong'. As such, the victim is often immaterial and interchangeable.

While we shall examine many of these issues further in the chapters on victimisation and perpetrators respectively, this brief consideration of academic definitions of hate crime serves to demonstrate some of the complexities and the range of issues that we face when we try to explain hate crime. But the problem of defining hate crime is further exacerbated by the fact that academic definitions, while useful in sociological and criminological terms, are far too broad and complex to be of much value in practical terms to criminal justice practitioners and legislators. Because of this, when considering official interpretations of hate crime, we face a host of different definitions.

Just as academic definitions of hate crime vary in their content, so it is for official definitions that in many cases not only vary between countries, but also within them. Because of this, a comprehensive overview is beyond the scope of this book. Instead we shall concentrate on a few illustrative examples.

The situation in the US is particularly interesting in this regard. The first official federal definition of hate crime emerged when the US Hate Crime Statistics Bill was proposed in 1985 and enacted in 1990. This stated that hate crimes are:

> Crimes that manifest evidence of prejudice based on race, religion, sexual orientation or ethnicity, including where appropriate the crimes of murder, non-negligent manslaughter, forcible rape, aggravated assault, simple assault, intimidation, arson, and destruction, damage or vandalism of property. (Public Law: 101–275)

Here, both the categories of prejudice and specific types of offences are delineated. However, to illustrate the complexity and diversity surrounding official definitions of hate crime, in addition to those prejudices stated in the Federal Act many individual US states have added significant numbers of categories to their own state legislation to include discrimination based on, for example, nationality, disability (both mental and physical), age, marital status, gender, political affiliation or beliefs, and economic or social status. As a consequence almost every US state has a different legal definition of hate crime. This is an issue that we shall consider further in Chapter 7.

Even within States definitions of hate crime can differ. For example, New York Bias Crime Law Section 485.05 states that:

> A person commits a hate crime when he or she commits a specified offence and either:
>
> (a) Intentionally selects the person against whom the offence is committed or intended to be committed in whole or in part because of a belief or perception regarding the race, colour, national origin, ancestry, gender, religion, religious practice, age, disability or sexual orientation of a person, regardless of whether the belief or perception is correct, or
>
> (b) Intentionally commits the act or acts constituting the offence in whole or in part because of a belief or perception regarding the race, colour, national origin, ancestry, gender, religion, religious practice, age, disability or sexual orientation of a person, regardless of whether the belief or perception is correct.

5

However, the New York City Police Department (2000: 1) recognises hate crime as:

> Any offence or unlawful act that is motivated in whole or in part by a person's, a group's, or a place's identification with a particular race, religion, ethnicity, sexual orientation or disability as determined by the Commanding Officer, Bias Incident Investigation Unit. Disability [is defined as] the possession by a person of any of the following: a physical, medical, mental or psychological impairment or a history or record of such impairment. This includes the sustaining by a person of any injury or damage to any system of the body including muscular, sensory, respiratory, speech, heart, reproductive, digestive, blood, immunity (i.e. AIDS) and skin. Also included among those who have a disability are recovering alcoholics, and former abusers of drugs and other substances who currently are not abusing alcohol, drugs, or other substances.

The police definition does not include gender or age, yet the State law does. Similarly, just as individual states and local law enforcement agencies differ on their understanding of hate crime, so it is for federal law enforcement agencies. For example, the Federal Bureau of Investigation (FBI, 1997) defines hate crime as:

> a criminal offence committed against a person, property or society which is motivated, in whole or in part, by the offender's bias against a race, religion, disability, sexual orientation, or ethnicity/ national origin.

Clearly then the situation in the US is complicated. The definitions of and the elements that would constitute a hate crime vary greatly both between and within federal, state and local agencies. Although consistent themes can be identified, for example the presence of prejudice and the offender's intentional selection of victims on the basis of certain identifiable characteristics, the specifics vary. This in turn can have huge implications for accurately measuring the size of the hate crime problem, as we shall see. Effectively, then, when we talk about hate crime, we could be talking about a number of very different things depending on where we happen to be.

In this country the situation is different to the US. Between 1986 and 1999, each of the 43 police forces of England and Wales collected information on racist incidents only under the Association of Chief Police Officers' definition, which referred to:

Any incident in which it appears to the reporting or investigating officer that the complaint involves an element of racial motivation; or any incident which includes an allegation of racial motivation made by any person. (ACPO, 1985)

Following the Stephen Lawrence Inquiry, the police service adopted the definition recommended by Sir William Macpherson and as such:

A racist incident is any incident which is perceived to be racist by the victim or any other person. (Macpherson, 1999)

This definition is held to be clearer and simpler than the original (Home Office, 2002) and purposefully removes the discretionary element from the police in determining what is and what is not a racist incident, a situation that contributed to the failure of the investigation into the murder of Stephen Lawrence.

However, since the publication of the Stephen Lawrence Inquiry the debate has widened beyond just issues of race to encompass the much broader concept of 'diversity' and 'hate'. As such, in England and Wales the Association of Chief Police Officers (2000: 13) defined hate crime as:

a crime where the perpetrator's prejudice against any identifiable group of people is a factor in determining who is victimised.

This is further broken down by the category of prejudice to include the definition of a racist incident described above, and similarly a homophobic incident is defined as:

any incident that is perceived to be homophobic by the victim or any other person. (ACPO, 2000: 13)

We shall explore the implications of this particular ACPO definition later in this chapter, but at this stage we should simply note that the definition allows for anyone to be a victim of hate crime, and for any offence to be recorded and investigated by the police as a hate crime.

In 2005, however, ACPO revised their definitions of a hate incident and a hate crime. A hate incident is now defined as:

> Any incident, which may or may not constitute a criminal offence, which is perceived by the victim or any other person, as being motivated by prejudice or hate. (ACPO, 2005: 9)

A hate crime is defined as:

> Any hate incident, which constitutes a criminal offence, perceived by the victim or any other person, as being motivated by prejudice or hate. (ACPO, 2005: 9)

This change is significant because it acknowledges that hate crimes are not always about hate, but about prejudice. This is a point to which I shall return later in this chapter.

It is important to note, however, that these definitions are those used operationally by the police to recognise hate crimes, yet they differ markedly from legislative definitions. Indeed, as we shall see in Chapter 7, hate crime as a distinct category of offence does not officially exist in British legislation. Instead, the key pieces of legislation in this regard recognise only offences motivated or aggravated by racial and religious prejudice (the Crime and Disorder Act 1998 as amended by the Anti-terrorism, Crime and Security Act 2001), and those related to homophobia and disability bias (the Criminal Justice Act 2003).

Under the Crime and Disorder Act (1998: Part 2, s.28) an offence is racially aggravated if:

(a) at the time of committing the offence, or immediately before or after doing so, the offender demonstrates towards the victim of the offence hostility based on the victim's membership (or presumed membership) of a racial group; or

(b) the offence is motivated (wholly or partly) by hostility towards members of a racial group based on their membership of that group.

Under the Act a 'racial group' refers to persons defined by reference to their race, colour, nationality or ethnic or national origins and in section 28(3a) includes membership of any religious group. Again, we shall explore the implication of the definition shortly, but note here the narrow nature of the definition in terms of the prejudices included (race and religion) as compared to the two ACPO definitions (any prejudice).

The complexities and implications of defining hate crime

Earlier in this chapter it was suggested that while defining crime in general is difficult enough, defining hate crime is a particularly complex task. The various definitions presented here, which themselves represent just a small sample of those that currently exist, are testament to that difficulty. But why is it that hate crime is so uniquely difficult to define and conceptualise? And why is it significant? We have already noted the importance of relative, historical and cultural issues in defining crime, but where hate crime is concerned, a number of other crucial points also bear heavily on this process. Here we shall consider some of these issues, and where relevant we shall do so with specific reference to the implications for the definitions of hate crime used officially in the UK.

What is hate?

The first problem relates to the word 'hate' and what, exactly, we mean by it. Despite the frequency with which the term is used, for the purpose of furthering our understanding of hate crime, the word *hate* is distinctly unhelpful. As Andrew Sullivan (1999) points out, for all our zeal to attack hate we still have a remarkably vague idea of what hate actually is, and despite the powerful and emotional images that it invokes it is still far less nuanced an idea than prejudice, bias, bigotry, hostility, anger, or just a mere aversion to others. When we talk about 'hate', do we mean all of these things or just the extremes of them?

If we look at the definitions presented in this chapter then we can see that none of them speaks of 'hate' as a causal factor. Rather, the definitions refer to prejudice, or bias, or *–isms*. Clearly, then, hate crime thus defined isn't really about *hate*, but about criminal behaviour motivated by *prejudice*, of which hate is just one small and extreme part. This is significant because prejudice is a far more expansive concept than hate, covering many varieties of human emotion. What we might think of as 'pure' hate is just a small part of this spectrum. The expansive nature of hate crime is a point to which I will return later in this chapter, and the complexities of prejudice will be the subject of the next chapter, but it is important to understand at this juncture that for the most part it is prejudice and not hate that we refer to when we talk about hate crime. This crucial distinction, as will become clear, has many important implications for understanding and in particular for responding to hate crimes.

What prejudices are unacceptable?

The concept of hate becomes increasingly muddied and confused when we try to make the distinction between those prejudices that are acceptable and those that are not, how strong those prejudices must be in order to become unacceptable, how they must be expressed, whether someone is prejudiced or whether they are not, or indeed how we can ever know for certain.

Let us apply this to the original definition of hate crime adopted by ACPO in 2000, above. This states that hate crime is any crime where the perpetrator's *prejudice* against any identifiable group of people is a factor in determining who is victimised. The problem here is that the word 'prejudice' is not defined or explained. Which prejudices are to be included? Which, if any, are to be excluded? The same is true for the 2005 ACPO definition, although some clarification is provided because the police are required to record incidents based on race, sexual orientation, faith and disability. But as we shall see, creating lists of 'acceptable' prejudices is itself problematic. Nevertheless, this issue of defining prejudice is important because, as Jacobs and Potter (1998) suggest, if everyone holds some form of prejudice then potentially every crime committed by one group against another could be labelled as a hate crime.

It is not unreasonable to suggest, they argue, that some form of prejudice on the part of the offender motivates all crimes against any victim, but clearly not every crime is a hate crime otherwise the concept would just be coterminous with crime in general. This indicates then that some prejudices must necessarily be socially and officially less acceptable than others. This unavoidable situation leads us to our next problematic and contentious issue, namely, which prejudices turn ordinary crimes into hate crimes?

The ACPO (2000, 2005) definitions imply that any prejudice on the part of the offender will constitute a hate crime. But as Jacobs and Potter have suggested, offenders probably have many prejudices, both conscious and subconscious, against people who are, for example, rich, poor, successful, unsuccessful and so on. If we start looking for prejudice in offending behaviour, they argue, then the closer we look the more we will find. Simply, because of its pervasiveness, prejudice of one kind or another is present in most forms of offending. Therefore, to allow a distinction to be made between *crime* and *hate crime*, we necessarily have to identify and select the prejudices we wish to challenge. The question is, then, what prejudices are we going to take action against? Or put another way, what groups are we going to protect?

As will have been apparent from the definitions outlined above, answering this question is a far from simple task. This is particularly true for legislation across the US where protected categories differ from state to state. In the UK the situation is different but remains complicated. In explaining their definition, ACPO (2000, 2005) states that a hate crime will include any incident which is perceived by the victim or any other person as being motivated by prejudice, which in itself can be based on any identifying factor, but in their *Guide to Identifying and Combating Hate Crime* (2000), particular reference is made to age, disability, faith, sexual orientation, gender, gender identity and race. This list, however, is held to be non-exhaustive. Interestingly, age is not specifically mentioned in the revised ACPO guide (2005).

While defining and stating these specific categories might be seen as a helpful step in clarifying what is and what is not a hate crime, other elements of the definition serve to complicate things considerably. For example, by adopting deliberately broad and inclusive definitions that include the phrases 'any identifiable group' and 'perceived by the victim or any other person', ACPO's definitions, adapted from the recommendations of the Stephen Lawrence Inquiry, unquestionably accept that anyone can be a victim of hate crime if they believe themselves to be so. But if anyone can be a victim of hate crime, and if any crime can be a hate crime, there is a danger that the very concept will effectively lose its meaning.

Moreover, a notable contradiction exists in the UK. While a broad definition is used in policing, in terms of the law the range of protected groups is considerably narrower. Legally, only crimes motivated by racial or religious prejudice are specifically recognised (homophobia and disability bias can be taken into account as aggravating factors at sentencing but are not separate crimes), and the specific term 'hate crime' is not mentioned at all in the statute books. In effect then, by recognising hate and prejudice in the widest sense the police service is potentially identifying and responding to categories of offending that have no legal recognition whatsoever, although the 2005 ACPO guide serves to clarify this situation a little by drawing particular attention to race, sexual orientation, faith and disability. But the point remains that if the police are seeking to respond to any prejudice or hate, then they may at times find themselves with motivations that are not clearly delineated by criminal law. This is an important issue to which I shall return in Chapter 11.

Of course the very notion of recognising and listing categories of prejudice is in itself problematic. Creating such a list is fraught with difficulties. The exclusion of some groups may give the impression that their victimisation is of less importance than those stated on the list, while including every conceivable minority group will ultimately cause the original intention of the focus on hate crime to be at best watered down and at worst lost altogether. Critics would also argue here that all victims should be protected from crime, so the question then becomes why should we seek to protect some more than others (Jacobs and Potter, 1998)?

If we are to protect certain groups more than others, then this necessarily raises difficult questions of how we decide what groups to protect. For example, how did we get to the position in Britain whereby crimes based on race and religion are specific offences, yet crimes based on other prejudices against other minority groups are not? Under the ACPO definitions this issue does not require much attention. The need to make these decisions is avoided by allowing for members of any identifiable group to be recognised as victims of hate crime if they perceive themselves to be so. Under the law, however, we can ask searching questions as to why only prejudices based on race and religion, and to a lesser extent homophobia and disability bias, are specifically singled out for additional protection while other identifiable groups (for example the elderly, the young, tall people, short people, obese people, left-handed people and so on) are not.

Writing of a similar situation in the US, Gerstenfeld (2004) suggests that legislative decisions regarding which prejudices to outlaw and thus which groups to protect are affected by a number of factors. Such factors might include economic, political and socio-demographic conditions within a jurisdiction, but they also might be influenced by media attention and the lobbying activities of advocacy groups and social movements. To this we might also add historical conditions relating to certain minority groups. If we consider the UK situation, each of these factors might reasonably have contributed to our legislative focus firstly on race and more recently on religion. We shall focus on these issues in greater detail when we consider the history of hate crime and its emergence as a contemporary social issue in Chapter 3.

Crimes and causal links

Jacobs and Potter (1998) suggest that there are two further issues that serve to complicate our understanding of hate crime. Firstly, we need to consider what types of behaviours are included in our definition. As we shall see in Chapter 2, prejudice can be expressed in a multitude of different ways, and decisions have to be made about where to draw the line between the acceptable and the unacceptable expression of negative attitudes. In other words we have to decide how strong an offender's 'hate' must be before it becomes unacceptable.

Secondly, we have to establish just how strong the causal relationship between the offence and the officially designated prejudice must be before we can call a crime a hate crime. In the UK, our definitions are particularly susceptible to the implications of both these issues. If we return to the ACPO (2000) definition, two phrases that have particular implications for our understanding of the problem in this regard are 'any incident' and 'a factor in determining'. We shall examine these in turn.

The first issue centres on the use of the word incident. Here hate crime is not just about crimes, but about incidents too. This is an important distinction to make because the two are very different things. An incident does not need to be a recordable crime. In England and Wales a hate incident may occur and be recorded by the police in the official statistics but not have the necessary elements to be classified as a notifiable offence at a later stage in the criminal justice process.

Put simply, an incident may be something that occurs that is perceived by the victim or any other person as being motivated or aggravated by some form of prejudice, but may not actually be a crime in the strictest legal sense. In England and Wales, at the reporting and recording stage of the policing process there is no evidential test that the hate incident has to pass. The definition is simply concerned with the prima facie test, rather than an evidential one (i.e. 'does this appear on the surface to be a hate crime?' rather than 'is there sufficient legal evidence for this to be classified as a notifiable offence?').

In practical policing terms, then, at the initial reporting and recording stage of the process the difference between a hate incident and a hate crime is irrelevant. Both are recorded. This lack of distinction between the two is significant primarily because if we add hate incidents to hate crimes, then the number of hate 'occurrences' that come to official attention will be vastly greater than if we were to just concentrate our attention on legally defined crimes. As we shall see when we consider the policing of hate crime, this situation has important implications for effectively responding to the problem.

The second issue relates to the strength of the causal link between the incident or crime and the officially designated prejudice. Clearly, for an ordinary crime to be transformed into a hate crime there has to be a causal connection between the offence and the offender's prejudice. As Jacobs and Potter (1998) suggest, if in our definition we require hate crime to be motivated only by prejudice to the exclusion of all other factors then we will not experience much hate crime. Conversely, if we are happy for prejudice to be only loosely related to the offence then a great many more offences will be defined as hate crimes.

Accordingly, the ACPO definition (2000) states that the offender's prejudice must be a *factor* in determining who is victimised, but it doesn't tell us just how much of a factor the offender's prejudice must be. The implication is that the slightest hint of prejudice will suffice, in which case a great many incidents can potentially be, and indeed are, officially labelled as hate crimes. The 2005 definitions, however, suggest that the prejudice must be a *motivating* factor. But again, the question remains as to how much of a motivating factor the offender's prejudice must be.

This is an issue that also extends to legal definitions in the UK. The Crime and Disorder Act 1998, as we have seen, refers not only to racially and religiously *aggravated* offences, but also to offences that are *motivated in whole or in part* by racial and religious prejudice. While the categories of prejudice are narrow, the scope for labelling a great many offences as hate crimes within those categories is also, in theory at least, wide. Here, the word 'motivated' refers to offences where the offender's prejudice is the *sole* or *primary* cause of the offence. On the other hand, aggravation refers not to the motivation behind the offence, but to some demonstration of hostility towards the victim around the time of the offence. Aggravating factors, such as racial slurs for example, are not the primary cause of the offence, but nevertheless represent an expression of prejudice that contributes as a subsidiary element to the crime. Both contribute to differing degrees to the transformation of crime into hate crime under definitions constructed in the UK.

The social construction of hate crime

Let us take a moment at this juncture to summarise some of the key points raised in this chapter. Western democracies in particular have 'created' a relatively 'new' offence that we call 'hate crime', but there is little consensus either nationally or internationally, academically or professionally, about what exactly hate crime is. At its most basic level hate crimes are offences motivated by prejudice: pre-existing criminal incidents or offences in which the offender's prejudice against the victim or the victim's group plays some part in their victimisation. But of course it is not that simple, and this basic definition masks a number of crucial issues that cannot be ignored or cast aside.

Because of this, in attempting to adequately conceptualise 'hate crime', we must consider a number of key questions: What prejudices when transformed into action are we going to criminalise? How will we know if these actions truly constitute a hate crime? What crimes are we going to include in our definition? Which groups will be acceptable to us as victims? How strong must the relationship between the prejudice and the offence be? Must that link be wholly or just partially causal? Who will decide? How will we decide? How can we guard against hatred without impinging upon people's basic democratic freedoms? And, of course, why is it important to consider these questions? The answer to this last question is crucial. As Jacobs and Potter (1998: 27) suggest:

> How much hate crime there is and what the appropriate response should be depends upon how hate crime is conceptualised and defined.

Consider the following theoretical model proposed by Jacobs and Potter illustrated in Figure 1.1. They suggest that hate crime is a potentially expansive concept that covers a great many offenders and situations.

The horizontal axis shows the degree of the offender's prejudice (high or low, or in other words prejudiced or not very prejudiced), and the vertical axis shows the strength of the causal relationship between the criminal behaviour and the officially designated prejudice (high or low, or strongly related or not strongly related). Both of these factors, and combinations of them, have important implications for understanding hate crimes.

As far as defining hate crime is concerned, cell I (high prejudice/high causation) is relatively unproblematic. Here we have offenders who are

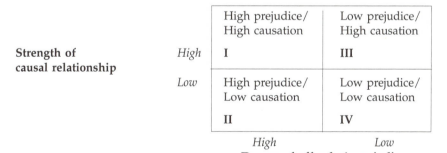

		High prejudice/ High causation	Low prejudice/ High causation
Strength of causal relationship	*High*	I	III
	Low	High prejudice/ Low causation II	Low prejudice/ Low causation IV
		High	*Low*
		Degree of offender's prejudice	

Figure 1.1 Labelling hate crime; the prejudice and causal components (Jacobs and Potter, 1998: 23).

highly prejudiced, and whose prejudice is a strong causal factor in their offending behaviour. These offenders are the ones that we probably associate most when we think of the word 'hate' in its most extreme form. As such this cell represents clear-cut hate crimes where there is little doubt that the offender hates his or her victim in the truest sense of the word. To illustrate this, Jacobs and Potter present a number of examples, including some of the historical activities of the Ku Klux Klan or of members of neo-Nazi groups. We might also include the perpetrators of two of America's most infamous hate crimes in this category. In Texas in 1997 John William King was one of three men who, as part of a bonding activity for an new white supremacist group, beat up James Bird Jr, an African American, and chained his feet to the back of a truck and dragged him for three miles until his body hit a culvert and was decapitated. In Wyoming in October 1998, Matthew Shepard was beaten to death in a homophobic attack and his body left hanging from a fence as a warning to others.

In a UK context we might reasonably include here David Copeland, the racist and homophobic neo-Nazi convicted of nail bomb attacks in Brixton, Brick Lane and Soho in April 1999 where he deliberately targeted, killed and injured members of London's ethnic minority and gay and lesbian communities. We might also include Robert Stewart, a violent racist who murdered fellow inmate Zahid Mubarek at Feltham Young Offenders Institute in London in March 2000. We might also consider the killers of black teenager Stephen Lawrence in South-East London in April 1993. In more extreme terms, this cell might also include the Nazi persecution of the Jews that culminated in the Holocaust. Jacobs and Potter (1998) argue, therefore, that if hate crimes included only cases like these, the concept would not be ambiguous, difficult to understand or controversial, nor would there be many hate crimes occurring because cases like these, generally, are rare.

However, it is when we consider the other three cells that things become more complicated. Cell II (high prejudice/low causation) refers to highly prejudiced offenders, such as those included in cell I, but whose offending is not strongly or solely motivated by prejudice. The hypothetical example Jacobs and Potter use to illustrate this is that of a neo-Nazi figure who shoplifts from a shop owed by a Jew, where the primary motive is to acquire the stolen goods, and not to target Jews. But is this a hate crime? Clearly the offender will be prejudiced against Jews, but it is wrong, Jacobs and Potter argue, to assume that all offences committed by prejudiced offenders against minority groups are primarily motivated by that prejudice. In the strictest sense such offences would not, and indeed should not, be hate crimes because they are not motivated by prejudice, but by some other motive, for example economics, or hunger.

Cells III and IV present particular challenges for defining and understanding hate crime. Cell III (low prejudice/high causation) contains offenders who are not particularly prejudiced, or whose prejudices may be largely subconscious but which nevertheless have a strong causal link to the offence. Jacobs and Potter use the example of Dontay Carter, a black American man who always targeted white men as his robbery victims. In this case, however, Carter targeted white men because he believed them to be rich and not because he had any other particular prejudice against their skin colour. Therefore his prejudice was based upon his perception of white men's financial status and not their ethnic group *per se*. Thus the causal link between his prejudice and his offending behaviour was strong, but his prejudice in terms of 'hating' his victims was not. Nevertheless, for Jacobs and Potter it is this group of offenders and this type of offence that dominate the US hate crime statistics. In other words, the strength of the motivation is often overlooked at the expense of the perceived causal relationship: a crime is committed by a member of one group against a member of another group and a hate crime is assumed.

Cell IV (low prejudice/low causation) represents many incidents or offences that are described by Jacobs and Potter as being 'situational' in that they arise from ad hoc disputes or short tempers, but are neither products of strong prejudicial attitudes nor are they strongly causally related to the incident in question. Consider two examples. The first was recounted to the author during ethnographic research with the Philadelphia Police Department in 2003. The case centred on a long-running neighbour dispute between a black family and a white family over the persistent playing of loud music. As the dispute came to a head the arguments became increasingly volatile during which racial epithets were exchanged. Did these constitute hate crimes? Ultimately not because the cause of the incident was determined by the police to be the playing of loud music, and not differences in ethnic origin.

The second case, also in the US, cited as an example by Jacobs and Potter, also involved a long-running dispute between two neighbours, one homosexual and one heterosexual, over the spilling of grass clippings by the gay man onto his neighbour's lawn when he cut the grass. As the dispute escalated the straight man responded on one occasion by shouting anti-gay epithets. As the argument developed the gay man sprayed his neighbour's son with water from the garden hose, and in response the son kicked and punched the gay man while yelling anti-gay comments. Ultimately the son was convicted of a hate-motivated assault. But again we can question the motive of the assault. As Sullivan (1999) queries, what exactly was the nature of this hate? Homophobia or, as he puts it, 'suburban property-owner madness'? The point is that under some definitions and interpretations these are hate crimes, and under others they are not. The number of hate crimes in society is therefore entirely determined by how hate crime is defined, conceptualised and interpreted. The problem is that the definitions currently in use ensure that the majority of officially labelled hate crimes are not motivated by hate at all, but by prejudice, which as will become clear is often an entirely different thing.

Applying the model to the US and the UK context

When we consider Jacobs and Potter's model it becomes clear that hate crime, like any other crime, is ultimately a social construct. Hate crime, however, is more susceptible to this process than other forms of crime because of the additional elements that have to be considered. As Jacobs and Potter suggest, when constructing a definition of hate crime, choices have to be made about the meaning of prejudice, the nature and strength of the causal link between the prejudice and the offence, as well as the types of crimes to be included. Our decisions in these choices will ultimately determine what is and what is not 'hate crime', and will naturally affect the size of the hate crime problem we will face, which will subsequently impact upon our response to it.

Consider the following illustration of this point. In 2001 the population of the United States officially stood at 284,796,887. In that year 11,987 law enforcement agencies recorded 9,726 hate crime incidents, of which 4,366 were racially motivated (FBI, 2002). In the same year the population of England and Wales stood at 52,041,915 and the 43 police forces of England and Wales recorded 54,351 racially motivated incidents alone (Home Office, 2002). Statistically, then, in 2001 England and Wales suffered almost twelve and a half times as many racially motivated incidents as the US, despite the population of the US being almost five and a half times greater than England and Wales. Indeed, West Midlands police recorded similar figures for racially motivated incidents to the whole of the US (4,058 incidents), and the Metropolitan Police recorded just under four times as many racially motivated incidents as the whole of the US (16,711 incidents).

Does this mean that England and Wales are vastly more racist places than the United States? Of course not. The most probable explanation for this enormous disparity lies in the construction and application of the definition(s) adopted on both sides of the Atlantic.

The broad definitions adopted by ACPO means that, superficially at least, any incident or crime could be a hate crime, and that anyone could be a victim of hate crime if they perceive themselves to be so. If we apply Jacobs and Potter's model to this then effectively the ACPO definitions cover all four cells. In other words any incident or crime can be a hate crime, any victim can be a hate crime victim, and any offender can be a hate offender. The distinction between crime and hate crime can therefore become very blurred.

Crucially though, the application of a narrow legal definition under the Crime and Disorder Act 1998, and the legal requirements for a successful prosecution mean that decisions do have to be made at various stages of the legal process. In this respect the distinction between a crime and a hate crime naturally becomes clearer as legal requirements have to be met if the hate element is to withstand legal scrutiny and a successful prosecution be achieved. In other words, prejudice as a motivating or aggravating factor has to be proved in court, but it doesn't have to be proved for a 'hate crime' to appear as such in the official police statistics. The narrower legal definition therefore has a 'culling' effect in determining the number of hate crimes.

In the US, in law enforcement terms more selective decisions are generally made regarding the strength of prejudice and causality before a crime is officially labelled as a hate crime. Where these issues are weak, the hate label is generally withheld and the crime remains exactly that, just a crime. Moreover, the focus is more concerned with crime rather than with incidents (Hall, 2004). We shall expand further on some of these issues in the chapter on policing hate crime, and as we shall see this can have serious implications for policing practice, and for the picture of intergroup relations that the official statistics paint.

A final issue to consider is that official and legal definitions on both sides of the Atlantic, and indeed the nature of hate itself, run counter to many of the academic definitions discussed in this chapter. This is because hate crime is not just a tool of the powerful nor is it just aimed at minority groups. Under the ACPO and CDA definitions, and many of those used in the US, it can also be a 'tool' of the supposed 'powerless'. Hate crime therefore cuts both ways, and often disproportionately so. As Sullivan (1999) highlights, FBI figures show that in America in the 1990s blacks were up to three times as likely as whites to commit a hate crime. In other words, hated groups may respond to their oppression with a hate of their own and be subsequently caught up in legislative efforts that are arguably designed primarily to protect them.

The question that arises here is whether or not this undermines the whole point of drawing special attention to hate crime in the first place.

If the attention and responses we now give to hate crime are intended to protect the supposed powerless from oppression by the members of the majority, then figures such as those from the FBI, and the nature of hate in general, pose something of a dilemma. We cannot wholly ascribe blame to one group and innocence to others, so if we try to regulate the hate of one group (i.e. the majority), then we are also forced to regulate the hate of others (Sullivan, 1999). The dilemma is that:

> If ... everyone, except the white straight able bodied male, is regarded as a possible victim of hate crime, then we have simply created a two-tier system of justice in which racial profiling is reversed, and white straight men are presumed guilty before being proven innocent, and members of minorities are free to hate them as gleefully as they like. But if we include the white straight male in the litany of potential victims, then we have effectively abolished the notion of a hate crime altogether. For if every crime is possibly a hate crime, then it is simply another name for crime. All we will have done is widened the search for possible bigotry, ratcheted up the sentences for everyone and filled the jails up even further. (Sullivan, 1999: 14)

Concluding comments

In this chapter we have briefly examined a small number of academic and official attempts to define hate crime. While some obvious themes emerge throughout it is clear that there is no consensus on exactly what is and what is not a hate crime. But does this really matter? Undoubtedly it does. It matters considerably.

Arguably, criminology is about seeking answers to seven basic questions: What is the problem? How much of it is there? Who is involved or affected? Where is the problem occurring? When is it occurring? Why is it occurring? And, crucially, what should we do to make the situation better? The answers to the last six questions are to a great extent determined by the answer to the first.

Effectively, everything that we associate with hate crime depends upon how we define and conceptualise it. The significance of accurately and effectively defining this phenomenon is therefore crucial. If in our definition we insist that hate crimes must be wholly motivated by prejudice to the exclusion of all other factors then society will not experience many such offences. Few offences can be said to be motivated exclusively and solely by hate. Conversely if we are happy for our definition to require just the slightest hint of prejudice for an offence to be classified as a hate crime then the number of crimes could become astronomical. At present in the UK, we find ourselves both at the latter end of this spectrum, and also somewhere in the middle. We have adopted the widest possible operational definition in policing terms, but a narrower one in terms of the law. Clearly, defining, conceptualising and understanding hate crime is a complex task that is fraught with difficulties.

Chapter 2

Prejudice and hatred

The last chapter identified a number of important issues that are central to an understanding of hate crime. First, the various definitions of hate crime show that this form of offending isn't always about *hate* but is predominantly about *prejudice*, of which hate is just a small part. It follows then that if we want to understand hate crime then we must first understand the nature of prejudice. This, however, is problematic. Just as there is little agreement about how we should define hate crime, so it is the same for prejudice. Jacobs and Potter (1998) point out that while prejudice has long been an object for study, sociologists and psychologists have been unable to agree on a single definition for it, nor agree on where it comes from or exactly what purpose it serves. Instead, we have a number of competing theories each seeking to explain the phenomenon in different ways, but none of them definitive or conclusive. The aim of this chapter is therefore to present an overview of current knowledge concerning the nature and origins of prejudice, and by doing so to highlight the inherent complexities surrounding the phenomenon and the difficulties this presents for understanding and responding to hate crime.

Defining prejudice and discrimination

Before we can explore the various issues associated with hate crime, it is important that we understand the foundations of hatred, namely the psychological concept of prejudice, and its relationship to discriminatory behaviour. The first requirement of this chapter therefore is to provide an appropriate definition of 'prejudice' and 'discrimination', and to distinguish between the two. The terms 'prejudice' and 'discrimination' are often used interchangeably, but it is important to be clear about the difference between them. For our purposes, prejudice can be described as a type of *attitude* towards members of a social group, while discrimination can be described as a *behaviour* or an *action* arising from that attitude and directed towards members of a social group. In other words discrimination is essentially 'prejudice in action' (Baron and Byrne, 1994).

As a separate entity, discrimination can take many forms. Its expression may often be restrained by, for example, laws and social pressures but where such forces are absent or weak prejudicial attitudes may be expressed in overt forms. The nature of these expressions is discussed in more detail below (see Allport's 'five-point scale') but as we will see in Chapter 4, even the subtlest forms of discrimination, whether direct or indirect, can have serious consequences for its victims. It can result in differential treatment or exclusion from services and provisions, and may extend further to include forms of aggression and violence.

The word 'prejudice' is derived from the Latin noun *praejudicium*, meaning *precedent*, and in the English language the term came to mean a premature or hasty judgment. More recently the term has also acquired its emotive sense of favourableness or unfavourableness now associated with such a judgment (Allport, 1954). According to one early definition, prejudice is

> a pattern of hostility in interpersonal relations which is directed against an entire group, or against its individual members; it fulfils a specific irrational function for its bearer. (Ackerman and Jahoda, 1950: 4)

However, Gordon Allport, arguably the most prominent of all researchers and writers on this subject, disagreed with the assertion that prejudice always holds some form of irrational function for the bearer. Instead Allport argued that prejudice often has a *functional significance*, but nevertheless is often simply a matter of blind conformity with some prevailing common ideology (and therefore has no functional significance whatsoever for the bearer). As such he defines prejudice as:

> an antipathy based upon a faulty and inflexible generalisation. It may be felt or expressed. It may be directed toward a group as a whole, or toward an individual because he is a member of that

group. The net effect of prejudice, thus defined, is to place the object of prejudice at some disadvantage not merited by his own conduct. (Allport, 1954: 9)

Under such a definition, prejudgments become prejudices only if they are not reversible when the holder is exposed to new knowledge or evidence relating to the object of his or her erroneous judgment. According to Allport a prejudice is actively resistant to all evidence that would unseat it. Therefore, the difference between ordinary prejudgments and prejudice is that one can discuss and rectify a prejudgment without emotional resistance.

However, Brown (1995) takes issue with both of the above definitions. He argues that by referring to an 'inflexible generalisation' or to an 'irrational function' these writers are making unwise suppositions. While at the time their definitions may have been wholly accurate given the existing level of knowledge, Brown suggests that to think of prejudice as being impervious to change or as having no rational function for its bearer is to fail to appreciate the variety and complexity of the forms prejudice can take and its tendency to be unstable in its nature and to change under certain circumstances. Thus, to take account of these issues, Brown (1995: 8) defines prejudice as:

the holding of derogatory social attitudes or cognitive beliefs, the expression of negative affect, or the display of hostile or discriminatory behaviour towards members of a group on account of their membership of that group.

Similarly, and more simply, Baron and Byrne (1994: 218) define prejudice as:

an attitude (usually negative) toward the members of some group, based solely on their membership in that group.

Here the definition implies that a prejudiced individual evaluates members of a particular social group in a specific manner simply because they belong to that social group, and thus the individual traits or behaviours of the target hold little significance for the prejudiced person. Baron and Byrne (1994) also suggest that prejudicial attitudes often function as schemas (cognitive frameworks for organising, interpreting and recalling information). They argue that prejudiced people process information about the object of their prejudice differently to other groups on which they hold no prejudicial views.

As such, information consistent with their prejudices tends to receive more attention, is cognitively rehearsed and reinforced more frequently, and tends to be remembered more accurately than other information. Therefore, in the absence of strong contradictory evidence, prejudice becomes a 'cognitive loop' that grows stronger and more deep-seated over time. Consequently, prejudice as an attitude can then move beyond a simple evaluation of a group to include negative feelings and emotions and stereotyping on the part of the bearer. This can in turn lead to negative actions or discriminatory behaviours directed towards the objects of the prejudice, although it is important to note that prejudicial attitudes do not always transform into discriminatory behaviour.

The origins of prejudice and discrimination

There are numerous competing perspectives that seek to identify and explain the origins of prejudice and discrimination. Arguably the most significant early contribution was that of Gordon Allport in his seminal work, *The Nature of Prejudice.* Although competing ideas have since been advocated, Brown (1995) acknowledges that Allport's work has come to be regarded as the departure point for all modern research into aspects of prejudice. Furthermore, Brown states that so significant was Allport's contribution that his theorising has provided the basis for programmes designed to improve race-relations in American schools for the past fifty years or so. Allport's work is encyclopaedic in its nature but it is important to begin with a brief overview of some of Allport's thoughts regarding the origin of prejudice before moving on to examining some more modern perspectives.

According to Allport (1954) prejudice is a normal and rational (that is to say, predictable) human behaviour by virtue of our need to organise all the cognitive data our brain receives through the formation of generalisations, concepts and categories whose content represents an oversimplification of our world and experiences therein. This process is essential to our daily living and the forming of generalisations, categories and concepts based on experience and probability helps us to guide our daily activities and to make sense of the world around us.

For example, as Allport suggests, if we see heavy black clouds in the sky we may prejudge that there is a high probability based on past experience that rain will fall and we adjust our behaviour accordingly (for example, by wearing a raincoat and taking an umbrella with us).

Similarly, for the most part, it is also easier for us to over-generalise about a subject or issue (for example 'all students are lazy'), or to quickly make an assumption that enables us to make life easier (for example, if we see a car being driven erratically it is easier for us to prejudge that the driver is drunk than it is to actually take the trouble to find out for certain).

Allport also suggests that we form certain concepts that have not only a 'meaning', but also provide a 'feeling'. Take, for example, the concept of a 'Londoner'. The vast majority of us will know what a 'Londoner' is, but our individual concept of a 'Londoner' may stir an accompanying personal feeling that we may harbour towards 'Londoners' in general even though it is unlikely that we will have met every single one. In this sense our oversimplification of the world leads us to one of Allport's more significant points: that the formation of our generalisations is just as likely to lead to irrational generalisations, concepts and categories as it is to rational ones.

Similarly, Allport suggests that in order to further simplify our lives human beings naturally homogenise, often for no other reason than convenience, which in turn creates separateness among groups. According to Allport, humans tend to relate to other humans with similar presuppositions for the purpose of comfort, ease and congeniality. However, it is this separateness, coupled with our need to form generalisations and categories, which lays the foundations for psychological elaboration and the development of prejudice. Allport argues that people that stay separate have fewer channels of communication, are likely to exaggerate and misunderstand the differences between groups, and to develop genuine and imaginary conflicts of interests. It is this, according to Allport, that contributes largely to the formation of 'in-groups' and 'out-groups' and therefore to the *potential* formation and development of in-group loyalty and out-group rejection and the subsequent *potential* expression of prejudice and discriminatory behaviour towards those out-groups.

Although this is a simplified account of the foundations of prejudice as defined by Allport (readers are advised to see Allport, 1954, for a comprehensive account), it is from this basis, he argues, that people develop their prejudicial nature, both positive and negative. Allport also believed that any negative attitude tends somehow to express itself in action, although the degree of action will vary greatly based upon the individual and the strength of the prejudice. To illustrate this Allport (1954: 14) provides a five-point scale to distinguish different degrees of negative action. *Antilocution* is simply the discussion of prejudices, usually with like-minded friends. *Avoidance* represents a more intense prejudice and leads the bearer to avoid members of the disliked group, although he or she does not inflict direct harm upon them. *Discrimination* is where the prejudiced individual makes detrimental distinctions of an active sort. Under conditions of heightened emotion prejudice may lead to acts of violence or semi-violence, categorised as *physical attack*. Finally *extermination* marks the ultimate degree of violent expression of prejudice. Perhaps the best example of this is the Hitlerian programme of genocide during the Second World War.

Allport is at pains to point out that most people never go beyond antilocution, and those that do will not necessarily move progressively up the scale, but it does serve to call attention to the range of potential activities that may occur as a direct result of prejudiced attitudes and beliefs.

While remaining inspirational and hugely significant, Allport's work is now somewhat dated and therefore it is necessary to examine some of the issues relating to the origins and development of prejudice in light of some more recent theorising, much of which has been influenced by Allport's original ideas, particularly those concerning 'in' and 'out' groups.

Unsurprisingly a large number of competing perspectives exist, many of which are complex. What necessarily follows, therefore, is a simplified overview of some of the key theories and concepts put forward to explain the origins of prejudice. For a more comprehensive account, readers are advised to see Brown (1995) and Baron and Byrne (1994).

Stereotyping

A further important concept relating to the development and spread of prejudicial views is that of stereotyping. Brown (1995: 82) states that:

> To stereotype someone is to attribute to that person some characteristics which are seen to be shared by all or most of his or her fellow group members. A stereotype is, in other words, an inference drawn from the assignment of a person to a particular category ... [Stereotypes] are embedded in the culture in which we are raised and live, and they are conveyed and reproduced in all the usual socio-cultural ways – through socialisation in the family and at school, through repeated exposure to images in books, television and newspaper.

Furthermore, Allport (1954) and Brown (1995) both suggest an additional explanation for the origin of stereotypes that they term the 'grain of truth' theory. Here, stereotypes derive from some aspect of social reality, regardless of how tenuous that link to reality might be. For example, if a university lecturer has a class that he or she deems to be particularly lazy then that view may be attributed by that lecturer to his or her other classes, and perhaps indeed to the student population as a whole, which while true for some students can by no means be applied to all. Thus Allport (1954: 191) defines stereotypes as:

> an exaggerated belief associated with a category. Its function is to justify (rationalise) our conduct in relation to that category. The stereotype acts both as a justificatory device for categorical acceptance or rejection of a group, and as a screening or selective device to maintain simplicity in perception and in thinking.

The second half of the last sentence of Allport's definition clearly indicates that stereotypes act as schemas (cognitive frameworks) which Baron and Byrne (1994) suggest exert a strong effect on the ways in which we process social information. Essentially, they argue, stereotypes lead the bearer to pay attention to specific types of social information consistent with their prejudice, and to actively refute information that is inconsistent with their beliefs. Thus stereotypes lead to biased processing of social information that in turn leads to a situation whereby stereotypes become self-confirming and this in turn ensures continued prejudiced attitudes.

Closely related to this cognitive aspect of stereotyping is the notion of *illusory correlations* (Baron and Byrne, 1994). These consist of perceived relationships between different variables where no such relationship exist. In other words, illusory correlations occur where relatively rare events draw our attention and are remembered more readily than common events. For example, if we take the former Home Secretary Jack Straw's comments of a few years ago that 'Scousers are always up to something' (BBC News, 1999) it is possible that an illusory correlation suggesting a strong link between people from Liverpool and criminal activity will emerge. While it is undoubtedly true that a proportion of Liverpudlians are involved in crime, the illusory correlation may lead people to assume that the relationship between Liverpudlians and criminal activity is actually higher than it is. Furthermore, people may draw the conclusion that Liverpudlians commit crime simply because they are from Liverpool, and not because of other social and criminogenic factors. As Baron and Byrne (1994) suggest, individuals pay just enough attention to sources of information to form an erroneous perception of the social world.

Realistic conflict theory

Arguably the oldest theory of prejudice, realistic conflict theory proposes that prejudice stems from competition between social groups for valued commodities or opportunities (Bobo, 1983). The theory states that as the competition for scarce economic resources intensifies, members of competing social groups will come to view each other in increasingly negative terms that if permitted to fester will develop into emotion-laden prejudice (White, 1977). Hovland and Sears (1940), for example, argued that competition for scarce resources was particularly applicable in explaining the widespread lynchings of black Americans in the south of the country during a period of particularly harsh economic conditions endured in the fifty years or so prior to their research (Hovland and Sears, 1940). Similarly, the popularity of the Ku Klux Klan has historically peaked in times when white interests have come under a perceived threat from 'outsiders'. More recent research has also supported the link between economic decline and the development of prejudice, and the subsequent hostility and violence. Interestingly, however, these research studies tend to suggest that prejudice is only inevitable when group interests are threatened, and that when an individual's interests are similarly challenged the development of prejudice is far less certain. The role of economics and social strain will be examined further in Chapter 5.

Social categorisation and group dynamics

Tajfel (1982) suggests that the need for individuals to enhance their self-esteem by identifying themselves with specific social groups is significant in the development of prejudice. This identification inevitably leads people to view their social group (their in-group) as somehow superior to other, competing social groups and, since all groups form and develop in the same way, prejudice can arise out of the resulting clash of social perceptions. For example, whites may see themselves as superior to blacks, men as superior to women, and so on and vice versa.

On a smaller scale, when we examine the perpetrators of hate crimes in Chapter 5, one of the striking features of the available literature is that hate crimes are often committed by young people in groups. The impact of group dynamics is therefore significant. Gerstenfeld (2004) notes this point. She draws attention to numerous psychological studies that have highlighted the influence of social situations on human behaviour, and in particular the importance of group conformity, to the extent that many hate crimes may not in fact be motivated solely by prejudice, but rather by pressure to follow the group.

The key processes here, she suggests, are firstly *deindividuation*, whereby people feel more anonymous as part of a group and therefore take less responsibility for their actions. Second, through *identification* an individual will assume the attitudes and behaviours of a group that they find attractive or admirable and want to be a part of. Third, individuals often *internalise* the beliefs of the group that they admire and want to be a part of. Gerstenfeld suggests that the group attitudes can become a permanent and important part of the individual's belief system, and can be extremely resistant to change.

She also suggests that *internalisation* can occur because of *cognitive dissonance*. Here it is held that people actively avoid inconsistencies in their belief systems. Where inconsistencies emerge then individuals must either change their beliefs or develop new ones to avoid such inconsistencies. In other words, where beliefs are challenged by, for example, exposure to new information about the subject of those beliefs, then the prejudiced individual will necessarily change their ideas in a way that allows the original prejudice to remain justifiable. The existence of cognitive dissonance is reflected in research evidence that suggests that hate offenders will often denigrate or dehumanise their victim, or see them as deserving of their treatment, so as to justify their behaviour towards them (see Chapter 5).

The processes associated with social categorisation and group dynamics are significant in the development of prejudice and therefore, as Gerstenfeld suggests, are important for understanding why some people commit hate crimes.

Social learning and authoritarianism

Social learning theories suggest that attitudes such as prejudice are learned in childhood through contact with older and influential figures who reward children (with, for example, love and praise) for adopting their views (Pettigrew, 1969). Indeed, Brown (1995) suggests that children as young as three years of age are aware of two of the major social categories, namely gender and ethnicity, and from that age children can readily identify with some categories rather than others, and can demonstrate clear attitudinal and behavioural preferences among these categories. Similarly, Baron and Byrne explain that children also adopt and conform to the social norms of the group to which they belong, resulting in the development and expression of prejudicial attitudes towards others.

Allport (1954) suggested that in this regard parenting styles played an important part in the development of a child's prejudice. Allport drew particular attention to parents with authoritarian personalities, whom he argued raised their children in a strict, authoritarian and conservative way, with an emphasis on the significance of authority, power and inequality in society. These values are then reflected in the child's attitudes and behaviours towards those they perceive to be subordinate or weak. In this sense, then, hate offenders are not born but bred. As we shall see in Chapter 5, some of the specific literature on perpetrators of hate crimes highlights the influence of parents and other elders, and of localised social norms on the development of a child's prejudice.

However, Brown (1995) argues that using a child's 'passive absorption' of existing prejudices in society as an explanation of the development of prejudice is perhaps a little too simplistic. He suggests that other factors relating to a child's social and cognitive development may in fact hold the key to a more comprehensive understanding of the origins of prejudice (for an explanation of these, see Brown, 1995). Furthermore, the suggestion that hate offenders develop and learn their hatred, for example from their parents, might partially explain hate crime, but it can never fully do so given that at some point in history that hatred must have developed in the individual by some process other than simply learning it. In other words, where did the first hater in the family acquire their hatred? Other factors must necessarily play a part.

Illustrating 'everyday' prejudice

Two recent English studies by the advocacy group Stonewall (2003, 2004) have identified a number of factors that appear to have a bearing on the development of prejudice. The findings of these studies illustrate a number of the theoretical points raised in this chapter.

The first study in 2003 comprised a survey of a representative sample of 1,700 adults throughout England. Of that number, 64 per cent expressed a prejudice against at least one minority group. The second study, conducted for Stonewall by Valentine and McDonald (2004), comprised a series of focus groups and single interviews with the aim of providing a deeper understanding of the factors that cause and sustain prejudice against minority groups.

The results of the research indicated five types of prejudice characterised by different levels of social acceptability and by varying forms of justification. The first category is that of *unintentional prejudice.* This form of prejudice includes attitudes or behaviours that while unwitting nevertheless demonstrate ignorance of diversity on the part of the holder. The second category, *cathartic prejudice,* is characterised by views that are recognised as being less positive about minority groups and socially unacceptable, but crucially that are in some way justified by the holder in order to render them acceptable.

The third category identified by the Stonewall study is that of *benevolent prejudice.* This is defined as the expression of positive views about minority groups that may in reality produce negative or discriminatory consequences. For example, some of the views expressed in the research illustrated caring stereotypes of disabled people, labelling them as vulnerable or helpless. While such views are not intended to offend they are often negatively received. Stonewall suggest that benevolent prejudices demonstrate a lack of understanding of the reality of belonging to a minority group and may indeed play an important role in the social exclusion of the group in question because such labels often imply incompetence and powerlessness.

The fourth category is *banal prejudice.* Stonewall suggest that this type of prejudice is evident towards all minority groups. It is defined as mundane or implicit examples of less positive attitudes that may be intentional or unintentional but nevertheless pass unnoticed. The final category is *aggressive prejudice*, which is defined as open and explicit animosity that is often backed up by the threat of violence.

The research also identified nine separate factors likely to affect the development of the prejudices described above. The first, *perceived economic injustice*, is an issue that I shall return to in greater detail in Chapter 5, but the Stonewall study suggested that resentment concerning the allocation of, and competition for, scarce economic resources (housing, jobs, benefits, and so on) is frequently used to justify negative attitudes towards minority groups. Similarly, concerns relating to a *perceived cultural injustice* are also important in the development of prejudice. Participants in the Stonewall study spoke of being 'invaded' or 'taken over' by minority groups, and often cited differences between 'us' and 'them' in relation to religion, language, morality, values and so on. Some participants felt that white English culture was being undervalued and shown a lack of respect, while public resources unjustly supported minority cultures. In a somewhat contradictory fashion, many participants attempted to negate their prejudice by declaring that it is acceptable for minorities to engage in their cultural or religious practices so long as this occurs in private and not in public. Public displays of 'difference' were frequently greeted with hostility.

A further influencing factor to which I shall return in the final chapter is a *lack of personal contact*. Stonewall found that the two groups identified as the most threatening (asylum seekers and travellers) were the only groups that most participants had never come into contact with. Conversely, disabled people were the subject of the least hostility, but were also the minority group with which the participants had had the most contact. The implication here is that contact, familiarity and knowledge of the object of one's prejudice will lead to a reduction in that prejudice. As we shall see in Chapter 12, however, this is a far from certain outcome. Rather, it is the quality of the contact that is important, and *negative encounters* with members of minority groups can lead to powerful negative stereotypes across the group as a whole. Significantly, however, the Stonewall study found that positive encounters did not lead to positive stereotypes of the whole group. In such instances that particular individual member of the minority group was viewed favourably, rather than the group as a whole. In other words, negative encounters affect prejudice to a far greater extent than positive ones.

The role of the *media* was also found to be crucial in the development of prejudice among the participants of the Stonewall study. While the interviewees denied that the media caused any of the prejudices outlined above, the researchers were able to identify a strong media influence. The results suggest that the media (particularly television and newspapers) provide much of the material that individuals use to justify their beliefs, and that these media stories are frequently held to be accurate and independent thereby corroborating the individual's view. The media were also found to encourage latent feelings, of which anger and disgust were common, and to produce a sense of powerlessness among the white majority group that nothing could be done about their concerns. Examples of this can be found throughout this book, and we shall specifically return to this issue in Chapter 12.

Closely allied to media messages is the role of *rumour* in the development of prejudice. Stonewall's study suggested that participants lacked trust in official sources of information and gave far more credence to informal sources and gossip from friends and acquaintances. This is significant because discussing similar views with like-minded others serves to justify and reinforce the prejudices in question. In other words, negative prejudice becomes justifiable because 'other people think the same way'.

Stonewall's findings relating to *intergenerational prejudice* challenge many of the social learning theories. The results suggest that contrary to previous studies prejudice is *not* passed down through families and that intergenerational differences in views are common. The extent to which this finding is generalisable is, however, unclear. Some of the studies examining the perpetrators of hate crimes point to the influence of elder family members, friends and acquaintances on the development of negative prejudice in the young. This is an issue we shall explore further in Chapter 5.

The penultimate influencing factor that Stonewall identify relates to *the Church*, although little is said other than that some participants in the study identified the Church as promoting prejudiced and intolerant views. As we shall see in Chapter 3, however, religious views have been significant in the history of hate crime.

The final factor that Stonewall identify as important is that *prejudice serves positive ends for the prejudiced person*. For example, Stonewall suggest that homophobia may reinforce an individual's view of themselves as a good Christian, or that prejudice against asylum seekers enables the individual to reinforce their sense of community belonging. In other words, prejudice serves a rational function for the holder that in turn enables the justification of that prejudice.

The problem of hatred

In the last chapter I posed a simple question: *what is hate?* The theories and ideas presented in this chapter do not allow for a simple answer. Hate crimes as they are currently socially and legally constructed are rarely motivated by pure hate, but rather by prejudice, and this presents a number of problems. First, we do not know for certain what prejudice is, nor where it comes from, nor how it develops. But we do know that prejudice is entirely natural to the human condition and is perhaps even definitive of it. As Andrew Sullivan (1999) suggests, we are social beings. We associate and therefore we disassociate and one can't happen without the other. Humans necessarily differentiate.

Second, there are many kinds of prejudice that vary greatly and have different psychological dynamics underpinning them. This has important implications for responding to hate crimes, as we shall see in Chapter 12. Third, because prejudices are independent psychological responses they can be expressed in a bewildering number of ways, ranging from a mild dislike or general aversion to others to extreme acts of violence. But as Green, McFalls and Smith (2003: 27) suggest:

> It might take the better part of a lifetime to read the prodigious research literature on prejudice … yet scarcely any of this research examines directly and systematically the question of why prejudice erupts into violence.

When we talk about hate, we are really referring to prejudice, but despite the wide research that has been conducted into prejudice as a psychological phenomenon, we still cannot say with any degree of certainty why it is that prejudice leads to violent behaviour. If we don't know why prejudice results in violence, then we cannot fully know what causes hate crimes to occur. If we do not know what causes hate crimes to occur, how can we respond effectively to them?

Fourth, prejudice serves different functions for different people, and while these may not be entirely rational, they usually have their reasons and cannot be understood or condemned without knowing what these reasons are (Sullivan, 1999). We can condemn the crime, but not so easily the prejudice.

So when we talk about *hate crimes*, what is it that we mean by the word *hate*? If we define prejudice narrowly to include just emotionally intense hatred, then hate and hate crimes are fairly easy to understand. But if we define prejudice broadly, as we generally do, then understanding (and also responding to) hate crime becomes more complicated, and many of the problems outlined above become very real concerns. The word *hate* in effect becomes a catch-all term for a host of human emotions, behaviours and experiences. Should *hate* then refer to all of these or just some of them? As Sullivan (1999) argues, if hate is to stand for every variety of human prejudice then the war against hate will be so vast as to be quixotic. Yet if hate is to stand for a specific prejudice or set of prejudices then in the US it is probably unconstitutional, and elsewhere simply illiberal. A single, simple word, 'hate', in the context of hate crime in truth relates to a multitude of human emotions, beliefs and behaviours that should not and cannot be simply encapsulated in a single word.

The modern words we use to describe different varieties of hate are also unhelpful in explaining this wide range of human emotion. Terms such as racism, homophobia and anti-Semitism, Sullivan suggests, tell us the identities of the victims, but nothing of how they feel, and nothing about the identities, beliefs or feelings of the perpetrators. Such terms indicate and allege the existence of power structures in society but say nothing about individuals or the workings of human nature.

Furthermore, if prejudice is normal, can we, and indeed should we, attempt to regulate it? Crimes, yes, but prejudice? If everyone naturally has prejudices, then every crime might reasonably be a hate crime thus defined. And in any case, how do we prove that a person's prejudice, however strong, is the motivation behind a crime? And finally, how do we identify and decide which prejudices are unacceptable? As Jacobs and Potter suggest, victims as a whole are a protected group, but the very notion of hate crime, our specific focus on it and our differential response to it means that some victims are now more protected than others. But how did this happen? We shall consider this further in the next chapter when we examine the history of hate crime and its emergence as a contemporary social issue, but for now we should be clear that by intentionally selecting prejudices for official sanction, our response to prejudice is in itself prejudiced and discriminatory.

Concluding comments

The chapter has presented an overview of some of the key theorising regarding the nature and origins of prejudice and discrimination. Just as there is no single definition of prejudice, so we find there is little consensus for theories that seek to explain this phenomenon. Clearly, prejudice underpins hatred as a human emotion. However, it is important to note that it is not a crime to hold prejudicial views nor is it a crime to hate. Indeed, unless that prejudice manifests itself into some form of physical or verbal action how would we know that an individual harbours negative views towards another? Significantly, however, as noted by Allport (1954), prejudicial views will almost inevitably be expressed in word or deed at some point in time.

But, as Gaylin (2003) argues, to suggest that *hatred* is normal to the human condition is too simplistic an argument to sustain. After all, he suggests, even given the opportunity and freedom to hate or express hatred without obstruction or sanction, most of us would still not do so. Yet when this does occur, we do not know enough about prejudice to say how or why.

While prejudice is seemingly normal and universal, hatred, it seems, is not. But in our definitions of hate crime we often fail to make a clear distinction between prejudice and hate. We label offences as 'hate' crimes, but the application of this label is determined by whether or not an offence was motivated or aggravated by *prejudice*, or wholly or partially by deliberate hostility towards a particular group. There is little talk of hate anywhere and there is a danger that by focusing on prejudice rather than on hate as an extreme and problematic element, that in fact we are targeting the wrong thing, if indeed it can be targeted at all.

As Andrew Sullivan further suggests, the difference between hate and prejudice and prejudice and opinion and opinion and truth are so complicated and blurred that attempting to regulate 'hate' as we have defined it is fraught with practical and moral difficulties. Yet despite this, everything we have covered in this chapter is conveniently covered by this single word. So when we think about hate crimes, we need to ask some searching questions about what it is we really mean when we talk about 'hate'. Simply, the word 'hate' oversimplifies the problem, and tells us little about 'hate crime'.

Chapter 3

A history of hate crime

If hatred is underpinned by prejudice, and prejudice is a natural and possibly unavoidable part of the human condition, then it seems reasonable to suggest that negative human behaviour motivated by prejudice and hatred will be as old as humankind itself. In other words, actions that we have recently come to label as 'hate crimes' will have a lengthy history that extends far further back than society's contemporary interest in them. As we shall see, this is indeed the case. By citing examples from across the world to illustrate that these crimes can indeed be traced back over many centuries, this chapter will examine a selective history of hate crimes, before exploring the reasons behind the rise of hate crime as a contemporary social problem.

Hate crime: a modern phenomenon?

As we have seen, the term 'hate crime' and societal interest in it are relatively recent developments. One might perhaps assume therefore that hate crime is only a relatively modern social problem. This is not the case at all. Hate crimes, although not always termed as such, have a long and pervasive history.

In her examination of hate crimes in the United States, Carolyn Petrosino (1999) provides an interesting comparative analysis of past and present hate crimes. By defining hate crimes as 'the victimization of minorities due to their racial and ethnic identity by members of the majority', Petrosino selects a number of historical events suffered by Native Americans, African Americans and Asian immigrants. These events, which include lynching, slavery, near genocide and other significant prejudice-based actions, are selected on the basis of their moral offensiveness, racial or ethnic bias, intentional harming, and differential or discriminatory responses by the criminal justice system to the event. In her article Petrosino classifies 'historical' events as those that occurred before the emergence of hate crime legislation in the US in the early 1980s. Most of the events upon which her research is based, however, occurred during the seventeenth, eighteenth and nineteenth centuries.

By comparing historical events with contemporary hate crimes, Petrosino finds a number of striking similarities, and these are contained in Table 3.1. Petrosino explains that Factors A–D in the table concern the prevailing attitudes of the times and indicate a social and political environment that facilitated division and acts of intolerance against minority groups. Factors F and G relate to the identities of perpetrators and victims, while factor J denotes the links between organised hate groups (such as the Ku Klux Klan) and legitimate political organisations. The remaining factors are self-explanatory.

Table 3.1 illustrates that there are many similarities between historical and contemporary hate crimes that make for interesting reading. Many of these factors will be discussed throughout this book but it is worth taking a moment here to consider these findings.

Perhaps the most striking similarity is the presence of white racism in American society (Factor A). Petrosino argues that racism was as prevalent in the past as it is today, if indeed not more so, and evidence of this was found in institutional and cultural practices, with government policies encouraging institutional racism which in turn gave credence to existing prejudicial social attitudes. In other words, government actions in the past, most notably discriminatory legislation, served to 'legitimise' racist sentiment in wider society. This is significant, she suggests, because the existence of widespread racist attitudes is a powerful predictor of the occurrence of subsequent hate crimes.

Despite the research being of American origin, Factor A in fact links very closely with the findings of Rae Sibbitt (1997), whose analysis of race hate perpetrators remains one of the most comprehensive British analyses of hate offenders to date. In her study, as we shall see in Chapter 5, Sibbitt argues that racist violence is in part a logical and predictable expression of racist attitudes in society at large. Moreover, the presence of widespread prejudicial attitudes towards minority groups in Britain also has a lengthy history. In his biography of London, Peter Ackroyd (2000) presents evidence of prejudice, suspicion and brutality towards immigrants in the city dating back to the twelfth century. Put simply, prejudice in society towards minorities is nothing new, and neither is

Table 3.1 Comparisons between historical and modern hate crime factors

Common items from historical events	Historical events[a]	Modern events
Factor A: Perpetrator group reflected ideals similar to the mainstream	x	x
Factor B: Perpetrator group believed the target group to be inadequate, inferior and undeserving (culture of hate in place)	x	x
Factor C: Diversity not well tolerated	x	x
Factor D: Targets were identified as anti-American, blamed for the ills of the country, inflation, unemployment, crime, loss of morality	x	x
Factor E: Perpetrators rarely punished	x	–[b]
Factor F: Perpetrators were primarily white males	x	x
Factor G: Targets were primarily people of colour	x	x
Factor H: Hate crime was characteristically violent	x	–[c]
Factor I: Targeted groups have constitutional protections by federal and state law	–	x
Factor J: Hate groups were affiliated with legitimate political parties (or sought affiliation)	x	x[d]

a An event is considered historical if it is pre-hate crime legislation.
b Punishment is relatively lenient.
c Much of it is crime against properties, yet incidents of violence are increasing
d For example, extremists infiltrated the Buchanan and Dole organisations and the David Duke and Tom Metzger early runs on Democratic and Republican tickets.

Source: Petrosino (1999: 35).

hostility towards them. This should come as little surprise given the view expressed in the last chapter that prejudice is a normal human trait.

The *nature* of these prejudicial attitudes is reflected in Factors B, C and D. In light of the issues discussed in the previous chapter, it should come as little surprise that the majority, or *in-group*, view minorities, or *out-groups*, as 'inadequate, inferior and undeserving'. This fits neatly with many of the theories regarding the nature of prejudice, in that people will often naturally view those who are different to themselves in these, or similar, unfavourable terms. In turn, this may be expressed by some individuals through negative action of some kind directed at the subject of the prejudice, which become justifiable to the offender through the dehumanisation of their victim.

Factor C, according to Petrosino, has also held constant over time in the US. The extent to which this holds true for the UK is, however, more difficult to ascertain. Despite evidence of both historical and contemporary hostility towards 'outsiders', Roxburgh (2002) suggests that it is precisely the acceptance and embracing of diversity relative to other European countries that has played a key role in restricting the political success of Far Right organisations in Britain in recent times (see Chapter 6). However, as we shall see later in this chapter, Bowling and Phillips (2003) suggest that the period between the Second World War and the late 1970s was one of the most violently racist periods in British history. So while the expression of negative prejudice has existed over a long period of time in Britain, the extent to which we can say that *diversity* as a concept has not always been well tolerated here is perhaps open to some degree of debate.

Factor D illustrates the extent to which minority groups have been used as scapegoats for perceived societal problems in the US. This situation is mirrored in the UK, and both the history of scapegoating and the importance of (often erroneous) perception and stereotyping is highlighted by Ackroyd (2000: 707–8) who, in relation to Ashkenazi Jews arriving in London in the eighteenth century, notes that:

> … they were not welcomed, principally because they were poor. It was suggested that they would 'deluge the kingdom with brokers, usurers and beggars'; once more emerges the irrational but instinctive fear of being 'swamped'. They were also accused of taking jobs from native Londoners, although, since they could not be apprenticed to Christian masters, the fear of usurping available employment was a false one. But, in London, such fears have always been widely advertised and believed; in a society where financial want and insecurity were endemic among the working population, any suggestion of unfair labouring practices could arouse great discontent.

Ackroyd also notes similar hostility to Irish immigrants, traditionally typecast as the poorest of the poor, dating back to the early seventeenth century:

It is a question, in the modern term, of 'stereotyping' which afflicts all migrant populations. The irony, of course, is that certain groups seem unable to escape this matrix of false expectations and misperceptions ...This has always been one of the cries against the immigrants of London: that they are lazy, living off hand-outs like beggars, and thus demoralising the resident population. The assumption here must be that immigrants are a threat because they undermine the will to work, and provide examples of successful idleness; they are also receiving help or charity which, paradoxically, the native population claims by right to itself.

Ackroyd (2000) also suggests that identical stereotypes have been applied to modern-day immigrants in London and indeed similar views were common in the Stonewall study discussed in the previous chapter. As we shall also see in Chapter 5, the blaming of minority groups by the majority for social problems, and the perceived competition for scarce resources is often used as an explanation for the commission of hate crimes, or more appropriately for the creation of a climate from which hatred and bigotry can emerge. Ackroyd's statements above also raise the issue of an ironic paradox, namely that immigrants are often despised by members of the majority population because they are 'lazy scroungers' and simultaneously because they 'take all the jobs'.

Arguably the best contemporary example of negative stereotyping and blame in Britain is that of the widespread hysteria concerning asylum and illegal immigration in recent years, during which much of the media reported that these individuals were usurping finite resources at the expense of the native population and were involved in crime and other immoral and illegal activities. The climate of hostility is perhaps best reflected in the public protests held in opposition to immigration and the establishment of immigration centres for asylum seekers across parts of Britain over the past few years. Similarly, as we shall see in Chapter 6, the perception that immigrants in particular are 'culturally polluting' white areas and threatening the future of white people and white culture is a key ideology adopted by organised hate groups to justify their beliefs and actions.

With regard to the punishment of offenders in the US (Factor E), Petrosino argues that little has changed over time. Her analysis of historical evidence suggests that perpetrators acted with impunity and were rarely punished. As we shall see below, part of the reason for this was that the beliefs held by perpetrators were often shared by those in positions of power in the post-Civil War reconstruction era, and therefore many hate offences went unrecognised and unpunished.

Today, hate offenders and offences are recognised across all US jurisdictions, yet despite the enactment of legislation allowing penalty enhancements for hate crimes (Chapter 7) punishment remains relatively lenient. Reasons for this, as we shall see in Chapters 5 and 7, include the age of offenders, the nature of their offences and inherent difficulties in the successful application of the law. Similarly, in Britain there is evidence to suggest that legislation aimed at punishing racial and religious hatred is not being used as effectively and widely as it might. In addition, because of the high attrition rate in the criminal justice system in this country for hate offences, many hate offenders escape with little or relatively lenient punishment, or indeed without punishment at all (see Chapter 7).

Two other historically consistent factors relate to perpetrator and victim characteristics (Factors F and G). Petrosino identifies that perpetrators in the US are, and have been, predominantly white males, and victims are, and have been, typically non-white. Historically, this has also been the case in Britain, and successive sweeps of the British Crime Survey over the past twenty years or so have consistently demonstrated the disproportionate victimisation of ethnic minority groups across the country. The clarity of this situation is somewhat clouded by official police statistics, however, largely because of the modern definition of hate crime in this country that allows anyone to claim they are a victim.

Factor H indicates that hate crimes in the US are characteristically less violent today than they were in the past, although Petrosino warns that the violent nature of contemporary hate crimes is increasing. In the UK, statistical sources generally indicate that the vast majority of today's hate offences are what we might call 'low-level' offences of harassment and intimidation and that violent hate crime is relatively rare in comparison (see Chapter 4). There is, however, plenty of evidence to illustrate the violent nature of hate crimes in the past. For example, Jones (2000) refers to a number of lynchings and violent riots against blacks in Britain since the end of the First World War, and specifically highlights the extreme violence (and in particular murder) directed towards blacks between the early 1970s and the late 1990s.

However, while statistically the number of hate crimes has generally been increasing in the UK in recent years (most notably following the recent changes in definitions and police recording practices), the extent to which they are also becoming more violent, and more frequently violent, than they have in the past is difficult to determine. For example, recorded police statistics for racist incidents in 2002/3 showed an increase in racist harassment and racist incidents involving wounding, but a decrease in criminal damage and common assault when compared with the previous year (Home Office, 2004). Even when we take into account the limitations of statistical data (see Chapter 4), evidence of a real sustained increase in violent hate crimes is difficult to ascertain, particularly when we compare these statistics with evidence of the violence of the past.

It seems unlikely, however, that Britain and America are more violent today than they have been in the past, although we should perhaps take account of the fact that the documented hate of the past is arguably more clear-cut and easier to recognise and understand than the crimes labelled as 'hate' motivated today. But as Andrew Sullivan (1999: 10) contends, 'anyone who argues that America is as inhospitable to minorities and women today as it has been in the past has not read much history', and the same could be said for Britain. This of course raises questions as to why it has suddenly become necessary to take specific action against hate crimes. One suggestion is that contemporary concern with hate crimes may be a symbolic attempt to repair the damage of the past.

While the constitutional element of Factor I does not apply to the UK, the wider issue of protection under the law certainly does. In the UK, as we shall see below, specific legal protection against discrimination was not afforded to minority groups until relatively recently. Indeed, to date this protection remains selective and partial in terms of who and what has legal recognition, and is the subject of an ongoing and controversial academic and political debate, particularly in the US, but also to a lesser extent in the UK (see Chapter 8).

Finally, Petrosino highlights the desire held by hate groups to be associated with legitimate political parties (Factor J). We shall discuss the concept and process of 'mainstreaming' by hate groups in greater detail in Chapter 6, but the move by some hate groups towards mainstream politics has been, and remains, central to an understanding of organised hatred both in the US and in the UK, where this has been an area of significant activity and diversification in recent years.

To summarise, Petrosino's work illustrates a number of important themes, many of which are just as applicable to the UK as they are to the US: that the hate crime 'problem' is not a distinctly modern phenomenon and dates back to at least the seventeenth century (and much further in the UK); that hate crime has deep historical roots; that hate crime was at least as prevalent in the past as it is today; that most hate crimes relate to racial prejudice; that crime, victim and perpetrator characteristics have remained broadly similar over the past 400 or more years; and that there are many distinct parallels that can be drawn between past and present-day hate crimes over a range of indicators. In other words, criminal behaviour underpinned by negative prejudice has a legacy that extends far further back than contemporary societal concern with 'hate crime'. Petrosino's research and the examples included here (and also elsewhere in this book) lend support to our earlier contention, namely that hate crime is nothing new while society's response to it is.

The emergence of hate crime as a contemporary social issue

Perhaps the best way to chart the rise of any social problem is through the process by which it achieves legal recognition which represents the ultimate official acceptance of the need to respond. It is through this lens that I shall examine the rise of hate crime as a contemporary social issue, first in the US, and then in Britain.

Accounts of the historical origins of hate crime laws differ. Some authors suggest that such legislation has its strongest roots in the post-Second World War period in America and can be directly attributed to the success of the civil rights movement and the resulting 'identity politics' (Jacobs and Potter, 1998). While this is undoubtedly a significant area of interest for us, other authors have suggested that the origins of hate crime legislation can be traced back much further to the post-Civil War period and the creation of the US Constitution, and in some cases even further back than that. Indeed, the earliest legislation to bear any resemblance to modern hate crime laws was passed as far back as 1649 when the predominantly Catholic colony of Maryland enacted the Act of Tolerance which extended religious freedom to all who believed in Jesus Christ and the Trinity, and included provisions for the execution of those that did not (Streissguth, 2003).

However, the most significant historical period for our purposes is the time from the end of the US Civil War onwards and as such it is here that we shall begin in particular with an examination of the detailed historical accounts provided by Brian Levin (2002), Tom Streissguth (2003) and others, followed by Jacobs and Potter's (1998) consideration of the significance of the post-Second World War Civil Rights movement.

Brian Levin (2002) traces the birth of hate crime legislation to the time of the US Civil War and the drafting of the Constitution. He asserts that:

The recent emergence of a hate crime category on the legal

45

landscape came about only after other foundational issues relating to free expression, federalism, and the role of status characteristics were addressed ... the seeds for recognising and eventually protecting on the basis of status are found in a history that often, and conversely, used status as a pretext for unfair treatment and the deprivation of rights. (2002: 227–8).

The 'unfair treatment' to which Levin refers relates to the fact that, despite the Declaration of Independence stating that 'all men are created equal', early America was in all reality a society based on status with various rights not extended to poor white males, blacks, Native Americans and women. Of particular significance to Levin's historical analysis of hate crime legislation is the concept of slavery. While the original Constitution legitimised slavery, for Levin the subsequent effort to abolish it and thereby extend equal rights and status protection to hitherto unprotected groups represents a critical period that can be directly related to the development of the hate crime laws we see today.

While the practical worth of early challenges to slavery and other repressive acts was limited by the lack of willingness of both federal and local courts to recognise status-based equality, Levin points to three crucial Constitutional amendments that would ultimately have a profound effect on the plight of those persecuted for being 'inferior':

New, sweeping Constitutional and statutory reforms cut off the traditional legal and political methods Whites relied upon to deprive Blacks of their rights. Although their initial success was fleeting, these new, egalitarian postwar reforms laid the foundation for changes that extended into the latter half of the next century, including the emergence of hate crime laws. They represented a newfound validation of federal authority in the area of criminal law and supremacy of national power over that of the states to protect minorities from the harms of race-based violence and discrimination. (2002: 231)

This federal authority of which Levin speaks refers particularly to the Thirteenth, Fourteenth and Fifteenth Amendments to the US Constitution. The Thirteenth Amendment, ratified on 6 December 1865, officially abolished slavery. The Fourteenth Amendment, ratified on 9 July 1868, conveyed citizenship on 'all persons born or nationalised in the United States' thereby affording equal status, equal protection and civil rights to hitherto unprotected groups. Finally, the Fifteenth

Amendment, ratified on 3 February 1870, extended the right to vote to citizens previously denied because of their race, colour or because of their status as slaves. Crucially, each of the Amendments contained provision for Congress to enforce them through legislation. In theory then, the traditional relative autonomy of individual states to deprive minority groups of various rights and sustain discriminatory practices was undone.

Further to this, Levin highlights the significance of this 'enforcing' legislation and illustrates in particular the Force Act of 1871 which allowed for the imposition of criminal penalties for those who interfered with the Fifteenth Amendment, the Ku Klux Klan Act also of 1871 which allowed for the criminal punishment of government officials who interfered with protected civil rights or deprived citizens of the equal protection afforded to them under the Constitution, and the Civil Rights Act of 1875 that allowed equal access to public places and amenities regardless of colour, race or status.

Such legislation was significant because many southern states in particular were keen to hang on to the status-based society that existed prior to the Fourteenth Amendment, and consequently were refusing to recognise the Constitutional rights of traditionally disadvantaged groups. Moreover, the laws were an attempt to enforce a 'colour-blind' justice system, combat the vigilante actions of the Klan and end the viciously discriminatory practices of local criminal justice systems and public officials, most notably in the south (Streissguth, 2003). In essence then, these Amendments and supplementary laws laid the theoretical and practical foundations for modern hate crime legislation, but more than that, the debate that raged over the extent of state and federal control at this time would continue to characterise the progress of civil rights and hate crime legislation into the modern era.

Of course legislating against a set of behaviours is no guarantee that such actions will automatically cease and this was the case following the Amendments to the Constitution. In practice little changed for a considerable period of time and the dominant prejudices and status-based social hierarchies of American society prevailed. Indeed, these hierarchies were in effect upheld by the decisions of both federal and local courts throughout America, with only a handful of notable exceptions. This situation, according to Levin, had the rather curious effect of both increasing hatred and increasing the desire to respond to it:

Neither the Supreme Court nor the majority of the White American public was ready for the exercise of equality that many

Reconstruction-era laws promised … The fact of the matter is that the law and judicial decisions of the times reflected the prevailing supremacist social and political attitudes of much of the White American populace. These attitudes in turn led to a new wave of hatred and violence that continued into the next century. The continued violence prompted new attempts to curtail not only the brutality, but also the groups and messages that promoted it. (2002: 232–3)

In seeming stark contrast to the spirit of the Constitution, many southern states responded by introducing so-called 'Jim Crow' laws in the late 1870s. These laws had the effect of separating the black from the white population, thereby ostracising blacks in almost every area of public life. However, the laws survived constitutional challenges (and prevailed in many southern states until the 1960s) on the grounds that the facilities provided for blacks were 'separate but equal' to those available to whites (Streissguth, 2003). Nevertheless, such actions represented the continuing power of whites over blacks in a way that resembled the pre-Constitutional era, and effectively presented blacks as 'inferior' to whites.

The new wave of brutality to which Levin also refers accompanied the enactment of 'Jim Crow' laws and relates in particular to the lynching of Black Americans, increasingly common from the 1870s onwards, and later the emergence of race riots directed against the same, most notably in southern states as the Klan in particular sought to return to the 'old days' through the use of violence. Again, state legislation aimed at curtailing lynching was rarely enforced in the 16 states in which it was introduced between the 1890s and the 1930s, and federal legislation in respect of this failed to make the statute books at all owing to Senate opposition on three separate occasions between 1922 and 1940 (Foner and Garraty, 1991b, cited in Levin, 2002).

Although still fairly limited, greater success was achieved following a resurgence in the violent activities of the Ku Klux Klan from around 1915, with numerous states across the country enacting anti-Klan laws to meet this rising and spreading threat and, crucially, with the Supreme Court striking down a number of challenges to these laws. So abhorrent were some of these violent acts which characterised the 'hate landscape' well into the 1960s that:

The national media coverage given to Klan violence and police brutality against innocent African Americans decisively turned the social and political leanings of the nation toward heightened civil rights enforcement and legislative reform. (Levin, 2002: 235)

Thus the process that had begun with the US Constitution and had survived initial resistance and opposition in public and political circles had with the aid of extreme hate violence laid the foundations for the hate crime laws we find today.

While the issues identified by Levin and described briefly above clearly laid the foundations for hate crime legislation in the US, a significant factor in the process was the emergence and success of the civil rights movement in the 1960s and the resulting 'identity politics'. Jacobs and Potter (1998: 5–6) state that:

> the term 'identity politics' refers to a politics whereby individuals relate to one another as members of competing groups based upon characteristics like race, gender, religion, and sexual orientation. According to the logic of identity politics, it is strategically advantageous to be recognised as disadvantaged and victimised. The greater a group's victimisation, the stronger its moral claim on the larger society ... The current anti-hate crime movement is generated not by an epidemic of unprecedented bigotry but by heightened sensitivity to prejudice and, more important, by our society's emphasis on identity politics.

The civil rights movement, they suggest, forced a shift in thinking in relation to the treatment of certain minority groups. Indeed Jacobs and Potter (1998) argue that the resulting Civil Rights Act of 1968 can be considered a precursor to modern hate crime laws. They suggest that section 245 of the Act marked the beginning of the modern civil rights movement by specifically enumerating federal, state and local activities and protecting participants involved in those activities from victimisation and discrimination on the grounds of certain prejudices and bigotry.

Simply, then, Jacobs and Potter argue that by raising the issues of disadvantage and discrimination based on certain prejudices held in American society, the civil rights movement played a central role in the emergence of identity politics (the fight for recognition as a disadvantaged minority group) that characterise American, and now also to a lesser extent British, society and politics today.

Of course the civil rights movement focused on the plight of ethnic minority groups; however, the resulting identity politics can be seen as a catalyst for the emergence of claims by other disadvantaged minority groups to be officially recognised as such and afforded equal rights, status and protection. This in turn has the effect of fuelling the attention paid to the situation and victimisation of minority groups thereby maintaining discrimination as a social and political issue in need of national attention. This increased official recognition of minority groups, and the resulting political lobbying and subsequent symbolic legislation, can be viewed as a key motivating factor in the rise of hate crime as a social and political issue, as can the political appeal of championing a disadvantaged group.

In relation to these issues, Jacobs and Potter (1998) also note something of a domino effect characterised by a general shift in social attitudes relating to prejudice and a greater tolerance and understanding of diversity in society among the majority population. Conversely, however, this rise in public awareness has, according to Jacobs and Potter, also resulted in an apparent escalation of 'hate' attacks, thereby reinforcing the need for strong legislation, although the extent to which this apparent escalation can be verified is debateable given the findings of Petrosino's research above.

In essence, then, the emergence of hate crime as a contemporary social issue in the United States can be traced back to the Constitution and its goal of achieving status-based equality for all American citizens. The process clearly stumbled at a number of junctures along the way but progressive and gradual changes to the social, political and legal horizons, and notably the success of the civil rights movement since the Second World War, have played a key role in challenging attitudes and discrimination in a number of social spheres.

Despite having a longer history of hate motivated violence, and despite subscribing to various anti-discrimination legislation for several decades (see Chapter 7), the focus on hate crime in Britain is much more recent than in the US. Indeed, the emergence of hate crime as a contemporary social issue in Britain is somewhat married to the recent history of race and racism in this country.

As we have already seen in this chapter, crimes motivated by racial prejudice in Britain have a long history, yet official recognition of the problem can be traced back to as recently as the early 1980s. Bowling and Phillips (2003) suggest that this is largely because the period from the Second World War to the late 1970s, as we have already noted, represented one of the most viciously racist periods in British history during which many British people strongly resented and resisted the immigration and integration of blacks and Asians into the country. Despite evidence to the contrary, the British government persistently denied the racist content of much of this violence and attempted to downplay its impact on ethnic minority communities (Bowling and Phillips, 2003).

Bowling and Phillips state that evidence of racist victimisation collected by campaigning groups in the late 1970s and early 1980s eventually led the government and the police to officially acknowledge the severity of the situation in a Home Office report published in 1981. This suggests that the 'identity politics' that Jacobs and Potter see as central to the modern concern with hate crime also played a role in its emergence in Britain. But the problem of racism was further highlighted in the early 1980s by public disorder across the country between minority groups and their supporters and the Far Right and the police (Bowling and Phillips, 2003).

In addition, the re-emergence of victimology as a significant social science in its own right, and in particular the subsequent development of victim surveys, began to reveal the extent, nature and impact of racist victimisation. Similarly, the problem of racist victimisation was further highlighted by other surveys, studies, inquiries and official reports throughout the 1980s and the 1990s. Together, these issues ensured that racism could no longer be ignored, particularly as earlier official denials of the problem were justified by an apparent lack of reliable information (Bowling and Phillips, 2003).

However, arguably the most significant single event that was ultimately to propel the problem of violent racism to the top of the political and social agenda was the murder of black teenager Stephen Lawrence in April 1993. At approximately 22:30 on the evening of 22 April 1993, 18-year-old Stephen and his friend Duwayne Brooks were subjected to an unprovoked racist attack by five white youths in Well Hall Road, Eltham, South-east London. Stephen Lawrence was stabbed twice during the attack and died shortly afterwards. The police investigation failed to bring the killers to justice and was later to be condemned as flawed and incompetent and the police labelled as institutionally racist (Macpherson, 1999). At the time, however, the Conservative government rejected a request from Stephen's parents for a public inquiry into their son's death and the failure of the police investigation.

In the same year that Stephen Lawrence was murdered, the first calls for racially motivated violence to be made a specific offence were made by the Commission for Racial Equality, but these calls were also rejected by the Conservative government, as were the Commission's calls for a strengthening of existing anti-discrimination legislation. Despite these rejections, John Major, the then Prime Minister, strongly condemned racism in a speech to the Board of Deputies of British Jews and tackling racist offending was also named as the top priority of the Metropolitan Police Service in London (Bowling and Phillips, 2003).

Nevertheless, Bowling and Phillips (2003) note that in reality very little practical action occurred for a number of years. However, they suggest, support for action against racism was present among a number of Labour backbench Members of Parliament, and with the then Shadow Home Secretary Jack Straw, who expressed hopes in the run up to the 1997 general election that, if elected, a public inquiry into the death of Stephen Lawrence would be possible. Following their landslide election victory, Jack Straw announced a full public inquiry into the matters arising from the death of Stephen Lawrence to be conducted by Sir William Macpherson of Cluny.

The Stephen Lawrence Inquiry was by no means the first report to critically examine the issues of race, policing and criminal justice. However, Sir William Macpherson's report into matters arising from the death of Stephen Lawrence has been described as 'the most radical official statement on race, policing and criminal justice ever produced in this country' (McLaughlin, 1999: 13).

The Stephen Lawrence Inquiry was divided into two parts. Part one was concerned with the matters arising from the death of Stephen Lawrence and part two with the lessons to be learned for the investigation and prosecution of racially motivated crimes. While many of the findings of the inquiry will be examined in Chapter 10, it is sufficient for our purposes here to note that the inquiry concluded that the investigation was 'marred by a combination of professional incompetence, institutional racism and a failure of leadership by senior officers' (Macpherson, 1999: 46.1). The inquiry team made 70 recommendations, including a new Ministerial Priority for all police services:

> to increase trust and confidence in policing among minority ethnic communities. (1999: Rec. 1)

In accepting the findings of the inquiry, and by accepting the vast majority of the inquiry's recommendations, the issue of race was placed firmly at the top of the political agenda. Crucially, however, the inquiry went beyond policing to, and made a number of recommendations for, responding to racist violence in much broader terms through, for example, the education system. This meant, of course, that the focus on racism wasn't simply restricted to the police, but also to other organisations. The inquiry, and the sharp public focus that it drew, necessitated governmental action against racism as a matter of urgency.

As we shall see in Chapter 10, the inquiry resulted in a number of significant changes to policing policies and practices. One key change was the adoption of the new definition of racially motivated offending that was discussed in Chapter 1 of this book, and also the publication of the Association of Chief Police Officers' Guide to Identifying and Combating Hate Crime (2000). In identifying the post-Lawrence era as a window of opportunity for change, and with a desire to improve standards of service delivery to minority groups other than just those identifiable by race, the ACPO guide incorporated the other strands of diversity noted in Chapter 1. This approach has led to the wider definitions of 'hate crime' that we also examined in Chapter 1.

In addition to announcing the inquiry into Stephen Lawrence's death, the Labour government also acted where the previous government had failed to do so, by implementing its pledge to make racially motivated crimes a specific offence with the introduction of the Crime and Disorder Act in 1998. Burney and Rose (2002) suggest, however, that political pressure for specific legislation had been growing since the 1980s. They highlight the fact that two private member's bills, the last in 1992, had been unsuccessful and despite the Parliamentary Home Affair Committee's endorsement of the need for specific legislation in 1994, the then Home Secretary Michael Howard rejected them on the grounds that such offences could be adequately dealt with by existing criminal law (a point to which I shall return in Chapter 8).

Nevertheless, following the election of the Labour government in 1997 it was concluded that racially aggravated incidents were sufficient in volume and seriousness to warrant specific legislation to tackle them. The Act caters only for racial (and by later amendment religious) prejudice, and according to Iganski (1999a), in addition to being a direct response to public and political concerns regarding a consistent rise in racist incidents in England and Wales throughout the 1990s, was also consistent with the implementation of similar legislation in many European countries as a result of identical fears.

The original Crime and Disorder Act 1998 has been widened to include religiously motivated offences through the Anti-terrorism, Crime and Security Act of 2001 and lesser provisions to incorporate crimes motivated by homophobia and disability bias were enacted in the Criminal Justice Act of 2003. Furthermore, the Serious Organised Crime and Police Bill before Parliament in 2005 contains proposals for a new offence of incitement to religious hatred. These laws will be the focus of further attention in Chapter 7, along with their American equivalents.

Concluding comments

This chapter has demonstrated that offences that we now label as hate crimes have a long and pervasive history, and countless more examples than just those that are included here can be readily found. In addition, it would appear that many of the characteristics of hate crimes have remained broadly constant over time. In short, hate crime is nothing new. What is relatively new, however, is societal concern with hate crime, and this chapter has suggested that there are a number of different reasons underpinning the emergence of hate crime as a contemporary social problem in need of specific attention.

In Britain, the legislative widening of the net beyond the original provisions for race contained within the Crime and Disorder Act is a complex combination of 'identity politics' and the need to respond to widespread concerns resulting from national and world events. Notable events that have influenced the inclusion of other prejudices in legislation include, for example, the racially and homophobically motivated nail bombings in Soho in London in 1999 (see Chapter 1) and also the attacks on the US on 11 September 2001 and the subsequent focus on religious extremism and retaliatory attacks on members of the Muslim faith.

One key issue that has also contributed to contemporary concern with hate crimes that was briefly touched upon in this chapter is that of the disproportionate victimisation of minority groups. While 'identity politics' has to a certain extent played a key role in the recognition of the plight of some minority groups in British law, much of this fight for recognition is based on very real concerns about disproportionate victimisation. Part of the justification for introducing specific legislation against hate therefore, as we shall see in Chapter 8, is the suggestion that hate crimes have a greater impact on the victim than similar crimes committed without the hate element. A consideration of hate victimisation will therefore be the subject of the next chapter.

Chapter 4

Hate crime victimisation

In Chapter 1 we examined various attempts to define and conceptualise hate crime, and suggested that the outcomes of these would have considerable bearing on just how much hate crime there is in society. With this issue firmly in mind, in this chapter we shall explore various attempts to measure the extent of hate crime victimisation and examine the many complexities associated with doing so.

In addition we shall look at attempts to uncover information concerning other aspects of victimisation: who is victimised, how often, when, where and in what ways? Furthermore, we shall seek to uncover the impact that hate crime has on its victims and the wider community, and also to establish just how confident we can be about accurately answering these questions with the information presently available to us.

As such this chapter will firstly examine the extent and nature of hate crime in the United States, followed by the corresponding picture in England and Wales. The limitations associated with measuring hate crime will also be examined. The chapter will then move on to discuss the emerging body of qualitative research that is beginning to shed light on the apparent unique impact of hate crime both on individual victims and the communities to which they belong.

The extent of hate crime in the US

Barbara Perry (2001) suggests that there are few endeavours so frustrating as trying to estimate and establish the extent of hate crime. Part of the reason for this, as we saw in Chapter 1, is that hate crime is essentially a social construction and that the size of the problem depends almost entirely on how we define and conceptualise it (Jacobs and Potter, 1998).

In the United States the collection of national hate crime data has been a legal requirement under the Hate Crime Statistics Act (HCSA) since 1990. The data is collected and published annually in the Uniform Crime Report (UCR) Program by the Federal Bureau of Investigation (FBI). The FBI collects data from law enforcement agencies across the US on eleven criminal offences (murder and non-negligent manslaughter, forcible rape, aggravated assault, simple assault, intimidation and robbery, burglary, larceny-theft, motor vehicle theft, arson, and destruction, damage and vandalism to property) committed against persons, property or society that are motivated in whole or in part by one of five officially designated prejudices (race, religion, disability, sexual orientation and ethnicity/national origin) (FBI, 2003).

While the original intention of the HCSA was to provide an accurate picture of hate crime across America, Perry (2001) suggests that that there are numerous shortcomings associated with the data collection that ensure that the figures are far from accurate. Unsurprisingly given our discussion in Chapter 1, the key limitation that Perry identifies relates to the narrow definition used by the HCSA. Only data relating to the five prejudices and eleven offences are officially collected, meaning that other criminal offences and non-criminal incidents are not counted, and neither are offences motivated by prejudices other than the five listed. In this sense only certain hate crimes are counted, while other offences that might have a strong claim to be included are not.

In addition, Perry questions inconsistencies between the agencies reporting offences to the UCR. What is and what is not classified as a hate crime varies greatly across different US states and Perry suggests that this has important implications for law enforcement agencies in terms of collecting and recording relevant data for the UCR. In short, the way that hate crime is defined by different jurisdictions greatly affects what, and how much of what, is recorded in the official figures. This situation is further amplified by inconsistencies in the extent of law enforcement training and their subsequent ability to recognise offences as being hate motivated. In other words, hate motivation is subjective and open to interpretation, which in turn affects what appears in the statistics.

Furthermore, the UCR figures are also susceptible to the limitations that affect all official crime statistics. Most significant, as we shall see in more detail later in this chapter, is the issue of underreporting and the resultant 'dark figure' of hate crime. Official statistics consist predominantly of incidents reported to the authorities by the public. This of course means that incidents that occur but are not reported to the authorities are unlikely to appear in the official statistics and will therefore remain largely unknown. This is crucial because there is evidence to suggest that this 'dark figure' of unreported crime is significantly higher for hate crimes than for other types of offences for a variety of reasons that we shall explore in due course (Weiss, 1993; Perry, 2001).

A final limitation of the UCR figures identified by Perry concerns qualitative shortcomings. By this she means that little is known about the qualitative elements of hate crimes because the statistics simply provide us with quantitative information. In other words, the statistics tell us that a certain number of defined 'events' occurred, but very little else in qualitative terms about these 'events'.

Nevertheless, despite these identified shortcomings and the need to question both what is counted and how it is counted, the official figures are not without their uses. Perry suggests that the UCR represents the most comprehensive database of hate crimes in the US and is potentially useful in identifying general trends and patterns. With this in mind, let us briefly examine the latest available UCR data.

The FBI (2003) state that 12,073 law enforcement agencies reported 7,462 hate crime incidents involving 8,825 offences (under UCR counting rules an incident can involve more than one offence) in 2002. Of these 7,462 incidents 48.8 per cent were motivated by racial bias, 19.1 per cent by religious bias, 16.7 per cent by sexual orientation bias and 0.6 per cent by mental or physical disability bias. Of the total number of offences, 67.5 per cent were crimes against the person, 32 per cent were crimes against property, and 0.6 per cent were crimes against society.

By offence category the UCR data shows that intimidation represented the most common offence (35.2 per cent of the offence total), followed by destruction/damage/vandalism (26.6 per cent), simple assault (20.3 per cent), aggravated assault (11.7 per cent) and the remaining offences collectively totalling 6.3 per cent.

Of the number of offences committed, 4,393 were motivated by racial bias of which 67.5 per cent were motivated by anti-black bias, 20.2 per cent by anti-white bias and 6.1 per cent by bias against Asians or Pacific Islanders; 4.6 per cent of the racial offences targeted groups comprising mixed races and 1.5 per cent targeted American Indians or Alaskan Natives (FBI, 2003).

In terms of religiously motivated offending, 65.9 per cent of the 1,576 reported offences were motivated by anti-Semitism and 10.8 per cent by Islamophobia; 13.8 per cent were motivated by bias against unspecified religious groups, 3.7 per cent were anti-Catholic, 3.6 per cent were anti-Protestant, 2 per cent against groups of multiple religions, and 0.2 per cent motivated by anti-atheism or anti-agnosticism.

The UCR data shows that in 2002, 1,464 offences were motivated by bias against sexual orientation. Of this total 65.4 per cent were targeted against male homosexuals. Of the remainder, 17.7 per cent were motivated by anti-homosexual violence, 14.1 per cent by anti-female homosexuality, 1.8 per cent by anti-heterosexual bias and 1 per cent by anti-bisexual bias.

Of the 1,345 offences motivated by bias against ethnicity or national origin, 44.7 per cent were motivated by anti-Hispanic bias with 55.3 per cent of offences relating to other anti-ethnic/national origin bias. In contrast, just 47 offences were motivated by disability bias, with 57.4 per cent of that number motivated by mental disability bias.

Other information contained in the 2002 UCR indicates 11 hate motivated homicides (4 attributed to race, 4 to sexual orientation, 2 to ethnicity/national origin and 1 to religious bias), 8 forcible rapes and 130 hate motivated robberies. Furthermore, the UCR shows that 29.5 per cent of hate crime incidents occurred at homes or residences, 20 per cent in roads or streets, 10.6 per cent at schools or colleges, 6.2 per cent in parking lots or garages, 21.6 per cent occurred in a variety of locations and in 12.3 per cent the location was unknown.

To summarise, the 2002 UCR demonstrates that race is the most common motivation for hate crime in America. African Americans represent the largest victim group, followed by Jews and homosexual males. The statistics also show that hate crimes are predominantly offences against the person rather than offences against property, and involve disproportionate physical intimidation and individual harm to victims as compared with comparable non-bias street crimes (Perry, 2001). Interestingly, however, the statistics also suggest that the majority of hate crimes are what we might term 'low-level' offences (intimidation, harassment, common assault, criminal damage, etc.) as opposed to what might on the surface be deemed to be more serious crimes (murder, robbery, rape, etc.). Moreover, previous UCRs have demonstrated that many of these issues have remained broadly consistent over a number of years (Perry, 2001).

Nevertheless the UCR statistics represent an underestimation of the 'true' volume of hate crime. This is demonstrated by data collected by various victim advocacy groups across the US. For example, in their annual audit of anti-Semitic incidents, which draws upon official figures and information provided by victims, law enforcement officers and community leaders, the Anti-Defamation League counted 1,559 incidents in 2002, and 1,557 in 2003. Similarly, the Antiviolence Project, an advocacy group for the lesbian, gay, bisexual and transgender (LGBT) community, estimated 1,903 homophobic incidents in 2002, as opposed to the 1,464 counted by the UCR in that year, and recorded a rise of 8 per cent to 2,051 incidents in 2003.

The extent of hate crime in England and Wales

In England and Wales the situation is different to that in the US. Whereas the US publishes official national hate crime figures, here we do not. Annual figures pertaining to racially motivated offending are published under section 95 of the 1991 Criminal Justice Act, but other forms of hate crime are not counted as they are in the US. As such, despite the limitations of the national US figures, it is even more difficult to establish anything like an official national estimate for the UK. That being said, however, the 43 police forces of England and Wales separately record hate crimes under the ACPO definitions (most commonly those relating to race and homophobia), recommended by, and adopted after, the Stephen Lawrence Inquiry (see Chapter 1).

Once again, the definition of hate crime plays a crucial role here. The broad generic definition refers to any prejudice (unlike the US which specifically identifies five) and any incident (which need not be a crime) and gives no indication of how strong the causal link between the prejudice and the offending behaviour must be. The two definitions of race and homophobia effectively remove the need to establish any causal link at all because an offence is officially recorded as a 'hate crime' if anyone believes it to be so. The result is that the number of officially recorded hate crimes in England and Wales is vastly different to the US, thereby rendering any useful comparison effectively impossible.

The latest figures show that the 43 police services in England and Wales recorded 48,525 racist incidents in 2002/3. In comparison, 12,073 US law enforcement agencies recorded 4,393 racist incidents over a similar period. The situation in England and Wales is complicated further by the legal recognition of racially aggravated offences within the Crime and Disorder Act 1998. Within these tighter definitional confines (see Chapter 1) the police recorded 31,034 racist *offences*. Of these, the statistics show that 54 per cent were offences of harassment, 14 per cent other wounding, 14 per cent common assault and 18 per cent criminal damage (Home Office, 2004). Thus, while the total figures are vastly different, the pattern in terms of offence type is not too dissimilar to that experienced in the US.

The breakdown of incidents over time also reveals some interesting insights into the social construction of hate crime victimisation. The appendix at the end of the book shows the recorded racist incidents for all police force areas between 1996/97 and 2002/3. Upon examination of the data, two points are immediately apparent. First, there is a huge geographic variation in the numbers of incidents recorded by the police. Broadly speaking, recorded racist hate crime is disproportionately present in metropolitan areas, most notably in London, the West Midlands, Greater Manchester and West Yorkshire, with rural areas recording far fewer incidents. The most obvious explanation for this is the greater concentration of minority groups in large cities, but it may also reflect different police practices and priorities.

The second interesting point relates to the sudden increase in recorded racist incidents between 1998/99 and 1999/2000. The most notable rise occurred within the Metropolitan Police area that saw recorded incidents rise from 11,050 to 23,346 incidents in the space of a year. In that period the Stephen Lawrence Inquiry was published, the new definitions cited in Chapter 1 were adopted and police attention was firmly on these types of crimes, as we shall see in Chapter 10. The combined result was that recorded incidents of racist hate crime rose sharply, demonstrating the sensitivity of hate crime to external influence and change.

Also of interest here is the percentage change from 2001/02 to 2002/03 with the various police forces experiencing considerable variation in their recorded figures. Overall there was an 11 per cent decrease in recorded racist incidents, but some police forces experienced significant increases. Most notably, Dorset Constabulary saw a 277 per cent increase, Humberside a 250 per cent increase and Wiltshire a 177 per cent increase, although the total number of incidents is still relatively low. Conversely, the two Yorkshire constabularies saw the largest percentage decrease (75 per cent and 71 per cent), followed by Staffordshire and Cheshire (59 per cent and 55 per cent respectively). However, referring back to Barbara Perry's criticisms, the statistics tell us nothing of why these changes have occurred in these areas.

Beyond these details, however, the official section 95 statistics for England and Wales tell us very little about racist victimisation, and nothing officially exists, at least not that is nationally collated, in terms of other forms of hate offending. For this we have to turn to the figures collected by individual police services which are not collected nationally. Also, because hate crime data are not always readily published by police services, and not all forces have historically recorded hate crimes other than those involving race or homophobia, it is difficult to establish the extent of recorded hate crimes across the 43 police services. Instead, we shall consider some of the data collected by the Metropolitan Police Service (MPS) to serve as an illustrative example.

In the 2003/4 financial year the MPS recorded 15,319 racist incidents of which 13,203 were notifiable offences (Hall, 2004). By category of offence, 10,484 were offences of violence against the person, 25 were sexual offences, 193 were robberies, 2,128 were offences of criminal damage and 372 were classified as other notifiable offences. In relation to these offences, 14,786 victims were identified, of which the largest victim group were Indian/Pakistani (4,810), followed by African/Caribbean (4,388), White European (3,230), Dark European (996), Arabic/Egyptian (441) and Chinese/Japanese (310), with 611 unknown.

In the same financial year the MPS recorded 1,536 homophobic incidents of which 1,245 were notifiable offences. Of these 929 were offences against the person, 185 were criminal damage and 131 other notifiable offences. There were 1,375 victims identified, with White Europeans formally by far the largest victim group (988) and African/ Caribbeans the next largest (156).

Again, while these figures give us quantitative data, they do not produce much qualitative information. However, research by Docking, Kielinger and Paterson (2003) has examined in further detail the information contained within the MPS's crime records. In addition the research took a 'snapshot' of one day (22 March 2001) and examined the data collected on that day. The results have revealed some interesting findings concerning common themes and patterns associated with hate crime across London.

Briefly, the general results show that male victims of racist incidents report proportionately more incidents involving violence whereas female victims report more incidents involving threats and harassment. They also show that in the majority of racist incidents *where the police have recorded* the relationship between the victim and the suspect (66 per cent) the suspect is not known to the victim. However, in examining the data on the 'snapshot' day, information *provided by the victim* suggests the two-thirds of incidents are perpetrated by people known to them, most notably by school children (in 18.4 per cent of cases), neighbours (18.4 per cent), colleagues (14.3 per cent) and local youths (8.2 per cent). The general exception to this is in the case of GBH or murder, which are more likely to be committed by strangers.

The research also reveals that almost two-thirds of racist incidents occur at or near the victim's home, at or near their place of work, and at or near their school. In other words racist victimisation generally occurs as victims go about their daily lives. Furthermore, more than a fifth of racist incidents occur between 3 pm and 6 pm, and of these a third of suspects are under 16 years of age. As we shall see in Chapter 5, this finding is consistent with other research concerning the age groups of hate offenders. In addition, almost half of the victims were described as 'school children' in the crime reports, and a further one in seven victims worked either in schools or shops (Docking, Kielinger and Paterson, 2003).

Docking, Kielinger and Paterson suggest that for recorded racist incidents the commonly held belief that suspects are often not known to the victim is inaccurate. In contrast, their research shows that suspects are in fact usually known to the victim. Their research also demonstrates that the victim was with their family or with others in more than half of the recorded incidents that occurred, and as we shall see later in this chapter, this has important implications in terms of the pervasive impact of hate crimes.

In addition to racist incidents, Docking, Kielinger and Paterson's research also examined faith hate crimes. Between January 2002 and March 2003 the MPS recorded 394 faith hate incidents. Of these almost half related to Islamophobia and a third to anti-Semitism, and predominantly involved violence, threats or harassment, or criminal damage. Five per cent of incidents were directed at buildings as opposed to individuals, but the latter had similar characteristics to racist incidents. Sixty per cent of incidents targeted males and two thirds resulted in no physical injury, while 40 per cent of incidents occurred in or near the victim's home. Interestingly, however, 80 per cent of incidents were committed by unknown perpetrators, perhaps reflecting the targeting of public or religious buildings. Finally, 60 per cent of incidents were classified as faith hate crimes because of their specific verbal or written content (Docking, Kielinger and Paterson, 2003).

Finally, and crucially, the research also revealed key information about repeat victimisation. Initial information contained in the sample of crime reports suggests that 12.6 per cent of victims had reported a previous racist incident in the previous 12 months. However, subsequent additional information and information from victim's own accounts show that 63 per cent of racist hate crime victims were repeat victims. Docking, Kielinger and Paterson suggest that this implies that the level of ongoing and potentially escalating incidents experienced by victims is much higher than the level of repeat victimisation recorded in the official police statistics. Indeed, repeat victimisation is a key issue to which I shall return shortly.

Clearly, then, despite the limitations of official statistics, they are not without their uses. However, as has already been suggested with the UCR figures, official crime statistics are a poor measure of the 'true' extent of any crime, and to uncover some of this 'dark figure' of unreported crime we must again turn to other sources.

The most comprehensive estimate of crime available in the UK is the British Crime Survey (BCS) that records people's experience and perception of crime using a representative sample of respondents (Home Office, 2004). The BCS estimates that 206,000 racially motivated incidents occurred in 2002/03, of which 135,000 involved personal crime and 71,000 involved crimes against households (Home Office, 2004). Clearly, when compared with recorded police figures, the BCS findings support the view that racist hate crime is vastly underreported to the authorities.

However, to estimate the extent of other forms of hate crime we have to search elsewhere. Useful information can often be obtained through victim advocacy groups. For example, with reference to homophobic hate crime, Stonewall (2004) state that their 1995 study of violence against lesbians and gay men involving over 4,000 respondents demonstrated that one in three gay men and one in four lesbians had experienced at least one violent attack between 1990 and 1995. The study also found that the problem was worse for young lesbians, gay men and bisexuals. For those aged under 18, 48 per cent of respondents had experienced violence, 61 per cent had been harassed and 90 per cent had experienced verbal abuse.

Stonewall (2004) also state that a national survey conducted in 1999 found that 66 per cent of 2,500 respondents had been victims of a homophobic incident but that only 18 per cent of these had been reported to the authorities and significantly, that 70 per cent were fearful of reporting future incidents. Similarly, Stonewall cite a study by GALOP (2001) that found similarly high levels of incidents committed against lesbian and gay black and minority ethnic groups. The sample size is not stated but nevertheless the study found that 68 per cent had experienced homophobic abuse and 81 per cent had experienced racist abuse.

The extent of other forms of hate crime is arguably more difficult to assess. Because societal focus has predominantly been on issues of race and more recently homophobia, data for offences motivated by other forms of prejudice is harder to come by and not so comprehensively collected. Attempting to assess the extent of such crimes is therefore extremely difficult. In terms of offences of elder abuse, for example, the largest survey undertaken in the UK by Jenkins, Asif and Bennett (2000) examined 1,421 calls made to the Action on Elder Abuse confidential telephone helpline over a two-year period between 1997 and 1999. The study found that two-fifths of calls reported psychological abuse, one-fifth each reported physical and financial abuse, 10 per cent of calls related to cases of neglect and 2 per cent to sexual abuse, with many calls reporting multiple types of abuse. The study also revealed that women are three times more likely to be abused than men.

It is certainly true that victim surveys produce valuable data that is useful in filling some of the gaps left by official statistics and provide key insights into hitherto unknown aspects of hate victimisation. However, methodological complexities ensure that they do not solve all our problems. In particular, as in the surveys cited above, they often involve small samples and, as with other hate crime statistics, rely on subjective judgments about motivation. In addition we cannot be certain that these studies are always measuring the same thing as the official statistics, or indeed as each other, thereby making comparisons difficult.

Hate crime as a 'process'

There is, however, a further problem that is inherently and unavoidably related to the very nature of hate crime that considerably complicates our attempts to establish its true extent. This, as Bowling (1999: 158) explains in relation to racist hate crime, is that crime in general, and hate crime in particular, should be viewed as an ongoing *process* rather than as a series of isolated, distinct and separate incidents:

Conceiving of violent racism as processes implies an analysis which is dynamic; includes the social relationships between all the actors in the process; can capture the continuity between physical violence, threat and intimidation; can capture the dynamic of repeated or systematic victimization; incorporates historical context; and takes account of the social relationships which inform definitions of appropriate and inappropriate behaviour.

Put simply, crime victimisation doesn't begin and end with the commission of an offence, and this is especially true of hate crime. Hate victimisation may involve one crime or, more likely, a great many crimes to the extent that it is not always clear where one ends and the next begins. It may also involve actions that border on being criminal offences but might not be easily defined or recognised as such. As we shall see, there is evidence to suggest that these events can nevertheless have a disproportionate effect on the victim and their community, and that the fear and intimidation that results will transcend far beyond just the moment when the incident or incidents occur.

As Bowling (1999: 189) explains in his study of racist victimisation in Newham:

> During the year January 1987 to January 1988, fifty-three incidents targeted against seven families in two streets were recorded by the police ... The overwhelming majority of the incidents consisted of verbal abuse and harassment, egg throwing, damage to property, and door knocking. Conceived of as individual instances of offensive or threatening behaviour, and employing any kind of hierarchy of seriousness using legal categories, many of these incidents would be regarded as minor. However, in the context of the life of any individual family and most clearly in the life of a locality the repeated incidence of harassment is bound to have a cumulative effect.

This example of course does not include those incidents that occurred but were not reported to the police, and also highlights a fundamental mismatch between the nature of many 'hate' crimes and the workings of the criminal justice system, which is a key issue to which I shall return in Chapter 11.

By extracting incidents from this process, Bowling suggests, as the criminal justice system and crime surveys attempt to do, hate crime is reduced to collection of solitary 'events' when in fact the victimisation process transcends far beyond that tightly defined time slice. Thus attempting to measure hate crime in terms of isolated incidents will present us with a figure of some sort that can be used for various counting purposes, but as hate crime is a process and not simply a collection of discrete incidents fixed in time and space, that figure is effectively useless as a measure of the *true* extent or nature of hate crime victimisation. Hate crime victimisation is more than just an incident or a collection of incidents; it is an ongoing process with a cumulative effect. Therefore, to understand the real nature – and in particular the impact – of hate crime victimisation, we have once again look to other forms of qualitative research.

The impact of hate crime

In their guidance to police officers the Association of Chief Police Officers (2000: 11) state that:

> Hate crime can have a devastating effect on the quality of life of its victims, those who fear becoming victims and the community. That is why we must give it priority.

Indeed, the widely held view that hate crimes have a disproportionately greater impact on victims than 'normal' crimes is one of the central justifications for both the recent recognition of hate as a distinct form of criminal behaviour and the imposition of harsher penalties for hate offenders. However, as Paul Iganski (1999b) points out, while there has been much speculation about what the distinct harms of hate crime might be, there has in fact been relatively little empirical research undertaken into the impact of hate crime victimisation.

In addition, Perry (2003) suggests that the existing literature on hate crime victims has tended to be rather broad and non-specific in its focus, and has concentrated largely on generic factors relating to victimisation. Nevertheless, this body of literature is beginning to grow in terms of its depth and scope, and is providing some valuable insights into this area of hate crime. As such, in this part of the chapter we shall examine some of the recent research studies into the qualitative aspects of hate crime victimisation.

Arguably the most comprehensive study of hate victimisation to date is that conducted by Herek, Cogan and Gillis (2002) who examined victim experiences in cases of homophobic hate crime in the United States. The research built upon an earlier pilot study conducted in 1997, which found that hate crime victims experience greater long-term post-traumatic stress disorder symptoms, including higher levels of depression, anxiety and anger, when compared with victims of similar non-hate motivated offences. Significantly, the 1997 research also found that some hate crime victims took up to five years to overcome the effects of the crime, compared with two years for victims of comparable non-hate offences.

The larger 2002 study supports and extends the earlier findings. Herek, Cogan and Gillis (2002) found that hate crimes based on sexual orientation most frequently occurred in public locations and were perpetrated by one or more males unknown to the victim. However, the researchers point out that victimisation is not confined to these dynamics and that members of sexual minorities are effectively at risk of victimisation wherever they are identified as being gay, lesbian or bisexual. Herek, Cogan and Gillis also state that while hate and non-hate personal crimes did not significantly differ in their general severity, they were struck by the physical and psychological brutality of the hate crimes they encountered. The effect of this greater brutality, they suggest, is twofold. Firstly, as was the case in the pilot study, victims generally suffered greater psychological distress that persisted over a longer period of time than non-hate victims. These findings are consistent with other studies on hate victimisation by Erlich (1992) and Garofalo (1991).

Secondly, the research also found that hate crime victimisation extends far beyond the immediate victim and has consequences for the entire gay community. Because they are motivated against an impersonal characteristic over which the victim has little or no control, Herek, Cogan and Gillis argue that hate crimes act as a form of terrorism in that they send a 'message' to other members of the community who share the same traits or belong to the same social group as the victim that they are not safe either. In this sense then, ACPO (2002: 11–12) are justified in their view that:

> Hate crime victims feel the added trauma of knowing that the perpetrator's motivation is an impersonal, group hatred, relating to some feature that they share with others ... A crime that might normally have a minor impact becomes, with the hate element, a very intimate and hurtful attack that can undermine the victim's quality of life ... In any close community, the impact of hate crime on quality of life extends to the victim's family, broader circle of friends, acquaintances and the whole community. For every primary victim there are likely to be numerous secondary victims. The perception of the victim is the reality that determines the impact of hate crime on quality of life. This is of paramount importance. Assessing the gravity purely by the physical extent of what has happened can be meaningless.

Other studies have also indicated a 'unique' impact associated with hate crime victimisation. McDevitt, Balboni, Garcia and Gu (2001) surveyed a sample of victims of hate and non-hate motivated aggravated assaults in Boston in an attempt to establish the extent to which hate crime has a differential impact. In terms of behavioural reactions the study found no significant difference between hate and non-hate victims in their post-victimisation behaviour. The majority of victims of both groups stated that they paid more attention to where they walked and that they tried to be less visible following the incident, and some stated that they had subsequently become more active in the community.

However, McDevitt *et al.* (2001) uncovered significant differences between hate and non-hate victims in terms of their psychological reactions. Overall, the study found that hate victims experienced adverse and intense psychological sequelae more often than non-hate victims, were found to have greater difficulty coping with their victimisation, and experienced problems with their recovery process because of increased fear and more frequent intrusive thoughts. In addition the research suggests that hate crime victims experience increased fear and reduced feelings of safety than non-hate victims following an attack, largely, McDevitt *et al.* suggest, because of concern over the likelihood of future attacks often based upon the experience of repeat victimisation in the past. With regard to other consequences of victimisation, the research found that hate victims were more likely to lose their job, suffer health problems, experience more post-incident traumatic events, and have greater difficulty in overcoming the incident.

More recent research by Craig-Henderson and Sloan (2003) argues that victims of racist hate crime experience a range of unique reactions and are different from both crime victims generally and also victims of other forms of hate crime in at least two ways. The first is that because race hate victims are targeted specifically because of their race (or ethnicity), the characteristics of which are always visible and easily recognised, victims are unable to take comfort in the belief that the offence was simply random and could have happened to anyone. Rather, they are forced to view their experience as an attack on their identity. The researchers suggest that this differs from other victims of crime, and indeed many other victims of hate crime, because their race (or more broadly, the reason for their victimisation) cannot be hidden from the view of others and therefore the attack cannot be easily attributed to other factors.

Craig-Henderson and Sloan (2003) argue that the second factor that distinguishes race hate victims from other hate crime victims is that they are almost always members of extremely negatively stereotyped or stigmatised social groups. Furthermore, the recognition of these factors is predominantly present in the motivation of offenders and is usually pervasive and resistant to change. It could reasonably be argued, however, that all victims of hate crime are the subjects of negative stereotypes so the extent to which this is conclusively and solely attributable to race hate victims is open to debate. Nevertheless, the researchers highlight the additional issue that anti-black hate crime in particular also has the potential to invoke emotions that relate to a lengthy history of racism and discrimination, both in terms of criminal behaviour towards blacks and discrimination in other areas of their lives such as employment and housing and so on.

While most of the studies referred to above are American in origin, many of the findings are supported by a British study examining the impact of racist victimisation on the lives of those that experienced it. Chahal and Julienne (2000) found that victims were significantly hindered or affected in several key areas of their lives. Most notably problems were associated with the victim's relationship with their partner or spouse and their children, the frequency and duration of visits from friends and family members, disruption to their routine activities and their use of space (both public and private), their general health and well-being and their overall feelings of security and safety.

But beyond this, as suggested by many of the research studies, hate crime is also a *message* crime. Essentially the victim is interchangeable and it is some feature over which the victim has no control that is the target for the offender, rather than the individual traits of the victim themselves. Therefore the perpetrator, through his or her crime against an individual or small group, is telling a particular wider community that they are different, unwelcome and that any member of that community could be the next victim. As such, hate victimisation creates an *in terrorem* effect that extends beyond the individual victim and is projected to all community members creating a sense of group vulnerability and community tension and fear.

This situation, while problematic enough in its own right, can lead to other problems in society, as identified by Levin (1999: 18). His research in the US reveals that:

> hate crimes involve a heightening of tension along already fragile intergroup lines, and a heightened risk of civil disorder. Even in the absence of explosive civil strife, the lessening of trust and a change of behaviour among affected groups in a community creates a distinct harm to the public interest.

While this research draws upon the American experience, the race riots that took place in Oldham in England in May 2001 serve as a useful example for a British context in terms of revealing the fragility of intergroup lines. Levin also points to evidence suggesting that the wider impact of hate crimes increases the risk of further civil disorder through retaliatory attacks along intergroup lines, and also through an increased risk of copycat offending. In short, hate crimes are held to be socially divisive.

69

While this emerging body of literature is revealing some interesting insights into various aspects of hate victimisation, the argument that hate crime victimisation is somehow different is not without its critics. Andrew Sullivan (1999), for example, argues that all crimes victimise more widely than just the individual victim. In many cases, he suggests, a random murder may invoke more fear and terror in a community than a specifically targeted murder because the whole community, and not just a part of it, may feel threatened. Furthermore, Sullivan suggests, high crime rates of any kind will victimise everyone and spread fear and suspicion and distress everywhere.

Sullivan also argues that claiming that some *groups* are more vulnerable and more intimidated than others is somewhat condescending to towards minorities. He suggests that within any community the response to a crime or an incident will invoke many different responses that will vary considerably from fear and panic to mild concern or complete indifference. To suggest that an entire group will be disproportionately affected, he argues, is to make a rather crude and inaccurate generalisation. Finally, not only will there be differences within groups, but there will also be differences between groups, and equating the suffering of one with the suffering of another 'is to set up a contest of vulnerability in which one group vies with another to establish its particular variety of suffering, a contest that can have no dignified solution' (Sullivan, 1999: 14).

Similarly, Jacobs (1998) also questions many of the assumptions made about hate crime victimisation. Jacobs concurs with Sullivan in his contention that all crimes have repercussions beyond the immediate victim, often perpetuated by media accounts of acts of random violence that invariably impact upon people's perceptions of personal safety and their fear of crime. Jacobs also suggests that there is a need for greater empirical verification of both the social and psychological repercussions of hate crimes before we can draw any firm conclusions concerning the true impact of hate crime. The empirical claim for disproportionately severe impacts on individual victims has not been conclusively established and despite recent research suggesting otherwise, many of these studies are based on small samples and their findings cannot be easily generalised or proved to be conclusively accurate.

Furthermore, Jacobs also questions the conflict-generating and retaliatory potential of hate crimes, suggesting that while interracial hate crimes have the potential to result in intergroup conflict (and in the past have done so), this has rarely resulted from other forms of hate crime such as homophobia or anti-Semitic attacks. To suggest therefore that there will necessarily be a disproportionate probability of intergroup conflict as a consequence of hate crime is also an inaccurate generalisation.

Similarly, Sullivan contends that if hate crimes are socially divisive, then so are societal responses to them. By responding to a crime that treats groups differently in a way that also treats groups differently, our responses to hate crime similarly highlight social divisions along intergroup lines. This is a point to which I shall return in due course.

Concluding comments

In this chapter we have examined efforts to establish the extent of hate crime victimisation in both the US and in England and Wales. We have also examined some of the findings of an emerging empirical literature base concerning the apparent unique nature and impact of hate crime. Clearly many of the definitional issues discussed in Chapter 1 bear a heavy influence on what is counted, and the subjective nature of hate further influences how much of what is counted. If we add to this mix the methodological shortcomings of data collection methods and the very nature of hate crimes that effectively mean that counting incidents would tell us very little, even if we could count them accurately, then the difficulties in establishing how much hate crime really occurs become strikingly apparent. In simple terms, while we can identify trends and patterns, we have no idea about *how much* hate crime there really is. Nevertheless, Barbara Perry (2001) suggests that this is rather less important than the fact that we simply know that it does exist.

What is perhaps more important is that the failings of quantitative accounts of victimisation are increasingly being replaced in importance by qualitative research studies. In essence these are effectively 'fleshing out' the bare bones of numerical data thereby allowing us to gain a greater insight into this form of victimisation. While these studies are relatively small in number, and have various methodological and practical shortcomings, they are beginning to provide valuable information. And while the evidence is not conclusive beyond doubt and continues to attract critics and sceptics, the literature increasingly suggests that hate crime is indeed a unique form of offending that results in unique forms of victimisation. The continuance and furtherance of research in this area are crucial not just for our understanding of hate crime but also, as Iganski (2001) suggests, because understanding the harm caused by hate crime should help us to better help its victims.

Chapter 5

Hate crime perpetrators

Bowling (1999) suggests that academic and professional interest in issues of race and racism in relation to crime (and therefore, by analogy, the emergence of interest in hate crime) can be traced back to the early 1980s in the UK through two key events. The first was the urban riots of 1981, most notably in Brixton, that saw the emergence of race, prejudice and discrimination as significant social issues. The second was the re-emergence of victimology in the late 1970s and early 1980s as a significant social science in its own right, and the subsequent development of large social surveys that for the first time began to provide a wealth of data relating to the plight of the victim, and in particular the disproportionate victimisation of minority groups.

Together, these two events served to ensure that the victim was placed at the centre of the criminal justice, criminological and political focus, a situation that remains to date. While this is of course absolutely right and the victim of any crime should be of central concern to all parties in the criminal justice system, this focus on the victim has meant that the perpetrator as an actor in the equation has been largely ignored. This is particularly true for perpetrators of hate crime and poses something of a problem for criminology. The following two quotes from Ben Bowling adequately outline the consequent challenges now facing criminal justice professionals as a result of the predominantly victim-oriented focus. Firstly:

> There has been almost no research on perpetrators. While the most basic of descriptions have been formulated, they remain something of an effigy in the criminological literature ... The perpetrator is unknown and, consequently, the possibility for any

understanding or interpretation of his or her behaviour becomes impossible. (1999: 163)

And secondly:

> What is needed for the purposes of explaining [*hate crime*] is for attention to be turned away from an analysis of the characteristics of victims to focus on the characteristics of offenders: their relationship with those they victimise; the social milieux in which anger, aggression, hostility, and violence are fostered; and the social processes by which violence becomes directed against minority groups ... Criminologists operate with scant evidence about what is going on in the lives of these people. Instead, we have only a devilish effigy for symbolic sacrifice. (1999: 305 emphasis added)

Writing of this situation from the United States, Barbara Perry (2003) argues similarly. In addition to the impact of the victim-oriented focus of which Bowling speaks, Perry suggests that theorising about perpetrators is scant partially because hate crime, as we have seen, is 'new' to the criminological horizon, and also because of the lack of agreement that we noted in Chapter 1 about how exactly we should define 'hate crime'. In addition, Perry points to the fact that historically, when criminology has taken an interest in minority groups per se the focus has tended to be on their criminality rather than on crimes committed against them.

In spite of this, however, there are signs that this trend is beginning to reverse somewhat. There is a growing body of emergent literature on the subject of perpetrators and, while still small, this is starting to fill some of the gaps to which Bowling and Perry both refer. You will have noted from our discussion of definitions of hate crime that the words 'prejudice', 'discrimination' and 'bigotry' frequently appear, and, as Perry (2003) suggests, these concepts mark the starting point for this emerging theorising about the perpetrators of hate crime. But as we saw in Chapter 2, for all our theorising about these concepts, the existent literature tells us remarkably little about how prejudice transforms into actions that would constitute hate crimes. Because of this these concepts need to be placed within relevant psychological, criminological, cultural and political contexts if the motivations for hate crime are to be understood.

In light of this proposition this chapter will present an *overview* of current knowledge in relation to the perpetrators of hate crime. We will attempt, as far as is possible, to shed some light on the missing issues identified in the second quote by Bowling, cited above, and in so doing present something a little more useful than the 'devilish effigy' we have thus far been confined to. We shall, however, confine our discussion here to what we might term 'ordinary' or 'everyday' offenders, and save our consideration of *hate groups* for the next chapter.

Explaining hate crime: the failure of criminological theory?

While Gordon Allport (1954) hypothesised that all prejudice will likely manifest itself in physical action of one form or another at some point in time, it was also noted that not all prejudices will necessarily and automatically be transformed into an action or actions that would likely constitute a *crime*. It is also unclear from the literature as to why and how prejudice transforms into negative action. We know that it does, but we don't know with any great degree of certainty *how* it does.

It would seem reasonable to assume then, given that the ultimate purpose of criminological theory is to offer explanations for criminal behaviour, that the transformation from *prejudice* into *criminal behaviour* could be adequately explained by criminology. However, this is not the case. As Perry (2003: 97) points out:

> … criminology has yet to come to terms with the phenomenon we have come to know as hate crime. Existing theory tends to neglect either or both the structural underpinnings of hate crime, and the situated process that it entails.

In her book, *In the Name of Hate*, Barbara Perry (2001) presents a critique of criminological theory in relation to hate crime, and highlights a number of holes through which explanations of hate crime can slip. While there is not the space to trace Perry's critique in its entirety here, her account is, in my view, significant. For our purposes we shall concentrate primarily on the criminological theory historically most frequently used to explain hate crime, namely strain theory, before examining Perry's deconstruction of that theory, followed by a consideration of her own theoretical account of hate crime.

Strain theory

Many accounts of hate crime have their roots in Mertonian strain theory. Full accounts of Merton's theory are readily found in criminology textbooks so we will satisfy ourselves with a simple overview here. Merton (1949) believed that crime was a product of the mismatch between the goals by which western society judges 'success' (wealth and material possessions) and the means available to individuals to achieve those goals. While society by its very nature pressures everyone to achieve those valued goals, not everyone has the opportunity or ability to do so legitimately (for example through hard work, education and so on). Those who are unlikely to legitimately achieve the goals valued by society, Merton argued, would be placed under a 'strain' to achieve them through alternative means. In other words, it is achieving the goals that is important and not how you achieve them.

Given these pressures, Merton argued that people would adapt to their situation in different ways. Some would conform and 'play by the rules' and others would deviate from those rules. Of the four categories of deviants (ritualists, retreatists, rebels and innovators) we shall concern ourselves with *innovators*. These individuals, according to Merton, accept society's goals but reject the legitimate means of achieving them. Instead, because they are unable to legitimately achieve 'success' (for example, because of unemployment, poor education, poor skills and so on), these people will innovate and use illegitimate means that may prove more efficient for them to achieve the very same goals. In essence, then, the frustration, or strain, caused by the desire for 'success' and the inability to achieve it legitimately gives rise to criminal behaviour. Moreover, Agnew (1992, cited in Williams, 1994) suggests that this strain often gives rise to negative emotions including disappointment, depression, fear and, crucially, anger because of the situation they find themselves in.

If we relate this theory to hate crime then it is tempting to conclude that such offences are committed by people in response to a perceived instability (or strain) in their lives, for example through increased competition for jobs and other scarce resources caused by 'foreigners' and people's economic security being threatened by 'outsiders' (Perry, 2001). According to strain theory, then, hate crime is a way of *responding* to threats to the legitimate means of achieving society's proscribed goals; minority groups serve to increase the perception of strain that the majority population feel, and hate crime is a product of, and a response to, that strain.

Consider, for example, a small sample of studies cited by Sibbitt (1997). In outlining the role of social factors in shaping racist attitudes, the Association of London Authorities (1993) identified the key issues as unemployment, competition for housing, a lack of facilities for young people and the need for people to find scapegoats to blame for their situation and therefore for the *strain* in their lives. In addition, Sibbitt also draws upon a study conducted in Germany by Heitmeyer in 1993 that claimed hostility towards foreigners to be a product of social and political disintegration, the search for identity, experiences of powerlessness and isolation, and anxiety relating to social conditions, most notably in relation to jobs and housing. Likewise the results of a Scandinavian study conducted by Bjorgo (1993). Such arguments are also frequently presented and fuelled by the British tabloid press in their recent coverage of immigration and asylum in this country.

However, while strain theory may be suitable for explaining some hate crimes, or perhaps more suitable as a part-explanation, as a generic theory strain falls down at a number of critical points. Perry (2001: 37) argues that:

> ... there is no doubt that hate crime occurring in the historical (recession) and sociogeographical (inner city) context of economic instability may be in part a response to perceived strain. Those facing downward mobility may indeed lash out against scapegoats whom they hold to be responsible for their displacement ... However, not least of the inconsistencies here is that if strain accounted for hate crimes, then those most prevalent among the victims would instead be the perpetrators! Who is more disadvantaged – economically, socially and politically – than women and racial minorities? Yet these groups are much more likely to be victims than offenders.

In other words, if those experiencing the greatest strain should be those most likely to commit hate crimes, then minority groups should logically also be the largest perpetrator groups, but in reality this is not the case. While the intention of hate crime policy is sometimes subverted and blacks may in some instances be disproportionately represented on the official statistics as perpetrators, it is minority groups who are predominantly the victims of hate crime. Perry also points to the fact that hate crime is not just committed at times when strain and cultural tension may be present, nor is it always committed by those who are powerless in society and who are therefore most likely to perceive strain.

Indeed, Perry highlights the fact that hate crime crosses all class boundaries. She argues that the perpetrators of hate crime regularly include those who hold positions of relative power within society and not just those who are alienated or deprived. As we shall see in the next chapter, those in the highest positions of power have perpetrated some of the worst examples of hate crimes throughout history. Perry also highlights the professional backgrounds of the leaders of certain organised hate groups and, perhaps more close to home, the historical evidence relating to the secondary victimisation of minority groups by the criminal justice system, most notably by the police who hold a clear position of power within society. Furthermore, even where offenders are relatively powerless, through hate crime they are in fact exercising a degree of power over what they perceive to be 'subordinate' groups and in doing so are maintaining their 'rightful' place in a perceived hierarchy of power within society.

Doing difference (Perry, 2001)

Barbara Perry (2001: 46) argues that the United States (and therefore by analogy the UK):

> ... is a nation grounded in deeply embedded notions of difference that have been used to justify and construct intersecting hierarchies along lines of sexuality, race, gender, and class, to name but a few. In other words, difference has been socially constructed, but in ever-changing ways across time and space. Nonetheless, these constructions have reinforced similarly changing practices of exclusion and marginalisation.

In other words, there is essentially a form of classification in society with different categories of 'belonging'. For example, as Perry explains, one is either male or female, black or white or Asian, Christian, Jew or Muslim and so on. Here, the boundaries are held to be fixed and impermeable, and membership is usually given and not chosen. With these divisions, according to Perry, come assumptions about the members of each of the other categories. In creating an identity for itself, a group necessarily creates its antithesis. Again, similarly to Allport's findings, while one group perceives itself as dominant and privileged, so it also sees other groups as subordinate, disadvantaged and 'different'. Significantly, Perry (2001: 47) states that:

> ... difference has been constructed in negative relational terms. A dominant norm ... has been established, against which all others are (unfavourably) judged. This is the case whether we speak in terms of race, class, gender, sexuality, beauty, or any other element of identity. So it is those who are not white or male or Christian or moneyed who are marked or stigmatised as different.

So those who do not fit the 'mythical norm' of dominance and power in western society (i.e. those who are not white, male, young, financially secure, heterosexual, Christian, etc.) are categorised as 'different'. With the notion of 'difference', Perry argues, comes the assumption of inferiority and the assignment of a subordinate place in society. Thus we are left with a hierarchical structure of power in society based upon notions of 'difference', with the 'mythical norm' at the top and those who are 'different' assigned subordinate positions. According to Perry these hierarchies are reinforced through labour and employment, politics, sexuality and culture, the facets of which serve to continually construct, reinforce and maintain the dominant order.

Therefore, according to Perry (2001: 55):

> ... when we do difference, when we engage in the process of identity formation, we do so within the confines of structural and institutional norms. In so doing – to the extent that we conform to normative conceptions of identity – we reinforce the structural order. However, not everyone always performs 'appropriately'. Frequently, we construct our gender or race or sexuality in ways that in fact challenge or threaten sociocultural arrangements. We step out of line, cross sacred boundaries, or forget our 'place'. It is in such a context that hate crime often emerges as a means of responding to the threats. The tensions between hegemonic and counterhegemonic actors may culminate in violent efforts to reassert the dominance of the former and realign the position of the latter.

As such, through Perry's theory hate crime can be viewed as a 'tool' by which perpetrators attempt to reaffirm their perceived dominance when 'subordinate' groups attempt, for example, to 'better their lot' and threaten the 'natural' relations of superiority and inferiority within society. Such theorising, Perry contends, allows hate crime to be placed within the wider context of oppression that is found in a complex structure of power relations firmly and historically grounded in various notions of 'difference':

> In other words, hate motivated violence is used to sustain the privilege of the dominant group, and to police the boundaries between groups by reminding the Other of his/her 'place'. Perpetrators thus re-create their own masculinity, or whiteness, for example, while punishing the victims for their deviant identity performance. (Perry, 2001: 55)

However, structural theories of hate crime such as Perry's are not without their critics. The suggestion that hate crimes are expressions of power aimed at reaffirming the offender's perceived hierarchy of appropriate social positions masks a number of complexities associated with individual offences and offenders and indeed victims. There are effectively two problems. First, if hate crime is indeed used to sustain the privilege of the dominant group, then the implication appears to be that members of a dominant group can only ever be offenders, and conversely that members of minority groups can only ever be victims. Yet as we noted in Chapters 1 and 4, victims of hate crimes are often members of the dominant social group, and members of minority groups are often the perpetrators of hate crime. Such a reality clearly does not sit easily with structural theories.

Second, to suggest that every hate crime is always about maintaining power is arguably a little too simplistic. This notion of power can be expressed in a variety of ways, and to differing degrees to the extent that no two motivations for hate offences can ever be said to be truly identical. Andrew Sullivan (1999) suggests that structural accounts are far better at alleging structures of power than at delineating the workings and complexities of the individual heart and mind. Structural theories necessarily tell us very little about how the victims or the offenders feel, nor indeed who the offenders might be. Power may be the underpinning factor in many cases, but as we saw in Chapter 2, prejudice and hate are expressed in many different ways, and no two 'hates' are ever qualitatively the same. The varieties of human emotion and human behaviour encapsulated by the word 'hate' are far too varied to be defined or explained as straightforwardly as they are in structural accounts. To understand the specifics and complexities of hate offending, it is necessary to move away from theory and consider the findings of existing empirical studies.

Emerging research

In her review of the socio-psychological literature Kellina Craig (2002) identifies specific areas that relate to the characteristics of hate crime perpetrators, and in doing so notes the difficulties and limitations of theorising hate crime. Craig (2002: 120) suggests that:

> Although several explanations may be applicable to hate crime occurrence, no existing one can fully account for all types of hate crime. This is because the factors that contribute to hate crime

(i.e. perpetrators' motives, victims' characteristics, and cultural ideologies about the victims' social groups) differ markedly for each incident … Thus, in order to explain hate crimes, a consideration of all potentially relevant explanations is necessary.

Craig presents evidence from a range of disciplines that suggests that hate crime represents a unique form of aggression and has both symbolic and instrumental functions for the perpetrator. Symbolically, the victim represents a despised social group, and instrumentally because, as we saw in Chapter 4, hate crimes can alter the actions and behaviours of the group to which the victim belongs. Craig also identifies that many hate offenders will carry a deep-seated resentment of minority groups and their members, and committing hate crimes helps perpetrators to maintain a positive social identity by lauding their in-group through the denigration of an out-group, as suggested by social categorisation theory (see Chapter 2). Thus, she suggests, victims will often be the targets of extreme negative stereotypes.

Craig also presents evidence to demonstrate that this resentment may be fuelled by actual or imagined economic competition and frustration (note the link with strain theory), the presence of certain religious values, the greater presence of psychopathological traits among hate offenders as compared with other criminals, and the presence of authoritarian personality traits among a large number of haters.

Simply, then, hate crime perpetrators can effectively be motivated by one or more of a wide range of social, psychological, political, cultural and other factors. On the basis of Craig's research, the search for a single, universal causal factor for hate crime is likely to be fruitless. Rather, it is the interplay of a number of different factors that produces perpetrators.

This situation is recognised by Rae Sibbitt (1997) in her study of the perpetrators of racial violence and racial harassment in London. Sibbitt suggests that there are essentially two strands of theories to explain why certain people commit racially motivated offences. The first, she argues, links racist behaviour to crime in general in that the psychological and contextual factors that facilitate wider criminal and anti-social behaviour will also facilitate racist behaviour.

The second approach suggests that racial harassment is a logical and predictable expression of underlying racism in society at large. In this sense, then, prejudice is felt by a community towards a minority group, perhaps fuelled by perceptions of strain, but there is a context in which a minority of that majority will 'cross the line' and express their prejudice in some physical form, in this case through harassment and violence.

This approach assumes that the perpetrator is simply expressing the views that are felt but not necessarily criminally expressed by the wider majority community.

In addition to asking why these individuals 'cross the line', this also raises the question of how the wider community develop their prejudices. We have already discussed the 'normality' of prejudice, but Sibbitt presents historical evidence to suggest that, in particular, the rapid demographic changes in this country during the 1960s, coupled with the inability of some communities to cope with this change, has played a part in the development of community prejudice. The situation is somewhat amplified, Sibbitt suggests, by factors such as unemployment, economic hardship and/or deprivation, competition for scarce resources (for example, housing) and a lack of community facilities (particularly in relation to youth and leisure facilities). Thus strain is not always the sole cause of hate crime, but may instead provide a platform from which it can emerge. In this sense people will require a scapegoat upon which to blame the situation in which they find themselves. Here the problems experienced by certain communities are inevitably perceived as being not of their own making or a product of circumstance, but as the fault of certain groups who are seen as responsible for causing or intensifying these social problems.

Sibbitt (1997) therefore argues that it is the interplay of these *contextual* factors and the *psychology* of certain individuals that produces perpetrators. Offenders are likely to be involved in other forms of criminal or anti-social behaviour, of which hate offending is a part, and will operate with the passive support (or at least without the condemnation) of some sections of the wider community who share similar views but who are not necessarily inclined towards criminal behaviour themselves.

Sibbitt's research suggests that the perpetrators of racist offences span all age ranges, from young children to old age pensioners, and involve both sexes who often act in groups. In constructing an offender typology, Sibbitt suggests that the experiences of older people are crucial in providing a framework that shapes the hate-based attitudes and behaviours of others within a family or a community. Sibbitt suggests that the attitudes of younger offenders are often derived from those of their elders, although at this point we should remember the limitations of social learning theory considered in Chapter 2.

Nevertheless, Sibbitt argues that the pensioners involved in her study of two London boroughs, having witnessed periods of significant demographic change and deteriorating social conditions, often saw ethnic minorities as 'invading' both their country and, more broadly, their lives in general and thus viewed them as scapegoats for their, and the country's, problems. Despite in many cases being friendly with black neighbours, their general negative attitudes towards ethnic minorities were found to influence the attitudes of younger members of their family.

Sibbitt also found that the attitudes of elders profoundly affected the racist tendencies of the second group in her typology, 'the people next door'. These are adults who have grown up listening to the views of their elders and in turn racialise their own problems and insecurities, for example unemployment, housing and so on. Sibbitt suggests that such people will engage in racist behaviour where, for example, they perceive biased allocation of desired resources to minority groups, or as part of a general offending behaviour, or as retaliation for a perceived misdemeanour by a member of a minority group. Such action fits neatly with Barbara Perry's theory concerning hate crime as a tool for the 'correction' of 'inappropriate' behaviour by those perceived to be subordinate.

The 'problem family' represents a third category of offender. Such people, Sibbitt suggests, experience a number of problems, for example poor health and aggressive tendencies, and see themselves as persecuted and rejected by society. As such racist offending forms part of wider anti-social behaviour, particularly where community racism is already in existence.

A fourth and particularly problematic category of offender identified by Sibbitt is that of the '15–18 year olds'. Typically, these individuals have been subject to the views of their elders, and at school will likely have associated with older youths with racist attitudes and engaged in other forms of anti-social behaviour. On leaving school, Sibbitt suggests that these individuals will have a sense of limited prospects and will often find themselves with little to occupy their time, together with a need to develop some sense of identity for themselves. They may find it easy to attach themselves to far right ideologies that provide them with both a sense of belonging and with scapegoats for their plight. These people, according to Sibbitt's research, often engage in abusive and threatening behaviour, offend as part of a group and may be responsible for extremely violent attacks.

The '11–14 year old' category, the fifth in Sibbitt's study, had predominantly grown up in areas where racist attitudes were common and regularly expressed. Many of these children were found to have low self-esteem and to bully other children who they perceived to be weaker than them, primarily to gain status among their peers. Some of the bullying was racist in its content, and in particular ethnic minority children were bullied in areas where wider community racism was common, often in an attempt to impress others. Again, the racist behaviour occurred in a group context.

The final category of offender that Sibbitt identifies is the '4–10 year olds'. Again, racist language has been a part of their upbringing and is reflected in their own language. Indeed, racist views are held to be normal and may be regularly expressed by the child. Sibbitt found that 'offenders' in this category often engage in bullying which continues away from the school environment in the form of wider harassment and intimidation. Again, this type of behaviour may be related to a sense of boredom, and may also be positively reinforced by older family members.

Sibbitt's typology is useful because it sheds light on a number of the dynamic risk factors that inform racist offending. Despite Perry's identification of flaws in strain theory as a complete explanation for hate crimes, the research nevertheless highlights the role of localised perceptions of strain in the commission of hate crimes. Furthermore, Sibbitt's work lends empirical support to Perry's theorising concerning expressions of power and the significance of perceptions of appropriate positions within social hierarchies.

Additionally, Sibbitt's work, and in particular her discussion of the wider 'perpetrator community', illustrates many of the issues discussed in Chapter 2, notably concerning the formation of in- and out-groups, the presence of erroneous but widespread negative perceptions of 'the other' and the 'normality' of prejudice. In turn, the factors associated with community prejudice have important implications for criminal justice practitioners responding to perpetrators of hate crime, given that the individual's prejudice is likely to be entrenched in the wider community from which they were drawn and to which they will likely return having served a sentence.

A further offender typology has been developed in the United States by McDevitt, Levin and Bennett (2002). These researchers analysed 169 Boston police case files in an attempt to produce a typology of hate offenders based upon the motives cited in interviews by police officials, victims and some of the perpetrators themselves. The research of 2002 built upon their 1993 typologies, and concluded that while the underlying motivation for all hate offences is bigotry there are often additional motivating factors present in this type of offending behaviour.

Using indicators nationally accepted in the United States to identify the hate element of an offence (for example, the use of language by the offender, the perpetrator's offending history, the presence of 'triggering' events, the use of hate graffiti and the location of the offence), McDevitt, Levin and Bennett concluded that hate offenders can be placed into one of four categories based on motivation.

Of the 169 cases analysed, McDevitt, Levin and Bennett concluded that 66 per cent (or 111 of the total) of the offences, mostly committed by youths, were motivated by the thrill or for the excitement of the act. In other words, the vast majority of hate offences were motivated by the offender's desire for a 'thrill' often because they were bored or were seeking some form of 'excitement'. This finding supports Sibbitt's contention, above, that many younger racist offenders commit offences out of a sense of boredom and a need for excitement in their lives. The present researchers report that in 91 per cent of these 'thrill' cases the perpetrators left their neighbourhood to search for a victim and deliberately selected their target because they were 'different' to themselves. In a neat fit with Barbara Perry's theory, above, and with a number of the theories of prejudice described in Chapter 2, the researchers also suggest that many of the offences analysed in this category were underpinned by an immature desire to display power and to enhance the offender's own feeling of self-importance at the expense of others.

In 25 per cent (or 43 cases) of the cases analysed, McDevitt, Levin and Bennett categorised the motivation as being 'defensive' in its nature. In these cases, the offender committed hate offences against what he or she perceived to be outsiders or intruders in an attempt to defend or protect his or her 'territory'. Echoing the view discussed in Chapter 4 that hate crimes are 'message crimes', the researchers found that many 'defensive' offenders believed that minority groups had undeservedly moved into their neighbourhood and that their hate crimes served to send a message to the victim and other members of the victim's group that they are unwelcome and should relocate. McDevitt, Levin and Bennett suggest that defensive attacks are often associated with demographic shifts at a local level, particularly where neighbourhoods or communities begin to experience a transition from being dominated by one ethnic group towards a more diverse population. This mirrors the findings of Sibbitt (1997), above, who highlighted rapid demographic changes in the UK in the 1960s as a key factor in the development of community prejudice and resentment towards ethnic minority groups, a factor held by Sibbitt to underpin hate offences against these groups.

The third category of hate motivation identified by McDevitt, Levin and Bennett is 'retaliation', accounting for 8 per cent (14 cases) of the sample. This is based on the finding that a hate offence is often followed by a number of subsequent hate attacks. The researchers state that retaliatory offences are not a reaction to the presence of a particular individual or group, but rather are a reaction to a particular hate offence that has already occurred, be it real or perceived. Retaliatory offenders are therefore retaliating against, or avenging, an earlier attack. McDevitt, Levin and Bennett illustrate their point by citing an example from New York where the murder of a black man named Yusef Hawkins in a predominantly white neighbourhood was followed by the largest number of hate offences recorded in a month in the city's history. Many of these subsequent offences were determined to be retaliatory, with many offenders citing their desire to avenge Hawkins's death and re-establish their honour as one of the primary causes of their offending.

Perhaps the best example of retaliatory offending, however, can be seen in the escalation of offences committed against Muslims (or those mistaken to be Muslims) in both the US and Britain in the period following the terrorist attacks in the US on 11 September 2001 (NYPD, 2002; Hall, 2004). Both examples lend support to McDevitt, Levin and Bennett's suggestion that retaliatory offences based on revenge have the greatest potential for fuelling further offences resulting in a cycle of offending that is difficult to end.

The final, and thankfully rarest, category identified by McDevitt, Levin and Bennett is that of the 'mission' offender, representing less than 1 per cent (1 case) of the sample. Here the offender is totally committed to his or her hate and bigotry and views the objects of their hate as an evil that must be removed from the world. These offenders are those that would fit into Cell I of Jacobs and Potter's (1998) table (see Chapter 1). The researchers suggest that these offenders are often members of organised hate groups, and we shall consider these further in the next chapter.

While these typologies have been somewhat simplified here (see McDevitt, Levin and Bennett, 2002 for a comprehensive overview) and despite the study's methodological limitations, most notably the size of the sample and the use of police case files, the study has nevertheless provided some interesting supplementary information about the commission of hate offences, as illustrated in Table 5.1.

It is clear from Table 5.1 that the majority of hate offenders are young adults, as is the case for offenders generally. Here, however, the typology varies from that proposed by Sibbitt, who found that race hate perpetrators spanned a range of age groups. This discrepancy in the findings may, however, be more to do with differences in research methodologies and terminology. Sibbitt suggests that the older people

Table 5.1 Characteristics of hate crimes by offender motivation

Attack characteristics	Thrill	Defensive	Retaliatory	Mission
Number of offenders	Group	Group	Single offender	Group
Age of offenders(s)	Teens–young adults	Teens–young adults	Teens–young adults	Young adults–adults
Location	Victim's turf	Offender's turf	Victim's turf	Victim's or offender's turf
Weapon	Hands, feet, rocks	Hands, feet rocks	Hands, feet, rocks,	Bats, guns
Victim offender history	None	Previous acts of intimidation	Often no history	None
Commitment to bias	Little	Moderate	Moderate	Full
Deterrence	Likely	Unlikely	Unlikely	Most unlikey

Source: McDevitt et al. (2002: 311).

in her study were more likely to be involved in verbal harassment, the expression of opinion and the influencing of others rather than physical forms of offending. Such behaviour is unlikely to have been present as 'crimes' in the police case files examined by McDevitt, Levin and Bennett, in whose research physical forms of crime appear to feature more frequently. Given the 'normality' of prejudice, had McDevitt, Levin and Bennett used sources other than police files then they too may have found similarly to Sibbitt, but for hate crimes that are likely to be reported to the police it is perhaps unsurprising that in this typology the offenders are frequently young and that the offences are predominantly physical in their nature (note the use of weapons in the Table 5.1).

Also of interest, and in line with Sibbitt, is the suggestion that hate crime is often a group activity. Furthermore, hate offences often involve whatever 'weapons' happen to be at hand, and occur often with little or no victim–offender history. This lends support to the contention that hate crimes are impersonal and that victims are interchangeable, although we should note here the contrast with Sibbitt's findings concerning the victimisation of neighbours, above, and the findings of Docking, Kielinger and Paterson (2003 – see Chapter 4) that suggest that in many cases the victim and offender are in fact known to each other.

The final points of note in Table 5.1 relate to the last two categories. The offender's commitment to their hatred is a significant factor, particularly in relation to whether or not they can be deterred from their actions. Thrill offenders are not particularly committed to their prejudice, where in contrast mission offenders are fully committed to their erroneous beliefs. Defensive and retaliatory offenders fall somewhere in between the two ends of this spectrum. These latter findings serve to highlight the complexity of prejudice as a psychological phenomenon. In reinforcing the view expressed in Chapter 2 that hate is felt and expressed in different ways by different people to different degrees, it becomes apparent that when we talk about 'hate' as a motivation for criminal behaviour, we cannot always be referring to the same thing in every case. The hate of the mission offender, for example, is considerably different in its nature to the hate of the thrill offender, yet the term 'hate' that we apply to both sets of offenders and their offences does not discriminate between, or indeed acknowledge, such differences. Hate is hate, even though we know that in reality it isn't.

Just as there are different degrees of hate, so there are different degrees of culpability. The finding that hate crimes are often committed by offenders operating in groups rather than alone has also led McDevitt, Levin and Bennett to advance a 'continuum of culpability' to assist criminal justice decision-makers in determining the role of group members in the commission of an offence, and to develop sentencing options based upon that degree of culpability. Identifying differing degrees of involvement in an attack, and thereby different degrees of culpability for those operating in groups, not only serves to potentially aid prosecution decisions but also furthers our understanding of offender behaviour.

Just as there are four offender typologies, so McDevitt, Levin and Bennett have identified four levels of culpability in group offending. The most culpable group member is the 'leader', who may suggest to the group that they commit a hate offence for any of the reasons outlined above (for example, for the thrill or to retaliate). Members of the second category, 'fellow travellers', do not initiate the offence but once it is suggested are happy to comply with the leader, making them only slightly less culpable than the 'leader'. The third identifiable category is the 'unwilling participant', who while disapproving of the situation that is occurring, still does not actively attempt to intervene in the crime, or report it to the police. For these individuals, the need for acceptance and peer group approval is the key factor in the failure to intervene. The final category is that of the 'heroes' who actively attempt to stop the offence from taking place. McDevitt, Levin and Bennett suggest that this behaviour should be rewarded because their actions require immunity to social influence and a strong conscience in order to put the needs of a person they have never met before the desires of their friends or peer group.

In addition to providing academics with useful information about offenders, this typology is now widely used in law enforcement in the United States and has had numerous implications in terms of policy development in this area. As McDevitt, Levin and Bennett point out:

> One reason why the original typology has been so widely adopted by law enforcement is that, early on, it offered a way to categorize hate crime offenders and suggested some clues as to methods of identifying hate offences … Understanding different types of hate motivation and specific indicators associated with these have been shown to be useful in identifying and prosecuting hate crimes and providing appropriate services to hate crime victims … Tools that assist government agencies in understanding and effectively dealing with hate crime incidents may be our best effort toward curtailing this brand of violence. (2002: 315)

The determination of culpability is also of value because, the researchers contend, it allows criminal justice decision-makers to match offenders with suitable sentences, which as we shall see in Chapter 12, can be of great importance in rehabilitative terms.

Justifying offending

Further research conducted in the US by Byers, Crider and Biggers (1999) has also revealed some interesting insights into hate crime offending by drawing on Sykes and Matza's (1957) techniques of neutralisation, which seek to identify how perpetrators of crime justify their offending behaviour. Sykes and Matza found that offenders in general often attempted to justify their actions in a number of ways that mitigated their involvement and that these justification techniques provided useful information about the motivation of criminals.

In their study of hate crimes committed against the Amish, Byers *et al.* found that while some offenders showed little or no remorse for their actions, others attempted to justify or rationalise their behaviour by using a number of 'neutralisation techniques'. The first technique described by Byers *et al.* is that of *denial of injury.* Here offenders attempted to neutralise their behaviour by suggesting that no real harm was done to the victim, that the offence was in effect 'harmless fun' and that the victim should in any case be used to being subject to certain forms of abuse, all of which combined to make the offender's behaviour somehow acceptable.

The second identified technique was that of the *denial of the victim.* According to Byers *et al.*, this makes the assumption that the victim either deserved what they got or that the victim is effectively worthless and offences against them are inconsequential either socially or legally. Essentially, then, victims are somewhat dehumanised and seen as deserving of their victimisation.

The third identified technique is the *appeal to higher loyalties.* Here, offences may be committed through allegiance to a group. Offenders therefore may see their behaviour, and subsequently not reveal that behaviour or the behaviour of their peers, as a form of group bonding and security within their 'in-group'.

Fourthly, Byers et al. suggest that some offenders will engage in *condemnation of the condemners.* Here offenders attempt to neutralise their behaviour by questioning the right of their condemners to sit in judgment of them. This may be done by suggesting that those that condemn them are in reality no better, share similar views to the offender and given the chance in similar circumstances would act, or may have previously acted, in a similar way to the perpetrator.

The final technique relates to a *denial of responsibility*. Here, Byers *et al.* explain, offenders attempt to neutralise their responsibility for their actions by claiming other factors to be the cause of their behaviour, such as, the researchers suggest, the offender's socialisation and the way they were brought up. In other words, the blame for their behaviour lies somewhere other than with them.

Furthermore, Byers *et al.* found that many offenders broadly fitted the 'thrill' category described by Levin, McDevitt and Bennett, above, and also pointed to the importance of peer support, which has links to Sibbitt's work on the 'perpetrator community' by highlighting the significance of shared views and the reinforcement of those views. Offenders' attempts at justifying their actions also lend support to the view that victims are frequently dehumanised by their attackers, are subordinate to the offender and are somehow deserving of their victimisation. This in turn reflects Perry's notion of power, the expression of power and the use of hate crime as a method for maintaining perceived social hierarchies and for 'punishing' those who attempt to disturb the social order.

Concluding comments

In this chapter I have presented a broad overview of existing knowledge in relation to the perpetrators of hate crime. The chapter has purposefully concentrated on academic research and avoided official statistics on perpetrators. Police statistics tell us very little qualitatively beyond the age, race and gender of suspects. For this reason, police statistics have not been included.

But while the body of academic research continues to grow, it is clear that we are still some distance from a comprehensive understanding of why some people act as they do. Yet developing an accurate understanding of hate offenders is crucial if the criminal justice system is to respond effectively and appropriately. While we are fairly safe in our assumption that hatred as a human emotion has its roots in prejudice, we know that simply being prejudiced is not enough. We don't all act upon our prejudices in a negative way and certainly not in a way that would constitute a crime.

Rather, there has to be something more that transforms erroneous beliefs and negative emotion into criminal behaviour, and that 'something', as we have seen, could be one or more of a great many social, psychological, criminogenic and contextual factors. The interplay that occurs between these factors that ultimately produces perpetrators is complex and unclear, and would appear to be context-specific.

What is certain though is that the word 'hate' that is used as a 'catch-all' term in the current context in fact masks a myriad of human emotions and behaviours that manifest themselves in many different ways with varying degrees of consequence. Hate, as a single word might lead us to believe, is not a single emotion or behaviour, but instead stands for a variety of complex psychological phenomena that can be expressed in many different ways by different people. Why some people express 'hate' in the form of criminal behaviour is something that we do not yet fully understand.

Chapter 6

Extreme hatred

In the last chapter we saw that the majority of hate offences are committed by 'ordinary' offenders and not by members of organised hate groups as we might mistakenly assume. This is not to say, however, that hate groups and their members should be ignored or their role understated. Rather, in addition to the actual offences committed by their members, organised hate groups are of particular interest because of the influence they can exert on the beliefs and actions of non-members who, as we have seen, commit the majority of hate offences.

In this chapter we shall explore the nature and characteristics of organised hate groups. We shall begin by attempting to define what hate groups actually are, followed by a consideration of the common ideologies that permeate most hate groups and serve to 'legitimise' their beliefs and actions. The chapter will then examine existing hate groups in the United States before moving on to the history, activities and resurgence of the 'far right' in the UK and across Europe. While these represent a more virulent form of bigotry and hatred than has hitherto been discussed in this book, this chapter will also take this a step further with an examination of the most extreme of hate offenders and offences, namely those of genocide and mass hate.

Problems with defining and conceptualising hate groups

Terms such as 'hate group', 'organised hate', 'extremists' and 'the far right' are used fairly liberally and interchangeably to describe those individuals, separately or collectively, who are, or are perceived to be, purveyors of a more extreme form of hatred. The variety of terms used to describe these groups illustrates the point that defining hate groups is not an easy task.

Gerstenfeld (2004) suggests that there is no simple way to define (or indeed identify) a hate group and that very few academic attempts have been made to do so. The reasons for this, she suggests, are plentiful and relate primarily to the diverse nature of these groups. First, while such groups share many common features, they also differ markedly in a number of ways. Some are open in their declaration of hatred, others are not, and others will attempt to mask their extremism through the use of populist language and literature. In addition, different groups 'hate' different things and will express that hate in different ways. Second, what is, and what is not, a hate group is in many cases open to question and is therefore a matter of perception and opinion.

Third, Gerstenfeld suggests that some groups or organisations have factions that hold extreme views and other factions within that same organisation that do not. Fourth, it is often extremely difficult to distinguish between hate groups and other extremist organisations, such as terrorist groups. Here the distinction can become very blurred and some authors have argued that there is no discernible difference between terrorism and hate crime, and between terrorist organisations and hate groups. Indeed, the closer you look the more blurred the distinction becomes. Gerstenfeld also suggests that is it sometimes difficult to distinguish between hate groups and 'normal' street gangs, and indeed between hate groups and legitimate political bodies, as we shall see later in this chapter.

Because of these complexities is it perhaps better not to attempt to define hate groups at all, but rather to simply recognise them. In this regard, Gerstenfeld suggests a number of characteristics that are shared by all or most existing hate groups. First, each organised hate group will have bigoted viewpoints based on opposition to some other, usually minority, group or groups, coupled with the key aim of advancing their own interests at the expense of the interests of the groups they oppose. Second, she suggests, the groups are organised, although the degree, structure, complexity and formality of organisation will vary greatly between the groups. Groups typically will have a name, a leader and membership criteria, will publish literature and hold meetings and rallies, will adopt symbols and uniforms, and so on. Third, the majority of hate groups are white supremacist, and fourth, the majority will hold views from the far right of the political spectrum with religion and narrow interpretations of religious doctrines informing and underpinning many of their beliefs and ideologies.

Hate ideologies

In considering contemporary hate groups in the United States, Barbara Perry (2001), Phyllis Gerstenfeld (2004) and others have identified a number of common core ideological claims to superiority that are used by hate groups to 'justify' their beliefs and actions. In many cases these are just as applicable to hate groups here in the UK. While a detailed examination of these is beyond the scope of this book (readers are advised to see Perry, 2001; Gerstenfeld, 2004) it is nevertheless important to briefly consider these ideologies because they allow us to gain an insight into the motivations and belief systems that serve to justify and legitimise the behaviour and actions of the members of such groups.

Gerstenfeld suggests that arguably the most important of these ideologies relates to *power*. Historically, as we saw in Chapter 3, hate groups have tended to form, and grow in popularity, at times where the dominant group feels somehow threatened. Indeed the history of the Ku Klux Klan is characterised by such peaks and troughs in popularity when faced with perceived threats to white dominance.

The notion of power is particularly central to white supremacist discourse and the belief that power is rightfully theirs is based largely on the misguided premise that the white race is biologically superior to all other races. Specifically, Gerstenfeld suggests that such groups believe that the power of the white race is being stolen, for example by blacks through their criminal behaviour; by mass immigration and the taking of jobs and the 'swamping' of the white population; by a Jewish conspiracy to control government and the media; and by non-whites race-mixing and thereby 'polluting' and 'weakening' the 'pure' Aryan gene pool.

The second ideology that Gerstenfeld outlines is *racial separatism*. She suggests that most hate groups advocate either complete or at least partial racial separatism, with many members believing that their perceived superiority gives them the right to define what constitutes a natural citizen of their country and that entry into that country can only happen on their terms. Indeed this focus on racial separatism is not restricted to white supremacists, as non-white organisations are known to advocate similarly.

The third ideology relates to *religion*. Gerstenfeld suggests that while not all hate groups have a religious basis, for many it is the key to their belief system. For white supremacists the most important (but not always exclusive) religious sect is that of *Christian Identity*. Gerstenfeld points out that the teachings of Christian Identity are attractive to white supremacists because they provide these groups with a 'theological seal of approval'. The sect teaches that Aryans are God's chosen people and non-whites are sub-human, and that white people are descendants of Adam while Jews are descendants of Satan. These 'facts' provide a rationale for racist views, particularly given that Christian Identity teaches that Adam's descendants are engaged in an apocalyptic struggle against the descendants of Satan. Gerstenfeld suggests that in this sense white supremacists believe that they are literally doing 'God's work'.

Two other key ideologies that Gerstenfeld and others have identified firstly concern a common antipathy for certain groups, particularly Jews who are frequently perceived to be descendants of the devil and who are also involved in a conspiracy to take over the world, and non-whites who are perceived to be a wholly inferior race, and secondly, a common antipathy for certain beliefs and actions, in particular abortion, communism, feminism and political liberalism (Gerstenfeld, 2004).

Organised hatred in the United States

In their annual report, the Southern Poverty Law Center's (SPLC) Intelligence Project counted 751 active hate groups in the United States in 2003, estimating that they were collectively responsible for 471 hate incidents in that year. The Project, which lists organisations and their chapters known to be active throughout the year, is compiled using hate group publications and websites, reports from citizens and law enforcement agencies, field sources and news reports. The 751 groups are categorised under seven broad headings, and we shall briefly consider the SPLC's findings here.

Of the groups identified, 136 were categorised as *black separatist*. These groups, according to the SPLC's Intelligence Project, are characterised by their anti-white and anti-Semitic views. They are opposed to integration and racial intermarriage and advocate the separateness of blacks, in some cases basing their views on the belief that black people, and not whites or Jews or others, are God's 'chosen people'. Specific groups identified in this category include Nation of Islam, the New Black Panther Party and the United Nuwaubian Nation of Moors (SPLC, 2004).

The second category identified by the SPLC is that of the *Ku Klux Klan* (KKK), comprising 158 groups in 2003. Having been formed in December 1865, the KKK represents the oldest and most widely known hate group in the US, and historically one of the most violent. The SPLC state that although blacks have typically been the Klan's primary target, it also has attacked Jews, immigrants, homosexuals and, until recently, Catholics. The SPLC also states that while the Klan has typically seen itself as a Christian organisation, today's Klan groups are motivated by a variety of theological and political ideologies, many of which we discussed above.

Despite its lengthy history and worldwide recognition, the Klan's popularity and strength has waxed and waned periodically. As we noted in Chapter 3, the Klan enjoyed peaks in the immediate post-Civil War era in opposition to southern blacks in particular, and also throughout the 1920s in response to mass immigration, and also during the 1960s as the Civil Rights movement gained momentum. However, at present the KKK are somewhat fragmented and are a significantly weaker organisation than they have been in the past. Indeed, the SPLC has noted a steady demise of the Klan over the past 35 years or so, suggesting that they have been weakened by internal conflicts and splits, damaging court cases and government infiltration.

In addition, many factions of the Klan have also moved in different directions, with some maintaining an open, violent and militant approach while others have attempted to legitimise their activities by 'going mainstream'. From a peak of over 5 million members in 1925, the SPLC estimates that in 2003 there were between 5,500 and 6,000 Klan members, split among many disparate and fragmented groups, many of which are in dispute and disagreement with each other. In addition, the SPLC suggests that a number of groups have simply adopted the Klan name and therefore may not be 'true' Klan organisations.

The third category identified by the SPLC is that of the *neo-Nazis*. The 149 groups identified as being neo-Nazi draw their inspiration and beliefs from the Third Reich. As was the case with Hitler and Nazi Germany, neo-Nazis share a particular hatred for Jews, whom they see as the source of society's ills, but also extend their hate to other minority groups who are held to be inferior to Aryans. Such groups exist not only in the United States but also have particularly strong roots in Europe from where their ideology originally emerged.

The SPLC suggests that the links between US and European neo-Nazi groups are becoming increasingly stronger, aided by the Internet and the protection afforded by the First Amendment of the US Constitution. The latter allows such groups to publish material widely and freely without sanction, and the former provides an ideal vehicle to do so. Moreover, the SPLC states that many European neo-Nazi groups use US Internet servers to host their hateful sites thereby avoiding the risk of prosecution under European legislation. We shall consider neo-Nazis further in our consideration of organised hate in the UK, below, but in the US some of the key groups include the National Alliance, White Aryan Resistance, the American Nazi Party, Aryan Nations and the National Socialist Movement.

The SPLC's fourth category is the *racist skinheads*, comprising 39 groups in 2003. Perry (2001) states that these represent a less orderly, more loosely organised but more violent element of the neo-Nazi movement. The SPLC traces the birth of the racist skinheads to 1960s Britain, arriving in the US in the early 1980s. The movement on both sides of the Atlantic has split between its racist and anti-racist elements, with the former predominantly operating in small groups that regularly move from place to place (SPLC, 2004).

The fifth category is *Christian Identity*. The 31 groups identified by the SPLC are characterised by the belief that whites are 'God's chosen people' and that Jews are descended from Satan, while other non-whites are similarly unholy. Because of this, their interpretation of the Bible places whites above all others. The SPLC suggests, however, that despite Christian Identity being one of the central ideologies for white supremacists as we noted above, deep doctrinal disputes, the lack of a central church structure and a shift among white supremacists towards agnosticism and racist variations of neo-paganism have weakened the Identity movement and reduced the number of its followers in recent years (SPLC, 2004).

Neo-confederate groups, of which the SPLC identified 91 in 2003, are found predominantly in southern US states and support the traditional southern culture and celebrate the conflict between the Unionists and the Confederacy at the time of the US Civil War. But while not all are deemed to be hate groups, the SPLC suggest that some have nevertheless come to embrace racist attitudes and ideologies. In some cases, these groups advocate white separatism, opposing, for example, non-white immigration and interracial marriages because, in their view, such actions contribute to the destruction of 'white culture'.

In a move that perhaps signifies the diversity of hate groups, the remaining organisations are categorised as 'other'. Groups within this category have what the SPLC defines as a 'hodge-podge' of doctrines that do not fit particularly well with the ideologies of the other categories outlined above. Included within the 147 groups in this category are organisations such as the Council of Conservative Citizens, the Jewish Defense League and the European-American Unity and Rights Organisation.

From this brief consideration of the SPLC's Intelligence Report, it is clear that hate groups are extremely diverse. But while estimating how many hate groups exist is one thing, figuring out how many people are involved in such groups is quite another. Estimates of the numbers involved in US hate groups are difficult to ascertain with any great degree of certainty. Perry (2001) suggests that the membership of many hate groups is fluid with people moving between groups, and indeed holding membership to several at a time. Moreover, the interaction and cooperation between groups and their members further complicates the task of establishing how many people might be involved, as does the rather obvious point that the membership of a hate group (assuming people view themselves as belonging to a 'hate group') is not information that is always readily declared either by the individuals involved or by the organisations themselves. In other words, hate groups are rarely, if ever, open to outside scrutiny and examination, voluntary or otherwise.

Unsurprisingly, estimates of membership necessarily vary greatly for each category of group. The Anti-Defamation League (2004) estimates membership of Christian Identity groups to be between 25,000 and 50,000, and the Klan to number no more than a few thousand. Similarly, the SPLC (2004) estimates that the Council of Conservative Citizens has around 15,000 members. Estimates of the numbers of skinheads are more difficult to ascertain because of their distinct lack of organisational structure, but the consensus of opinion is that they number between 5,000 and 10,000 but are growing in size (Perry, 2001). The issue of membership is further complicated, however, by those Perry describes as 'armchair racists'. These are individuals who associate with hate groups in terms of, for example, receiving literature and attending various events, but who generally abstain from other hate group activities. Estimates of the number of 'armchair racists' tend to be around 150,000, although Perry suggests that this is probably conservative.

From this brief overview of hate groups in the US it is clear that such groups are many and varied, and because of this it is difficult to be certain how many groups exist and how many people are affiliated in one way or another. From the available evidence, however, it is possible to identify a number of interesting trends and patterns that have emerged in recent years. Perhaps the most alarming trend is the apparent increase in the number of hate groups. The SPLC counted 602 groups in 2000, rising to 676 in 2001 (an increase of 12 per cent), rising to 751 in 2003. The SPLC attributed the rise in 2001 almost exclusively to an increase in neo-Nazi and Confederate groups in the aftermath of the terrorist attacks of 11 September. The SPLC's Intelligence Report of 2002 stated that:

While the carnage of Sept. 11 left most Americans shocked, angry and more tightly knit as a nation, the reaction of much of the American radical right was markedly different. For many American extremists, it boiled down to one simple emotion: pure delight. In a year that saw significant growth in U.S. hate groups, the most remarkable moment of all came in the immediate aftermath of the September terrorist attacks. Figure after figure rose to applaud the murder of more than 3,000 of their countrymen, revealing as never before the militantly anti-American and pro-Nazi features of contemporary right-wing extremism ... The extremists' message – that the United States has become the spearhead of globalization and multiculturalism – has fuelled the rise of ethnic nationalism and the growth of hate groups in recent years.

This rise in anti-statist, anti-Semitic and Islamophobic sentiment in the post-9/11 climate is not the only trend to have recently emerged. The Anti-Defamation League (ADL) (2004) suggests that the nature of extremism in the US is constantly changing, and recent years have seen an increase in what it terms 'lone wolf' activism, namely extremists operating alone or in small groups. Recent trends also include the ascendancy of the Internet as an extremist tool; an increase in the use of 'white power' music as a recruiting tool; an increase in Holocaust denial; increasing numbers of women involved in hate groups; the opportunistic support by some sections of the far right for the anti-globalisation movement and the Palestinian cause; the convergence of the far right and some elements of the radical left; and, in support of the SPLC's assertion above, an increase in support for foreign anti-American terrorists (ADL, 2004). Furthermore, the SPLC (2002) suggest that post 9/11, many hate groups in the US and in Europe, including those that have traditionally been opposed to each other, are now seeking (and in many cases achieving) unity and solidarity in opposition to common enemies.

The 'far right' in the UK

In her study of the perpetrators of racist violence, Sibbitt (1997) questions the role and responsibility of organised hate groups and the 'far right' in Britain. She argues that if one examines the number of hate crimes that extremist organisations are *directly* involved in then in fact such groups play a marginal role with regard to the perpetration of hate offences. Of far greater significance, Sibbitt argues, is the role such groups play in influencing public opinion and behaviour. This view is shared by Gordon (1994, cited in Sibbitt, 1997: 13) who states that:

> ... it will not do to blame the organisations of the far right, although it may be tempting to do so. Of course such organisations stir up hatred against black people and Jews and their collective criminal record – for murder, arson and assault – speaks for itself. But the responsibility for racist violence cannot be laid solely or even mainly with them. The extent of racist violence is far greater than their small numbers.

The general thrust of this statement is supported by more recent research by Roxburgh (2002). He recognises the importance of maintaining a wariness of neo-Nazi groups such as Blood and Honour/Combat 18 in this country, but suggests that they are 'little more than ideologised hooligans' who are 'tiny in number' (2002: 244 and 245).

Indeed, an examination of the Blood and Honour/Combat 18 website reveals their own appreciation of the precarious situation they currently find themselves in:

> The simple truth is, that despite all the goings-on in and around our so-called Movement, there are, basically, only two real reasons for the existence of that movement:
> 1. Bringing down the ruling old order of our enemies;
> 2. Building a new order based on our own principles and ideas.
> And the sad truth is, that so far we have failed miserably on both accounts.

And similarly:

> No doubt the odds are against us, and a bookmaker would probably not touch us unless someone put a gun to his head. How can we succeed where the drilled divisions of Europe's best fighting youth, led by a person whose brilliant political visions and leadership the world has never before experienced were beaten by the Zionist-led legions of the hellish mud people? I know it is an unnerving question, but unfortunately it is one that has to be asked. We must be realists. (Blood and Honour, 2003)

Roxburgh (2002) suggests that the lack of popular support for such groups rests at least in part with the fact that they are too obviously and abrasively racist and bigoted and are too closely associated with the image of 'thugs' and 'hooligans' to have widespread support. A further issue relates to the split of such groups from their associates who in certain cases have moved towards mainstream politics. For example, the Blood and Honour website states that:

> The British National Party had a brigade of fearless stormtroopers guarding its meetings and demonstrations. They called themselves Combat 18 after our leader Adolf Hitler. Now, the BNP is led by an honest man of great integrity with more than a life-time of nationalist activities behind him. But he, or at least his associates, are content with playing the game of democracy where the odds of winning are worse than the mafia's crooked number racket. So when C18 had some ideas of their own, they were promptly given the boot. (Blood and Honour, 2003)

This latter point suggests support for Sibbitt's view that far right groups are more influential when they attempt to affect people's views than when they attempt to 'resolve' a problem through violence and intimidation. To this end, then, the movement towards mainstream politics and the distancing of some groups from overt violence is particularly significant. Before we examine this issue though, it is important that we don't simply overlook groups such as Combat 18. C18 of course still exists independently and despite their size and self-acknowledged problems, the threat, however small, and the ideological determination still remain, as can be clearly seen through the following quotes from the Blood and Honour website:

> So, although the situation is indeed desperate, we are not without chances. We must simply work on, seizing every opportunity to undermine, sabotage and destroy the anti-White forces, while recruiting, organising and training our comrades of all ages and White nations for the coming conflicts. WE must be brave, use our brains and be prepared for anything and everything, trusting the just truth and vital necessity of our cause.

And:

> Aryan man will rise again and take back his rightful position on earth. Or he will die fighting for it. There is no middle ground. There is only the solemn call of our forefathers and the glorious vision of the future. Together, as comrades-in-arms, we – the last of the traditional Aryan gladiators and berserkers, the latter-day

White knights and crusaders, the inheritors of the armed legions
of European National Socialist volunteers – throw ourselves into
the final battle for our race. (Blood and Honour, 2003)

In Britain, as in some cases in the United States, we have effectively
witnessed a split within far right groups between those that believe that
the greatest chance of 'success' (however so defined) is to move away
from overt extremism towards mainstream politics thereby appearing
more moderate and palatable to a greater audience, and those who
view such a shift in position as playing into the hands of those they
so vehemently oppose. The latter advocate aggression and violence to
achieve their aim, while the former view the democratic political arena
as the key to success and have moved towards mainstream politics as
a result.

With regard to the role of the far right in politics, Roxburgh (2002)
suggests that academic interest in the far right in Britain has tended to
focus not on the danger that it poses, but more on why its influence
is weaker here than almost anywhere else in Europe and the US.
Roxburgh suggests a number of possible reasons for this. Firstly, he
states, for at least a generation following the Second World War, Britain
was a nation with very little tolerance of extreme right-wing parties
having seen the world blighted by the effects of Nazism and fascism.
Even when extreme right-wing politics became somewhat 'palatable'
again, both the National Front and the BNP have rather failed in their
bids to become a national political force. In respect of this, Roxburgh
(2002: 227) states that:

The point is, the National Front's policies are of little interest to
anyone. The party exists not as a serious political force nowadays
but as a disruptive element, intent on whipping up racial tension in
the interests of furthering its 'white nationalist' goals. The British
National Party is slightly more sophisticated ... targeting only
those seats where it [has] a measure of support and [campaigning]
on a recognisable slate of policies.

However, even where the BNP has campaigned with what might be
superficially viewed as moderate, appealing and acceptable policies,
its national success has remained limited (0.2 per cent of the poll at
the 2001 general election). Roxburgh suggests that this is because of
the extent of tolerance of diversity, and the extent of diversity itself in
Britain today. Furthermore, Roxburgh points to the lack of charismatic

leaders among far right British parties as compared with their European counterparts, and the lack of an influential and effective public relations machine.

Roxburgh also highlights the nature of the voting system in this country that effectively serves to discourage people from wasting votes on parties that have little or no chance of winning a general election. However, while the BNP has not been a national threat, in many areas it remains a local one where its range of policies may be appealing to a disillusioned electorate. Indeed, recent national and international events have been followed by subsequent electoral successes by the BNP and have illustrated exactly this point.

In his examination of the electoral success of the BNP between 1999 and 2003, David Renton (2003) notes that the local council elections in May 2003 represented a significant breakthrough for the party with 13 BNP councillors elected, mostly in seats in northern England. These electoral gains built upon BNP successes in the 2002 local elections and signify a rapid rise in the party's fortunes. In seeking to explain this recent rise in popularity, Renton suggests that the most crucial factors have been external to the party itself. In other words, while the party has changed little in terms of its position, character and style or leadership since 1999, it has been aided by significant external events.

The first, Renton suggests, relates to the asylum 'crisis' that has periodically dominated media, political and public attention since the late 1990s. Widespread public concern regarding immigration and asylum and the alleged usurping of finite resources by such individuals has, Renton suggests, been fuelled by emotive media coverage, which has in turn led to government action that has done little to alleviate public concerns. Recent legislation that imposes restrictions on immigrants and asylum seekers has in effect solidified the popular perception that these people represent a serious problem in need of strict control. Renton suggests that this 'hysteria' over asylum and immigration was highly favourable to the BNP and their 'British first' position.

The second key event identified by Renton concerns an apparent sharp rise in race-hate attacks perpetrated against white people, predominantly by Asians, in the northern English town of Oldham in 2001. At the end of January, the local newspaper ran a story citing police sources that suggested a hugely disproportionate number of hate attacks were being committed against white victims. Renton suggests that the impression of an ongoing and growing racial tension persisted and escalated to the point where Oldham's white population was led to believe that they were victims of Asian instigated racism. Similarly, the Asian community perceived themselves to be discriminated against in many areas of their lives leading to heightened racial tensions in the town. The BNP seized this opportunity and following the now infamous Oldham race riots on 27 May, the BNP's leader, Nick Griffin, recorded the highest vote by a far right party in a British parliamentary election, polling 16 per cent of the vote in Oldham (Renton, 2003).

It is worth noting here that the statistics given by the police showed that 60 per cent (of 572 incidents) of racist hate crime victims in Oldham were white, while only 14 per cent of the town's population at the time was Asian. Renton therefore rightly questions where all these attacks came from. Of course we can only speculate, but the answer may *in part* be found in our discussion in Chapter 1 of the social construction of hate crime and the impact of the definition adopted in England and Wales. It is possible that the Oldham case represents an example of the potential for subverting the underlying principle behind hate crime and hate crime policy. If so, this illustrates particularly well that hate crime is indeed a social construction and is particularly vulnerable and susceptible to external influences. In other words, the size and nature of the hate crime 'problem' in Oldham may have been more to do with how hate crime is defined and conceptualised rather than an accurate reflection of intergroup conflict.

The third event that Renton suggests has been central to the success of the BNP relates to the 11 September 2001 terrorist attacks on the US. These attacks, and the subsequent 'war on terror' and the resulting focus on Muslims and Arabs as potential terrorists, gave new impetus to Islamophobia across the world. Renton argues that the widespread focus on Islam and its perceived links to terrorism, aided by significant media attention, played an important part in the success of the BNP in the 2002 local elections, particularly in areas of Britain where conflict between whites and Muslims over scarce resources was already occurring. Similarly, Renton suggests that the 'demonising' of refugees and asylum seekers, particularly by the tabloid media, has been crucial in providing a platform from which the BNP can gain public support. In particular, Renton points to the media-fuelled link between refugees and terrorism, and between asylum seekers and crime and the general degradation of the country. Indeed, the view that 'outsiders' are responsible for crime and other social ills, as we have seen, is an important tenet of hate ideology.

Finally, Renton suggests that recent government rhetoric on immigration has also helped the BNP. Despite effectively encouraging widespread public concern in relation to asylum seekers, refugees and the immigration 'crisis' in Britain, Renton argues that these fears have not been quelled by government responses to the 'problem'. Rather, the racist sentiment that has been stirred up has served to boost the BNP who for many appear to offer better prospects for solving the 'crisis' and alleviating the perceived 'strain' in their lives than the government.

In sum, the recent success of the BNP in Britain, according to Renton, is more a product of external events rather than internal party developments. Renton also suggests that while the rise of the BNP is a matter for immediate concern, there is no guarantee that the favourable social conditions that have aided the BNP will continue. Their internal state, he suggests, is weak and their membership is significantly less than that of the National Front during the 1970s (approximately 3,500 in 2003). In addition, he argues, many of the BNP's local cadres are long-standing neo-Nazis, and despite considerable efforts the recruitment of new generations has been small. The net effect is that the party lacks the level of active support to achieve wider and sustained electoral success.

Nevertheless, the adoption of the political approach, or 'main-streaming', represents a significant change in the approach and activities of many far right organisations not only in Britain but also across the whole of Europe and is perhaps a reflection of an appreciation of both the futility of adopting predominantly violent means to further their cause, and also the potential to reach a far greater audience by 'moderating' their views, heading down the 'democratic' route and exploiting contemporary societal concerns and fears.

The rise of the far right in Europe

It is not just Britain that has witnessed a rise in the political success of the far right. Eatwell (2000) notes that a variety of other European extreme right-wing parties have achieved considerable electoral gains since the mid-1980s. The most notable of these are the entry into government of Jorg Haider's Austrian Freedom Party in 1999 and the more recent success of the French National Front leader, Jean-Marie Le Pen, in coming second in the presidential elections in 2003. In the late 1990s various significant electoral successes were also achieved: in Germany by the German People's Union (13 per cent in 1998); in Switzerland by the Swiss People's Party (23 per cent in 1999); in Belgium by the Flemish Block (16 per cent in 1999); in Italy by the National Alliance and the Northern League (10 per cent in 1996); in Norway by the Progress Party (15 per cent in 1997); and in Denmark by the Danish Popular Party (7 per cent in 1998) (Eatwell, 2000). Curiously, the success of many of these parties appears to have occurred as many of them were seemingly trapped in a period of political and electoral obscurity.

Eatwell suggests that a number of theories have been put forward to explain this rise in popularity of far right political parties. One of the most popular is the *protest vote theory*, by which support for extreme right-wing parties is held to be a product of voters' dissatisfaction with mainstream parties. According to Eatwell this populist view is problematic because it necessarily assumes that there is little or no social structure to the extremist vote, which is often far from the case. He suggests that it is perfectly possible to make a protest and a rational choice when protesting in this way. For the protest theory to hold it is necessary for voters to choose a party that is not ideologically close to them and for them to have no interest in whether or not the party is likely to exercise influence. Eatwell contends that on recent evidence neither of these conditions appears to hold true. There are often plenty of other parties for whom a protest vote could be cast, so why are such votes predominantly given to far right parties?

The second explanation comes from the *single-issue theory*, which Eatwell suggests places emphasis on the attractiveness of anti-immigrant and immigration-related politics. This therefore assumes that extreme right-wing parties will flourish when there is widespread public concern about immigration. This is certainly a plausible explanation, particularly in the light of Renton's examination of the rise of the BNP in Britain, above. The problem with this as a satisfactory generic explanation for the success of far right parties is that most of these parties in fact have a wide range of policies, and are often supported for the whole package rather than just for their stance on a particular issue (Eatwell, 2000). From this position a third theory suggests that the success of the far right can be attributed to this 'winning formula' of policies that may appeal to a disaffected electorate.

Eatwell doubts this, however. For him, the evidence from European parties indicates no such 'winning formula'. Rather, he suggests that a more plausible explanation can be found in the *political opportunity structure* approach. This view contends that extremist parties will be electorally successful when mainstream parties cluster around the centre and fail to pick up on or adequately respond to the issues that are of particular interest or concern to voters. Eatwell suggests that the extreme right can be legitimised when political discourse becomes contaminated by its themes, particularly those relating to immigration. This theory can be neatly applied to Renton's final explanation for the success of the BNP, whereby voter disillusionment with the government response to Britain's immigration 'crisis' effectively served to boost the popularity of the party.

In sum, Eatwell attributes the rise of the extreme right in Europe to six related issues: the desire of people to find a sense of belonging; the belief that it is economically rational to support at least some right-wing policies; the influence of community norms; the perception of the party as legitimate; the perception that voting for the party is in some way efficacious; and finally that there is a loss of trust in the mainstream parties. Together, Eatwell suggests, the presence of these six factors helps to explain the recent political rise of the far right across Europe.

Similarly, Zaslove (2004) argues that the rise of the far right in Europe is a product of parties having a specific organisational structure, incorporating a charismatic leader, a hierarchical structure and populist discourse; mobilising tactics to penetrate and attract disillusioned and alienated voters; and a specific ideology incorporating 'anti-authority' and 'anti-globalisation' (both economic and cultural) messages and the scapegoating of 'outsiders' for existing social problems. Put simply, no explanation can singularly account for the political rise of the far right. Rather, as with other expressions of prejudice and hate, it is the combination of a number of factors.

But while Renton was fairly optimistic in his view that the necessary conditions for the continuing growth of the far right in Britain would not persist, Eatwell is far more cautious in his appraisal of the wider European picture. In noting political stirrings throughout Europe (and remembering that this was written before the terrorist attacks of 11 September 2001, which have undoubtedly made many of these issues more acute), Eatwell (2000: 424) warns that:

> … there exists in many countries a potential for significant further 'extreme right' growth or new breakthroughs … the rise of new generations of leaders, with no direct connection with historic fascism, together with new forms of discourse, makes it more difficult to tag them as beyond the pale. So, too, does the rise of issues, especially relating to new or feared immigration, which are often fudged by a politically-correct establishment … there are clear dangers of a major realignment of voters, with hostility to the current EU reinforcing existing hostility to mainstream elites and fears about the immediate economic future … The extreme right is coming in from the cold.

Genocide and mass hate

Thus far in our consideration of hate crime perpetrators we have concentrated on what might be termed 'ordinary' offenders, in the sense that their criminality is not especially different from that of other offenders, whether part of an organised group or not. The use of the word 'ordinary' is not intended to underplay the importance of the actions of these individuals, but rather to set them apart from the extreme expressions of hatred that we shall consider in the remainder of this chapter.

Consider these troubling figures from James Waller's book, *Becoming Evil* (2002). Since the Napoleonic Wars there have been an average of six international and six civil wars each decade, and from the end of the Second World War to the end of the twentieth century there were approximately 150 wars and just 26 days of world peace. In the twentieth century alone more than 100 million people were killed by their fellow human beings. While war is tragic enough, Waller suggests that the greatest catastrophes occur when the distinctions between war and crime fade, and the line between military and criminal conduct disappear.

During the twentieth century, he suggests, more than 60 million people were victims of mass killing and genocide. In other words, 60 per cent of the people killed during the various conflicts of the twentieth century were the victims of criminal, and not military, conduct. Specific examples that Waller cites include the near-complete annihilation of the Hereros by the Germans in South-West Africa in 1904, the Turkish assault on the Armenian population between 1915 and 1923, the Soviet man-made famine in the Ukraine in 1932, the Nazi extermination of two-thirds of Europe's Jews during the Second World War, the massacre in Indonesia in 1965, and mass killings and genocide in Bangladesh (1971), Burundi (1972), Cambodia and East Timor (1975–79), Rwanda (1994) and the Sudan (present).

According to Waller (2002: xi):

mass killing is the killing of members of a group without the intention to eliminate the whole group, or killing large numbers of people without a precise definition of group membership. Collective violence becomes genocide when a specific group is systematically and intentionally targeted for destruction.

Article II of the General Assembly of the United Nations Resolution 96 (I), ratified in December 1948, defines genocide as:

any of the following acts committed with intent to destroy, in whole or in part, a national, ethnical, racial or religious group, as such:

(a) Killing members of the group;
(b) Causing serious bodily or mental harm to members of the group;
(c) Deliberately inflicting on the group conditions of life calculated to bring about its physical destruction in whole or in part;
(d) Imposing measures intended to prevent births within the group ...

For an ordinary crime to become a *hate crime* necessarily requires the intentional selection of a victim on the basis of some group affiliation. Given this necessity, mass killing, and in particular genocide, undoubtedly represent the most extreme examples of hate crime.

But while I drew the distinction between 'ordinary' and 'extraordinary' offenders, the distinction is perhaps more appropriate for the crimes than for the criminals. Killing on a genocidal scale is clearly extraordinary, but Waller suggests that in order to understand 'extraordinary evil' we in fact have to understand its 'ordinariness'. The perpetrators of mass killing and genocide are extraordinary because of what they do, not who they are. According to Waller, to consider the perpetrators of mass killing and genocide simply as psychopaths or monsters is not sufficient to account for all the examples throughout human history. For example, Waller points out that up to 500,000 people took part in the Holocaust, and that up to 150,000 Hutus took part in the killing of at least 800,000 Tutsis in Rwanda. Not all of these perpetrators can be psychotic or sadistic or attributed some other extreme psychological label. Rather, Waller contends, it is more fruitful to understand the ways in which ordinary people come to commit extraordinary acts.

To this end Waller suggests a synthesis of a number of factors that he combines to produce a unified theory of offender behaviour, and one that makes for uncomfortable reading. The first prong of Waller's model focuses on three tendencies of human behaviour that we also examined in Chapter 2: *ethnocentrism* (the belief that one's in-group is superior to other groups), *xenophobia* (the fear of outsiders and members of 'out-groups') and the desire for *social dominance*. As we saw in Chapter 2, these factors are universal and, given the nature of prejudice, both normal and unavoidable. However, while these form the foundations of hatred, we have already noted that this is not enough, and that not everyone expresses these natural tendencies in a violent way.

The second part of Waller's theory therefore focuses on the factors that shape the identities of the individual perpetrators. Here three factors are held to be particularly significant: *cultural belief systems* (external, controlling influences, authority orientation, ideological commitment), *moral disengagement* of the perpetrator from the victim (facilitated by moral justification, euphemistic labelling of evil actions and exonerating comparisons) and *rational self-interest* (professional and personal).

The third strand of Waller's theory considers the role of the social context in influencing individuals. Of particular significance is the role of *professional socialisation* (built on escalating commitments, ritual conduct and the repression of conscience), the *binding factors of the group* (including diffusion of responsibility, deindividuation and conformity to peer pressure) and the *merger of role and person* (the significance of an organisation in changing a person within it). The final strand of the theory relates to the victims or, more accurately, how the victims are perceived. In this regard three further factors are significant: *us–them thinking, dehumanisation of the victim* and *blaming of the victim*, each of which have been considered in other chapters in this book.

Waller points out that his theoretical model is not an invocation of a single psychological state or event. Rather it represents an analysis of the process through which perpetrators are changed from an ordinary person to an individual for whom committing extraordinarily evil acts becomes a part of their new self. The model, he suggests, specifically explicates the forces that shape human responses to authority by looking at who the perpetrators are, the situational framework they are in and how they see 'outsiders'. By considering those factors that make humans the same (the nature of prejudice) and those factors that make humans different (thoughts, feelings and behaviours), contextualising these within cultural and situational influences and considering the psychological processes by which victims are excluded, Waller provides a framework which facilitates the commission of extraordinary evil by ordinary people. In other words, under Waller's model, the nature of prejudice leaves all humans capable of extreme hatred and extraordinary evil when activated by appropriate cues contained within the identities of the perpetrators, the social context and the perception of victims.

Rather than provide a definitive and conclusive account of why people commit acts of mass killing and genocide, Waller's model instead presents an account of the conditions under which such acts can take place. It is a complex interplay of a number of factors, and as such is similar to accounts of 'ordinary' hate crime. Simply, there is no single factor that causes people to commit crimes against 'outsiders', regardless of the scale of those crimes. What is certain, however, is that prejudice plays a central role as the underlying facilitator that is somehow triggered by other factors.

In this sense we might reasonably return to Sibbitt's (1997) contention from the previous chapter that racial violence is a logical and predictable expression of underlying prejudice in society at large. In the context of genocide, it is clear that the support, or at least the indifference, of many people is often required for such acts to occur. The negative prejudices and violent actions of a minority alone are insufficient for genocide to take place. Jones (2000) suggests, therefore, that the presence of an underlying negative prejudice within a society is a common theme in accounts of genocide.

Jones points out that where genocide has occurred, 'outsiders' who have not successfully assimilated into a society have often been blamed and made scapegoats for social problems experienced by the majority. The groups in question, which necessarily have to be physically vulnerable, are usually stereotyped in negative terms and are frequently subjected to dehumanising propaganda. For scapegoating to occur, the existence of social problems is crucial, and it has often been the case that an authoritarian government will emphasise particular values and beliefs and disparage cultural diversity, which serves to minimise the development of sympathetic views towards the scapegoat. From this position of widespread prejudice against a particular group, Jones suggests that leaders can attract support for their position, and joining a movement or embracing an ideology can provide powerless individuals with imaginary or real authority, which in a military context may include the power to commit violent acts against others. In this way, Jones argues that emotions, including fear and anger, can be channelled against a perceived enemy, and as disaffected individuals join together as a group (for example an army or militia movement) then the governing ideology provides a collective solution to a collective problem.

Perhaps the best example of the process that Jones describes is the Nazi persecution of the Jews during the Second World War that culminated in the Holocaust and the extermination of over six million Jews. For many centuries the anti-Semitic myth of a Jewish conspiracy to take over the world was passed down through the generations, and this widespread (latent) prejudice against the Jews provided the perfect opportunity to attribute blame for Germany's interwar social problems (unemployment, recession, inflation, homelessness, anxiety over the future, the need to attribute blame for the loss of the First World War and so on) onto a particular social group by an authoritarian government with a distinct anti-Semitic ideology. It is the presence of these facilitating factors that Jones suggests provided the justification for pogroms against the Jews leading ultimately to the 'Final Solution'.

Concluding comments

This chapter has examined the extremes of prejudice, and it is perhaps these things that immediately come to mind when we think about hatred in the truest sense of the word. I am not so naive as to believe that the explanations put forward in this chapter are anywhere near comprehensive. This chapter does not provide any firm answers as to why people engage in acts of extreme bigotry and hatred. I would argue that a single chapter could never do justice to any attempt to explain such extremes of human behaviour. But one general theme that is consistent with those of other chapters in this book is that even the most violent forms of hatred have their foundations in the prejudice that is naturally found within us all. It is when this is combined with other internal or external factors, as is the case with other expressions of hate, that the potential for extreme expressions of hatred arises. But again, the process by which this occurs is uncertain.

Nevertheless, the study of hate groups is important not just because of the violence and intimidation that their members engage in, but also because of their potential for spreading messages of bigotry and hate to an audience far beyond their immediate members, messages that have become much easier to spread thanks in particular to the Internet. It is also necessary to consider the diversification and mainstreaming of hate groups, as the political success that we have examined in this chapter arguably represents an important social barometer regarding issues of public concern.

The study of genocide and mass hatred is similarly important. The research presented in this chapter suggests that while such actions are extraordinary, the perpetrators often are not. Developing an understanding of the processes by which people come to inflict such atrocities on their fellow humans is crucial if future genocides are to be prevented. In sum, if we can begin to understand the conditions that give rise to hatred, then we will be better placed to take the first steps towards removing or resolving them. One such step can be found in the enactment of new hate-based legislation, and it is to the law that we now turn.

Chapter 7

Legislating against hate

Over the past 25 years or so the enactment of hate crime legislation in the United States has represented one of the most lively and significant trends in criminal law making (Levin, 1999). In Britain we have begun to follow suit by outlawing certain specific 'hate-motivated' offences, most notably through the Crime and Disorder Act 1998, but also through other more recent legislation.

Jacobs and Potter (1998) suggest that hate crime laws in the US generally fall into one or more of four categories. Firstly there are those that enhance sentences for hate-motivated offences; secondly, there are those that redefine existing criminal behaviours as a 'new' crime or as an aggravated form of an existing crime; thirdly, there are those that relate specifically to civil rights issues; and finally, there are those that concern themselves solely with matters of reporting and data collection. In Britain, where our legislation is more limited, we are primarily concerned with the first three of Jacobs and Potter's categories.

To the casual onlooker the creation of laws to respond directly to hate crimes might appear relatively uncomplicated (i.e. just another law protecting people from just another crime), but in fact they are hugely controversial and subject to much political, scholarly and indeed public debate. While the various arguments and controversies surrounding hate crimes legislation in the United States, the United Kingdom and elsewhere will be the subject of the next chapter, we will simply concern ourselves here with the specifics of the law as it currently stands in the US and Britain before examining some of the practical issues relating to the application of the law and the prosecution of hate crimes.

Modern hate crime legislation in the US

The Civil Rights Act 1968

In Chapter 3 we noted the significance of the Civil Rights Act of 1968 as being something of a catalyst for modern hate crime legislation. The Act prohibits interference with federally protected rights by way of violence or threat of violence because of a person's race, colour, religion or national origin (US Department of Justice, 1999). These protected federal rights include, for example, the right to vote and to obtain government benefits, the right to public education, to participation in state programmes, to obtaining employment, to participation in jury service and to interstate travel, and the right to the benefits of various types of public places and services (Levin, 2002).

Although this statute is not aimed at hate crimes per se, Streissguth (2003) states that it has historically been the statute under which hate crimes have been prosecuted. However, he also suggests that the high burden of proof required to secure convictions under the Act is responsible for the small number of crimes actually prosecuted (37 cases between 1991 and 2001). This, he continues, has in practice had the effect of handing responsibility for hate crime prosecutions over to local law enforcement, and has therefore played a significant role in the emergence and development of the state legislation that we shall discuss in due course. Indeed, it is this high burden of proof that, according to Streissguth, has led to the proposed Hate Crimes Prevention Act (see below) that contains provisions for lowering the evidential requirements of federal prosecutions.

The Hate Crime Statistics Act 1990

The term 'hate crime' was officially coined in 1985 by three members of the US House of Representatives sponsoring a Bill seeking a 'Hate Crime Statistics Act'. The Bill sought the annual collection and publication of hate crime data from various law enforcement and voluntary agencies across the United States by the Department of Justice and was something of a response to a perceived rise in the number of offences motivated by prejudice and bigotry and subsequent lobbying by a number of civil rights groups (US Department of Justice, 1997).

The 'Hate Crime Statistics Act' was ultimately passed by the United States Congress in 1990, and the FBI Uniform Crime Reporting system was designated by the Attorney General as the official method for the collection of hate crime data. The 1990 Act required the collection of data relating to offences motivated by race, religion, sexual orientation and ethnicity and thus represented the first official recognition of prejudice-motivated offending as a specific form of offending deserving of attention in its own right. The offences covered by the Act are homicide, non-negligent manslaughter, forcible rape, assault, intimidation, arson and destruction, damage or vandalism of property (US Department of Justice, 1997).

Jacobs and Potter (1998) state that the aims of this early legislation were fourfold. Firstly it was hoped that the collection of hate crime data would enable the criminal justice system as a whole to respond more efficiently and effectively to incidents of hate crime. Secondly, it was hoped that the Act would improve the law enforcement response by increasing their sensitivity to and awareness of incidents of hate crime. Thirdly, it was hoped that the Act would raise public awareness of the hate crime 'problem'. And finally, it was hoped that a clear message would be sent to the American public that crimes motivated by prejudice and bigotry would not be tolerated.

The Violence Against Women Act 1994

While there was considerable debate about whether or not to collect data on offences motivated by homophobia, the category of sexual orientation was ultimately included in the Hate Crime Statistics Act. Significantly, however, the categories of gender and disability were not. The failure to include gender as a distinct category within the Hate Crime Statistics Act sparked much heated debate. The rationale for omitting gender centred on a number of issues. Firstly, it was argued by opponents that statistics on rape and domestic violence were already collected by the federal government and therefore did not need to be included again. Secondly, the argument was made that in the majority of offences against women the victim was acquainted with their attacker. The reasoning here was that such offences could not be hate crimes because perpetrators predominantly targeted one woman whom they knew, and not women per se. In this sense then, the victim is not necessarily interchangeable as is the case for other forms of hate crime where the victim is targeted because of their membership of a particular group rather than their individual identity (Jacobs and Potter, 1998).

Jacobs and Potter also suggest that a further reason for the non-inclusion of gender in the Hate Crime Statistics Act was the fear that, because of the prevalence of misogynistic violence against women in the United States, that the inclusion of gender as a distinct category of hate crime would cause other forms of hate crime to be eclipsed in the figures.

In response, women's advocacy groups argued strongly that many forms of crime against women do not involve acquaintances and can only be explained by the offender's irrational hatred of women (Jacobs and Potter, 1998). In such incidents the victim clearly becomes interchangeable thereby transforming an 'ordinary' crime into a hate crime. As such, following the lobbying of Congress by various advocacy groups, the Violence Against Women Act was passed in 1994 as part of the Violent Crime Control and Law Enforcement Act. Congress found that:

> Crimes motivated by the victim's gender constitute bias crimes in violation of the victim's right to be free from discrimination on the basis of gender. (Public Law 102–322: 1994, title iv)

The Act includes provisions against violent crimes committed by offenders who cross state lines to offend and those who violate a protective order. In addition, the Act allows for civil lawsuits whereby victims can claim financial reparation from their attacker (Streissguth, 2003). Jacobs and Potter argue, however, that the symbolic significance of the Violence Against Women Act is far greater than its practical value as its success in achieving convictions has been limited. Nevertheless, the Act saw the inclusion of gender as a specific category of hate crime for the first time.

Hate Crimes Sentencing Enhancement Act 1994

Another crucial part of the Violent Crime Control and Law Enforcement Act 1994 saw the introduction of the Hate Crimes Sentencing Enhancement Act which allows for increased sentences of up to 30 per cent to be passed down on offenders committing hate crimes where it can be proved that offence was motivated by the perpetrator's prejudice against the victim's race, religion, colour, national origin, ethnicity, gender, disability or sexual orientation (Department of Justice, 2003). Note here the inclusion of disability as a distinct category of hate crime victimisation for the first time.

Church Arson Prevention Act 1996

In response to an increasing number of hate attacks on churches and other places of worship, the Church Arson Prevention Act established the National Church Arson Task Force to oversee the investigation and prosecution of these forms of hate crimes. The Task Force brought federal agencies from the Justice and Treasury departments into partnership with state and local law enforcement and prosecutorial agencies to enhance efforts to combat attacks against religious premises, and also allowed broader federal criminal jurisdiction to aid criminal prosecutions. In addition:

> The law enhances penalties for damaging religious property or obstructing any person's free exercise of religious freedom ... The law also provides compensation to churches that fall prey to arsons and extends Federal hate crime and crime victim protections to churches attacked because of the ethnic or racial composition of their memberships. (US Department of Justice, 1997: 18)

In addition, the Act allows for the federal guarantee of private loans of up to $5 million for the rebuilding of damaged or destroyed religious properties. Furthermore, in addition the Act also reauthorised (in effect renewed) the original Hate Crime Statistics Act of 1990 (US Department of Justice, 2003).

Hate Crimes Prevention Act 1999

Although introduced in 1999, and despite having been passed by the US Senate, at the time of writing the Hate Crimes Prevention Act (HCPA) has yet to be passed by the House of Representatives and formally introduced into law. While this delay is probably a product of other pressing concerns in American politics at the present time, the HCPA remains a potentially significant piece of legislation. As Streissguth (2003: 50) explains:

> ... the bill would expand the role of the federal government in hate crimes prosecution ... It would provide technical, forensic, prosecutorial, or any other form of assistance to state and local law enforcement officials in cases of crimes that are considered hate crimes under state law, or that (a) constitute crimes of violence; (b) constitute a felony under state law; and (c) are motivated by bias based on race, colour, religion, national origin, gender, disability, or sexual orientation.

In addition, grants would be available to assist local hate crime investigations and, crucially, the burden of proof that Streissguth suggests has hindered the prosecution of hate crimes under the Civil Rights Act 1968 would be lowered. Previously it was necessary for prosecutors to prove both that the victim's status was a causal factor in the commission of the crime and that the victim was targeted because (not while) they were performing a particular federally protected activity at the time of the offence (Levin, 2002). Under this Act prosecutors would no longer need to prove the latter.

Future federal legislation?

In addition to the federal legislation outlined above and the HCPA 1999 that has still to be ratified, a further number of relevant bills were introduced in 2003. Although not yet enacted into law these bills (the Equal Rights and Equal Dignity for Americans Act 2003, the Hate Crimes Statistics Improvement Act 2003, the Hate Crimes Prevention Act 2003 and the Local Law Enforcement Enhancement Act 2003) represent further efforts to legislate against hate crime and their progress through Congress can be tracked by accessing the US Department of Justice website at www.ncjrs.org/hate_crimes/legislation.html.

State legislation

Thus far in this chapter we have discussed federal legislation in the United States. While significant because such legislation outlaws interference with a person's right to engage in federally protected activities and uphold the federal, Constitutional and statutory civil rights of American citizens, it is quite different to state and local hate crime laws. As Jacobs and Potter (1998: 42) explain, federal laws

> … provide federal insurance that crime will be prosecuted if state and local law enforcement authorities default in carrying out their responsibilities.

At the state and local level, however, the situation is far more intricate. Most states have enacted their own forms of hate crime legislation, and it is at this level that the majority of hate crimes are dealt with. The first to do so (in the modern sense) was California in 1987, which closely replicated the Civil Rights Act of 1968. Many other states have since utilised a model of hate crime legislation produced in 1981 by the Anti-Defamation League. The model, which can be retrieved from www.adl.org, was created to assist states keen to outlaw criminal acts motivated by prejudice and essentially provides a template document where state legislators can 'fill in the blanks' to suit their individual requirements about which criminal acts and which categories of prejudice are to be included.

The relative legal autonomy of each state has, however, meant that different states have adopted different forms of legislation covering different criminal acts and outlawing different prejudices at different times. Thus what is a hate crime in one state may not be in another, and what is a protected group in one state may also not be in another. Jacobs and Potter continue by explaining that:

> There are significant differences in the ways that federal and state legislatures define hate crimes. A number of states ... treat hate crime as a low-level offence, such as intimidation or harassment. Other states have more general hate crime laws and sentence enhancements that mandate higher sentences for most or all crimes when motivated by prejudice. The statutes also differ as to which prejudices transform ordinary crime into hate crime and as to whether those prejudices must be manifest in the criminal conduct itself or can be proved by evidence concerning the defendant's beliefs, opinion and character. The diversity of hate crime laws means that we cannot assume that people are talking about the same thing when they discuss 'hate crime' or that hate crime reports and statistics from one jurisdiction can be compared with reports and statistics from other jurisdictions. (1998: 43–4)

Consequently, a detailed discussion of state legislation in this field is beyond the scope of this chapter. To highlight the magnitude of such a task, Streissguth (2003) provides a summary of state hate crime laws. He lists those states under headings that include provisions for age (4 states), violence and intimidation (45 states and the District of Columbia), civil action (30 states and the DoC), data collection (23 states and the DoC), gender (25 states and the DoC), institutional vandalism (42 states and the DoC), interference with religious worship (21 states and the DoC), law enforcement training (11 states), mental and physical disability (29 states and the DoC), political affiliation (4 states), race, religion, ethnic group (43 states and the DoC) and sexual orientation (28 states and the DoC). Some states appear in numerous categories, but many do not and thus there is a lack of uniformity across the states. Furthermore, Streissguth's categorisation is significantly different to that published by the US Department of Justice just six years previously.

This would suggest that in addition to the massive variation in legislation across the different states, the law is also in a seemingly continual state of change and revision across those states. This makes it difficult to keep up to date with current provisions in every instance and any similar attempt that I might include here will likely be out of date relatively quickly. In light of this the reader is advised to visit the website of the Anti-Defamation League who provide information on the current legal situation in each state in a simple tabular form. This can be found at www.adl.org/99hatecrime/provisions.asp#al and outlines the statutory provisions contained within each state's hate crime legislation, which, as you will see for yourself, vary greatly across America.

Anti-discrimination and hate crime legislation in Britain

From the account above, which is necessarily brief, it is clear that American legislation against hate crime is a complex and varied phenomenon (for a comprehensive account readers are advised to see the US Department of Justice, 1997 and 2003; Jacobs and Potter, 1998; Levin, 2002; Streissguth, 2003, and the Anti-Defamation League's website). The situation in Britain is different because specific legislation is of more recent origin and is significantly less broad than in the US. Furthermore, legislation does not vary in its content at the local level. In this section of the chapter I shall outline relevant anti-discrimination legislation and, in particular, that which has been introduced to combat hate motivated crimes as a specific and aggravating form of criminal behaviour.

Anti-discrimination legislation

Although specific 'hate' motivated offences are a relatively recent development in law in this country, the need for protection from discrimination has been recognised for a longer period. A number of acts and conventions have set out various legislative provisions aimed at challenging discrimination in a number of social arenas. The key pieces of legislation in this regard are Article 1 of the 1945 United Nations Charter, Article 7 of the 1949 Universal Declaration of Human Rights, Article 14 of the European Convention on Human Rights, the 1965 International Convention on the Elimination of All Forms of Racial Discrimination, the Race Relations Acts of 1965, 1968 and 1976, section 95 of the 1991 Criminal Justice Act, the 1998 Human Rights Act and the Race Relations (Amendment) Act 2000.

Each of these legislative provisions extends the principle of legal equality and protection from discrimination to varying degrees in different areas of social life, although predominantly along the lines of race (see Bowling and Phillips, 2003, for a critique). However, none of these acts or conventions creates a specific criminal offence of 'hate'. Indeed the term 'hate crime' does not specifically appear in any British legislation and therefore does not officially exist as a distinct category of criminal behaviour in itself. Instead, other, more recent legislation prohibits certain acts which are already outlawed in other legislation, but allows for increased penalties to be imposed by the courts when those acts are proven to be motivated or aggravated by certain officially designated prejudices.

Towards 'hate crime' legislation

The key piece of legislation in this respect is the Crime and Disorder Act 1998, which allows for enhanced sentencing for racially and, following amendment by the Anti-terrorism, Crime and Security Act of 2001, religiously motivated assaults, criminal damage, public order offences and harassment. These criminal acts are already legislated against by the Offences Against the Person Act 1861, the Criminal Damage Act 1971, the Public Order Act 1986 and the Protection from Harassment Act 1997 respectively. However, where these existing offences can be proved to be aggravated by racial or religious hostility then the Crime and Disorder Act allows for additional penalties to reflect the offender's prejudice towards the victim.

For example, section 20 of the Offences Against the Person Act 1861 provides a maximum penalty on indictment for grievous bodily harm of five years imprisonment. Section 29(1)(a) and (2) of the Crime and Disorder Act allows for an enhanced sentence of seven years imprisonment if it can be proved that the same offence was racially aggravated. Similarly, section 4(a) of the Public Order Act 1986 allows for a summary sentence of six months imprisonment for causing intentional harassment, alarm or distress. Under section 31(1)(b) and (4) of the Crime and Disorder Act the same offence attracts a sentence on indictment of two years imprisonment where it can be proved that the same offence was racially motivated (ACPO, 2000).

In addition to the categories of offences outlined above, section 82 of the Crime and Disorder Act 1998 provides a requirement for the courts to consider racist motives as aggravating factors when determining a sentence for any offence not specifically listed in the Act.

Under the Crime and Disorder Act 1998, Part 2, section 28, an offence is racially aggravated if:

(a) at the time of committing the offence, or immediately before or after doing so, the offender demonstrates towards the victim of the offence hostility based on the victim's membership (or presumed membership) of a racial group; or

(b) the offence is motivated (wholly or partly) by hostility towards members of a racial group based on their membership of that group.

Under the Act a 'racial group' refers to persons defined by reference to their race, colour, nationality or ethnic or national origins and, following amendment, in section 28(3)(a) includes membership of any religious group. The latter is significant because under a legal ruling laid down in *Mandla* v. *Dowell-Lee* [1983] 2 AC 548, Jews and Sikhs were included in the definition of a racial group but other faiths were not. The amendment therefore ensures inclusiveness among religious groups under this piece of legislation.

In short, the Crime and Disorder Act 1998 (CDA) effectively created nine new racially aggravated offences based upon pre-existing offences contained in other legislation. The CDA allows for sentence enhancement for offences where it can be proved that racial aggravation was present at the time of the offence, except where offences already carry a maximum life sentence. The Act also allows for the courts (with the exception of the magistrates' courts) to increase sentences for other non-specified offences aggravated by racial hostility. Thus some offences that would normally be summary only have become either-way offences (magistrates are able to commit racist offenders to the Crown Court for sentence) and maximum sentences have increased to the 'next level' on the sentencing tariff. The provisions for enhanced sentencing also include increased fines, community sentences and compensation (Burney and Rose, 2002) and require the courts to explicitly pronounce in open court that the offence was racially motivated.

But the Crime and Disorder Act 1998 was not the first piece of legislation to draw attention to the issue of 'hate'. However, the provisions contained within the CDA were in part necessary to overcome the practical difficulties associated with other legislation in this area. The promotion of racial hatred had already been outlawed by the Race Relations Acts of 1965 and 1976, and also by provisions contained within the Public Order Act 1986 and the Football (Disorder) Act 1991 and later revised by the Football (Offences and Disorder) Act in 1999.

Although there was no specific scope for sentence enhancement in any of this legislation (the courts may, however, have taken the racist element into account at the sentencing stage but increased penalties were not incorporated into the wording of the law), the significance of the racist element of crime was at least recognised. Section 17 of the Public Order Act 1986 in particular states that:

A person who uses threatening, abusive or insulting words or behaviour, or displays any written material which is threatening, abusive or insulting, is guilty of an offence if (a) he intends to stir up racial hatred, or (b) having regard to all the circumstances racial hatred is likely to be stirred up thereby.

Additionally, a subsequent amendment to that Act made reference to the intentional causing of alarm, harassment or distress, which was aimed at responding to racially aggravated behaviour.

However, the problems associated with this particular piece of legislation are highlighted by the fact that only 41 cases were brought for prosecution between 1990 and 1997. Iganski (1999a) asserts that this low number of prosecutions, and thus the limited effectiveness of the legislation, can be attributed firstly to the low incidence of offences covered by the Act, secondly to the limitations of the provisions of the legislation, and finally (and crucially), to the ambiguous language used to define what is actually unlawful.

Of particular concern for Iganski is the use of the word 'hatred' which he explains implies a rather severe sentiment that may in reality exclude other lesser or more subtle acts, behaviours or language (written or verbal) that may nevertheless lead to criminal behaviour and may still stir up racial hatred. In essence then, prosecuting 'hatred' is difficult, but prosecuting 'hostility' as the Crime and Disorder Act 1998 does, should (in theory at least) allow for a far greater breath of 'prejudice in action' to be taken into account. The focus on wider prejudice rather than hatred is therefore deliberate and supports the contention that hate crime isn't predominantly about 'hate'.

More recent legislation has sought to protect groups other than those identified by race or religion, and has incorporated offences other than those specifically stated by the Crime and Disorder Act 1998. For example, section 153 of the Powers of Criminal Courts (Sentencing) Act 2000 requires the courts to consider racial or religious hostility as an aggravating factor when deciding on the sentence for any offence which is not specifically stated under the Crime and Disorder Act

1998. This means that racial or religious aggravation can be taken into consideration by the court in sentencing for any offence.

Similarly, the Criminal Justice Act 2003 allows for homophobia and disability (mental and physical) bias to be taken into account as aggravating factors at sentencing, but stops short of making them specific offences in the same way that the Crime and Disorder Act 1998 does for offences relating to race and religion. Likewise, in Northern Ireland the Criminal Justice (No. 2) Northern Ireland Order, introduced in September 2004, while not creating any new 'hate' offences, does allow for hostility based on religion, race, sexual orientation or disability to be taken into account on conviction when sentencing. The Criminal Justice Act 2003 does, however, state that it is immaterial whether or not the offender's hostility is also based, to any extent, on any other factor. The expression of prejudice, however strong or in whatever way, is the key issue.

Finally, Part IV of the Serious Organised Crime and Police Bill before Parliament in 2005 proposes the expansion of existing incitement to racial hatred offences to create a new offence of *hatred against persons on racial or religious grounds.* The aim of the legislation will be to combat the activities of extremists who seek to incite hatred against groups either because of their religious beliefs or because of a lack of religious beliefs, and has been requested by key leaders in all major faith communities (Home Office, 2004). This proposed legislation is, however, the subject of much controversy, and the key concerns will be examined in the next chapter when we examine the moral debate surrounding hate crime legislation.

Hate crime legislation around the world

Of course, Britain and America are not the only countries to have enacted hate crime legislation. Canada, for example, has sentence enhancement provisions for offences motivated by prejudice against nationality, colour, religion, sex, age, sexual orientation and disability, both mental and physical. Furthermore, Canada has expansive hate speech laws, allows for punishment for those who advocate genocide and outlaws incitement to hatred and the communication of statements that promote hatred on the basis of colour, race, religion or ethnic origin (Levin, 2002).

Closer to home, Germany has legislation that outlaws incitement to racial hatred and limits its constitutional protection of free speech to only that which is truthful and does not contravene the human rights of others (Levin, 2002). Similar legislation outlawing incitement to racial hatred has been established to varying degrees in many other European countries, including France, Denmark, Switzerland and the Netherlands, and Holocaust denial is an offence in countries such as Austria, Belgium, France, Spain and, perhaps unsurprisingly, Germany (Iganski, 1999a).

Prosecuting hate crimes

Having laws to combat hate crimes is one thing. Successfully applying them is quite another. In this section of the chapter I shall examine some of the key issues associated with prosecuting 'hate' crimes.

Although statistics are hard to find, Jacobs and Potter (1998) suggest that the number of hate crime prosecutions in the US is low, and because of this most prosecutors have little experience in prosecuting hate offences. Although some cases are clear-cut, the prosecution of most hate crimes is difficult because of the need to prove beyond reasonable doubt that the offender was motivated by prejudice, and also because of the difficulty in proving that the prejudice was the cause of the offence. These two issues, Jacobs and Potter suggest, often make hate crime cases more difficult to prosecute than crimes committed without the hate element.

In England and Wales the Crown Prosecution Service (CPS) also recognises the inherent difficulty in proving bias motivation. In their *Guidance on Prosecuting Cases of Racist and Religious Crime* the CPS (2003) draws attention to the wording of section 28 of the Crime and Disorder Act 1998, which refers to both the *demonstration of* and *motivation by hostility*. The problem here, according to the CPS, is that 'demonstrating hostility' is not defined by the Act, and that the dictionary definition of 'hostile' includes simply being 'unfriendly'. Furthermore, this hostility, however defined, may be totally unconnected with the basic offence in question, and may have been committed for other non-racially or religiously motivated reasons. In this sense, then, the Crime and Disorder Act 1998 encapsulates prejudices and feelings far removed from 'hatred', that may in fact be unconnected with the commission of the crime. This rather reinforces the view that hate crime is rarely just about 'hate'.

The CPS further advise that proving *motivation* may be particularly problematic. In the absence of an admission of intentional racial or religious hostility by the offender, the CPS questions how this motive might otherwise be known. The CPS suggests that in some cases a potential solution to this problem can be achieved through the collection of background evidence that might be relevant to establish a motive and may be admissible as evidence. Evidence of membership of or association with a racist group or evidence of previously expressed racist views may, depending on the facts, be used as evidence in a prosecution. The problem here, as Jacobs and Potter (1998) have suggested, is that this latter approach raises questions about what exactly is on trial, the specific offence or the defendant's beliefs, values, character, statements and affiliations? If it is the latter then this raises some serious moral questions that we shall consider further in the next chapter.

A similar prosecutorial problem can also be found in the wording of Part III of the Public Order Act 1986. The prosecution is required to prove that racial hatred was *likely* to be stirred up, as opposed to it just being a *possibility*. Because of their politically sensitive nature, and to ensure consistency, any allegation under this legislation must be referred to the CPS's Casework Directorate for discussion prior to pursuing a prosecution. Furthermore, to ensure that racist and religious crime is properly prosecuted under all relevant legislation, the CPS has, among other initiatives, developed staff training programmes to raise awareness of the complexities of prosecuting this type of offending, and has put in place arrangements to collate and analyse information provided by the CPS Racist Incident Monitoring Scheme (CPS, 2003).

With regard to the actual number of prosecutions, between April 2003 and April 2004 the CPS prosecuted 3,616 defendants for racist and religious crimes, a figure that is vastly smaller than that recorded by the police. Of this total, 44 were for religiously aggravated offences. The majority of prosecutions related to public order offences and were dealt with in magistrates' courts (CPS, 2004). Of course, prosecution data only tells us so much about the workings of the law. While we can speculate on potential difficulties with the law, in practice the problem we face in assessing the effectiveness of 'hate' legislation in Britain is that the relative novelty of many of the provisions means that they have not been in effect for long enough to be evaluated meaningfully.

To date, the only detailed evaluation of the effectiveness of the Crime and Disorder Act 1998 is one commissioned by the Home Office and conducted by Burney and Rose (2002). Using a triangulatory approach, Burney and Rose's research methodology consisted of case studies of five police divisional areas, statistical analysis of various data sets and a secondary analysis of various surveys. Their work focused on the experiences and opinions of those involved in the process of applying the law, most notably police officers, prosecutors and sentencers, but also members of the community.

The research broadly supports the proposition that hate crime legislation has both expressive and instrumental effects (an issue that we shall discuss further in Chapter 8). The reassuring message to victims and the stern warning to potential offenders are evident in the research through the frequency and vehemence with which defendants deny racist intent and through the shame and stigma attached to a racist conviction. If this is true then one might further suggest that the legislation indeed has some deterrent effect, although it is impossible to know this with any degree of certainty given that it is not possible to measure what has not occurred.

Burney and Rose's work also supports Paul Iganski's (1999a) contention that the real value of hate legislation is to provide an impetus for the criminal justice system. They state that practitioners in each agency that they researched (police, Crown Prosecution Service, magistrates and other sentencers) believed that the legislation helped them to focus on the issue of racist hate crime more acutely and respond to it more robustly and more appropriately than had previously been the case.

Despite this, however, the research reveals a number of difficulties with the legislation and evidence that it is not currently being used effectively, and some of the key problems are illustrated by the relevant statistics. For example, of the 47,814 racist incidents recorded by the police in England and Wales in 1999/2000, of which 21,750 were held to be racially aggravated offences and of which the police detected 7,506, just 1,150 offenders were sentenced by the courts (Home Office, 2001). This high attrition rate suggests the existence of a number of problems at each stage of the criminal justice process.

Although the figures are a little misleading because of the mismatch between the definition of a racist incident at the reporting stage and the substantive elements required for a case to be prosecuted by law, a number of concerns still exist. Burney and Rose's research found that the wide definition of 'racial aggravation' had resulted in many cases being incorrectly prosecuted as racially aggravated offences (RAOs) where the racist element was secondary to some other motivating factor. While permissible in law, this does raise questions about the extent to which we are prosecuting 'hate' or some other expression of prejudice, and the extent to which such offences are truly *motivated* by hate. Unsurprisingly then the research also demonstrated that racially aggravated offence charges are frequently contested and, consequently, that they are twice as likely to be committed to the Crown Court for trial as equivalent basic offences.

Once at the Crown Court 83 per cent of RAOs attracted not guilty pleas as opposed to 47 per cent for comparable offences without the racist element. This would appear to support the view that the racist 'tag' is something to be avoided for defendants at all costs. Significantly, at the Crown Court, Burney and Rose found that RAOs have less than half the conviction rate of equivalent basic offences. The difficulty in securing convictions can perhaps be attributed to the difficulties associated with proving bias motivation beyond reasonable doubt that Jacobs and Potter raise, above.

In addition, the issue of cases coming to court where the racist element is at best marginal has a further potentially significant effect on the prosecution process. Under current legislation, if cases are brought as racially aggravated they cannot be tried as basic offences if the racist element is insufficient to convict. This also has the related effect of preventing sentencers from considering evidence of racial aggravation in basic cases (i.e. the racist element cannot be later added even if it subsequently becomes evident at trial). The net effect of these issues is that oftentimes defendants are either acquitted or, in many instances, the racist element of a charge is dropped before trial in order to increase the chances of conviction on the lesser, basic charge. Where the latter occurs, hate offenders may not be convicted of a 'hate crime', but of a lesser 'non-hate' offence. As we shall see in Chapter 12, this situation has important repercussions for responding appropriately to hate offenders upon conviction.

For those cases that are sentenced, Burney and Rose's research suggests mixed responses. In the magistrate's courts, they found that adult offenders convicted of RAOs are on average nearly twice as likely to receive custody on conviction and half as likely to be discharged, and that fines are 50 per cent higher. The sentencing is even more severe in youth courts where the risk of custody is trebled. On the other hand, however, the response of the Crown Courts is a little harder to examine, primarily because of the small number of cases sentenced in the Crown Court throughout the duration of the research and the difficulties in comparison with basic offences. Burney and Rose nevertheless conclude that Crown Court sentencing, as far as it is possible to tell, shows no significant average increase in sentencing for RAOs. The reasons for this, they suggest, may lie in the fact that many judges questioned in the research felt that too many minor RAOs were coming before the Crown Court, and that in any case sentencers already had a duty to sentence more heavily for racial aggravation and the new system sometimes imposed procedural restrictions that impeded that duty.

Some of the other issues identified by the research suggested that the enhanced penalties for RAOs have distracted attention away from the wide range of seriousness of offences that are committed. In other words, the belief of some practitioners is that all RAOs are very serious and should be tried in the Crown Court when they could in fact be dealt with perfectly adequately elsewhere. Furthermore, the research suggests, as we have already noted, that proving racial aggravation presents particular difficulties for prosecutors, with the question of *mens rea* being especially problematic, as does interpreting exactly what is meant by 'hostility' under the Act (a criticism acknowledged by the CPS, and one that is similar to that earlier levelled at the wording used in the Public Order Act 1996 by Paul Iganski).

So does this mean that the law is not working? On the available evidence definitive conclusions are difficult to draw. It should be remembered that the fieldwork for Burney and Rose's research was conducted at a time when the provisions of the CDA 1998 were still relatively new, and many of the difficulties exposed by the research could reasonably be attributed to inexperience on the part of practitioners – teething issues, perhaps. This is indeed recognised by the researchers themselves, and they make a number of suggestions for improvements based upon two principles: firstly that the CDA is used with greater finesse, and secondly that it is used more firmly.

Concluding comments

In this chapter we have, albeit briefly, outlined the current state of the law in both the US and Britain, and speculated upon future legislative activity in each jurisdiction. We have also had a glimpse of related legislation in a small selection of other countries.

It is clear that the law in the US is more advanced, more intricate, broader and distinctly more complex than in Britain. Legislation which purposefully enhances the penalties for crimes motivated or aggravated by certain officially designated prejudices is varied in the US, but here in the UK it is contained within a small but growing set of legislative measures which represent the closest thing to 'hate crime' legislation we have.

The problem with most of the contemporary legislation aimed at 'hate' crimes is that it is too recent to evaluate with any degree of success or utility. Perhaps, however, the time is now right to subject the provisions of the Crime and Disorder Act 1998 to further scrutiny to assess more accurately where we stand now that the law has been in operation for a number of years. It is probably to soon to do likewise with other relevant legislation.

However, the existence of hate crime legislation is not without its controversies. Indeed a fierce scholarly and political debate has engulfed their emergence, particularly in the US, but also to a lesser extent in the UK as well. A number of very serious theoretical, moral and practical questions have been raised, and we shall attempt to answer these questions in the next chapter when we consider what has become known academically as 'the hate debate'.

Chapter 8

The theoretical and moral debate

In the last chapter we examined hate crime legislation in the US and Britain as it currently stands, as well as briefly touching upon provisions in other countries. We noted that legislation has become firmly established on the statute books in many countries around the world. But the nature of our discussion thus far has somewhat masked a number of controversies that have also accompanied the emergence of hate crime laws, and have at times posed something of a threat to the very existence of such legislation, both in terms of theoretical and moral critiques and through practical legal challenges.

In this chapter we shall explore the debate that surrounds the legitimacy of hate crime legislation. While this is a debate that continues on both sides of the Atlantic, it has been much more fervent in the United States than it has been here in Britain. Nevertheless, many of the issues are extremely pertinent to our situation, and the underlying principles that provide the foundations for both sides of the debate are just as applicable to this country as they are to the US. Moreover, the debate provides a framework within which to consider the implications of extending hate crime legislation in the UK, and indeed makes it clear that outlawing hatred is a complex matter fraught with difficulties that have to be considered.

Following our consideration of the theoretical and moral debate, we shall move on to examine some of the key legal challenges brought against hate crime legislation, many of which represent practical incarnations of some of the arguments put forward by critics of hate crime laws.

The case for hate crime legislation

As Chapters 3 and 7 have made clear, the US has led the way in terms of legislating against hate crimes. Indeed, Levin (1999) highlights the fact that enacting laws punishing bigoted and discriminatory crimes has been one of the most popular trends in US criminal legislation over the past two decades. As Boeckmann and Turpin-Petrosino (2002: 207) explain:

> The juxtaposition of broad societal agreement on the values of equality and tolerance and the presence of intergroup tensions arising from long-standing differences in society as well as increasing ethnic and social diversity have created a new category of criminalised behaviour: hate crime. Hate crime laws represent official recognition of the harm of intergroup aggression and the importance of applying sanctions against it.

While the US has been legislating against hate for a number of years, legislative provisions outlawing racially and religiously aggravated crimes in Britain are a more recent development. This is clearly a significant move but the question that remains is, of course, why should we make hate a crime at all? In seeking an answer to this question, one finds that the arguments for legislating against hate are plentiful and have been advocated by proponents from a broad spectrum of social and political backgrounds. Here, then, we shall examine the main arguments for outlawing 'hate'.

We noted in Chapter 3 that the rise of hate crime as a contemporary social issue was driven by a number of different factors. A combination of the extent and nature of racist hate crimes, their seemingly increasing upward trend, coupled with increased public tolerance to issues of diversity and sensitivity to prejudice and the influence of identity politics has forced 'hate' crimes onto the statute books. Hate crime legislation has not only been enacted to counter this perceived growing threat to society, but also to send a strong symbolic message to perpetrators and victims alike.

The enactment of hate crime laws is a statement that these actions will no longer be tolerated and that serious penalties will be applied if such offences are committed. The increased sentences reflect not only the disproportionate harm inflicted upon the victim and the wider community that was discussed in Chapter 4, but also the implication that because an individual is deliberately targeting his victim on the basis of what they are, then there must logically be a greater degree of intent on the part of that offender. On the other side of the coin, legislation represents official acknowledgement that the suffering of victims has been recognised and that society takes this type of victimisation very seriously, considers it socially unacceptable and is no longer prepared to tolerate it.

Such messages can also be said to contribute to the strengthening of social cohesion because the marginalisation of groups afflicted by the effects of hate crime is officially recognised and countered. Such legislation thereby has the effect of promoting equality across society, something that hate crime necessarily seeks to destroy. Simply, then, hate crime legislation extends legal protection to traditionally disadvantaged, victimised and marginalised groups, and offers inclusion rather than exclusion.

In addition to the symbolic nature of hate legislation, one of the primary aims of such laws is the intended deterrent effect. The increased penalties for hate offences are meant to act as a strong and effective deterrent to offenders and potential offenders who intentionally target members of minority groups.

Furthermore, hate crime laws provide something of an impetus for the police and the wider criminal justice system to take these crimes seriously, to respond appropriately and to be accountable for those actions (Iganski, 1999a). In addition to sending a symbolic message to victims and offenders, enshrining hate crime in law as a distinct category of offending also sends a clear message to the police and the wider criminal justice system that this type of crime requires serious attention against which their performance will be judged. This situation is quite clearly demonstrated by the flurry of police activity at both a strategic and operational level following the introduction of the Crime and Disorder Act (CDA) at the end of September 1998 and the publication of the Stephen Lawrence Inquiry in February 1999, both of which set new paths for the police to tread with regard to hate crime (Hall, 2000).

In essence then the rationale behind hate crime laws is fairly common-sensical. They represent an official recognition of an apparent emerging and increasing threat to society, and signify the importance attached to combating this threat. The potential for increased punishment of the offender signifies an appreciation of the disproportionate harm that hate crime can have on the victim and wider communities and provides a deterrent to potential offenders by clearly stating that hate crimes will not be tolerated and that firm action will be taken against those that perpetrate them. Hate crime laws also promote social cohesion by officially declaring that the victimisation of 'different' groups is not acceptable in a modern democratic society, and their very existence provides strong symbolic messages.

So where then is the problem? Given the arguments for hate crime laws outlined above it may seem rather straightforward, unproblematic and sensible to legislate against hate crime as a distinct form of criminal behaviour. While this might be the case in theory, in reality the enactment of hate legislation is fraught with both moral and practical problems and remains a highly controversial issue in the United States and, to a lesser extent, here in the UK. As Miller (2003: 437) explains:

> The intuitions and motivating forces behind such hate crimes legislation seem as obvious and straightforward as they are laudable – at least on the surface. However, there lurk just beneath this placid surface difficulties – conceptual as well as practical – which muddy the waters considerably.

The case against hate crime legislation

Two of the most outspoken critics of hate crime legislation are James Jacobs and Kimberly Potter who, in their thought-provoking book *Hate Crimes: Criminal Law and Identity Politics* (1998), argue the case for abolishing hate crime laws altogether. Given their apparent extreme stance in this respect, it is therefore important that we examine their key arguments, together with those of others who argue similarly.

In essence, Jacobs and Potter challenge the foundations upon which the case for hate crime legislation is made on moral, legal, political and practical grounds. For them the alleged hate crime epidemic in America is simply not 'real'; it is a social construction. Indeed they argue that America is freer of prejudice and hatred now that it has been for the past century. Rather, the 'hate epidemic' is a product of heightened public sensitivity to prejudice, the success of minority groups in moving 'identity politics' into the realms of criminal justice, the acceptance of broad legal definitions that encapsulate comparatively meaningless low-level offences for which the strength of the hate element is debatable, and an irresponsible media which exaggerates the latter point. Ultimately Jacobs and Potter are of the opinion that there is nothing so unique to hate crime that means it cannot be adequately responded to by generic criminal law.

Jacobs and Potter are particularly questioning of the reasoning behind enhanced penalties for hate offending, and they attack this issue on several fronts. As we have already seen, under such legislation, offences with a 'bias motive' attract higher penalties than those without and, significantly, given that the crime is already illegal under other pre-existing legislation, hate crime laws punish the offender's motivation *in addition* to punishing the offence committed. In this sense, then, hate crime may be viewed as a 'thought crime' as it is only the offender's motivation that separates it from any other crime. The question that remains poses something of a legal and moral dilemma: is it right to impose extra sanctions for an offender's prejudice when he or she commits a crime that is already proscribed and therefore punishable by existing criminal law? If the act is likely to be illegal anyway, is it right to additionally punish the offender's thought process behind the commission of that act? And even if we decide that it is right (as we do when we distinguish between murder and manslaughter, for example), in the absence of an admission from the offender, how can we accurately judge that thought process? In other words, how can we be sure that an offender is prejudiced and that the offence was motivated or aggravated by that prejudice?

A second problem for Jacobs and Potter concerns the extent and effectiveness of the supposed deterrent effect of such laws. For example, if an individual is prepared to carry out an offence that already carries a proscribed punishment, how can we be certain that simply increasing the potential for punishment will cause the offender to rethink? Jacobs and Potter argue that at best the deterrent effect will be marginal, and this problem has historically been amplified by the relative ineffectiveness of law enforcement agencies in apprehending, prosecuting and convicting hate crime offenders, and the imposition of lenient sentences when they do.

In Britain, Iganski (1999a) also questions the deterrent effect of hate legislation. He argues that the logic behind the assumption that legislation will deter offenders is both contorted and difficult to sustain, and is difficult to measure empirically. Iganski argues that there is little empirical evidence to support a correlation between sentence and deterrence and that in any case the sentence available for a basic offence should be sufficient in itself without the need for an additional penalty for the racist element. Furthermore, he rightly points out that what may act as a deterrent to one person will not necessarily amount to the same thing for another.

The 'moral, educational and general deterrent message' contained within hate legislation is also questioned by Jacobs and Potter. They argue that generic criminal law already sends a strong message about which behaviours are right or wrong and therefore the value of specific education or deterrence in this respect is highly questionable. In addition, for the most part the worst hate crimes are already punishable by the maximum available sentence and it is therefore simply not possible to enhance the sentence further.

Thirdly, Jacobs and Potter (1998) highlight conflicts over the inclusion of certain prejudices and the exclusion of others, and conflicts over labelling individual hate crimes. We have already noted the extent of definitional problems and the impact they can have on the 'hate crime problem', and this issue is exaggerated by the lack of uniformity across the United States in legislative terms. What is an offence in one state may not be in another, and where two states outlaw a hate crime, the punishment may in all probability vary greatly between them.

Similarly in Britain, 'hate' legislation specifically outlaws racially and religiously motivated offending, and contains lesser provisions for homophobia and disability bias, yet makes no mention of other prejudices. Critics argue that what we are effectively saying to society is that the victimisation of some groups is more important than others, and that these victims are somehow less deserving of similar protection under the law. In these circumstances the symbolic message of legislation may be a negative one. Identifying what to officially legislate against is therefore problematic and controversial and, rather ironically, is an act of discrimination in itself. On the other hand, if we include all identifiable groups in legislative protections then hate crime laws will simply be coterminous with generic criminal law.

Other problems associated with hate crime laws, according to Jacobs and Potter, include the negative picture of intergroup relations that such legislation produces, in particular the 'message' that social relations in a country are in such a bad state that an official response is not only required but is essential. Furthermore, publishing crime statistics that they believe do not reflect the reality of the situation simply serve to highlight the poor state of social relations. Andrew Sullivan (1999) builds upon this argument, suggesting that legal attempts to repudiate a past that treated people differently on the basis of some personal or group characteristic may only serve to create a future that permanently does exactly the same.

Legislation and crime statistics therefore have the potential to be socially divisive, rather than encouraging cohesiveness as proponents would claim. In the UK this situation is reflected in an emerging tendency for white people to report their perceived victimisation by non-whites as a hate crime whereas the motivating factor is in truth likely to be otherwise (see Chapter 11). This is a situation that has resulted because of what McLaughlin (2002) describes as a determined effort to subvert the meaning of new policy on racist incidents through the mobilisation of white resentments. In other words, divisions are being highlighted and the strength of social cohesion is being tested by the introduction of new legislation that illuminates group differences and a perception of preferential treatment for minority groups.

Jacobs and Potter also challenge both the 'greater intent' argument, and the notion that hate crime has a greater impact upon the victim and the wider community. With regard to the former, while the principle of linking punishment to motive is viewed as perfectly legitimate, Jacobs and Potter question the idea that prejudice is more morally reprehensible than other motivations for crime such as greed, power, spite and so on. Simply, is the motivation behind hate crime really any worse than the motivation that propels any other crime? Or put another way: are hate offenders really more to blame than offenders who commit similar types of offences when their motivations might be different but just as reprehensible? In criminal law offenders are already punished according to their degree of culpability (for example, murder is punished more severely than manslaughter), so why make specific provisions for hate crime?

With regard to the 'greater impact' argument, Jacobs and Potter question the extent to which this can be justified. They are highly critical of the research that has underpinned this view, claiming it to be dependent upon dubious empirical assumptions that produce assertions that cannot be substantiated. They also question the 'unique' impact that hate crime has on the wider community, arguing that to suggest that many of the 'low-level' offences spread 'terror' through communities is simply exaggerating the reality of the situation.

Furthermore they point out that hate crimes are hardly unique in spreading fear throughout a community. It was suggested in Chapter 4 that all crimes have the potential to spread fear throughout whole communities, and if this is the case, as it undoubtedly is, why is it that hate crime is singled out on this basis? Ultimately, other crimes, and not just hate crimes, have an impact upon innocent third parties, yet these are not specifically legislated against with enhanced penalties in the same way that hate crimes are.

Another contentious issue concerns the view that legislation is required to address a hate crime 'epidemic'. The existence of an 'epidemic' of hate crimes, and the additional contention that they are becoming increasingly violent, is difficult to assess because of the dubious reliability of relevant statistical data. Given the discussion in Chapter 3, however, the idea that hate crimes are more violent now than in the past seems particularly unlikely. Of the 7,462 hate crime incidents reported to the FBI in 2002, eleven were either murder or non-negligent manslaughter.

An 'epidemic' also seems unlikely. FBI figures suggest that hate crime trends have remained broadly consistent over a number of years, and although they are undoubtedly lower than the true incidence of hate crime, the fact that there is no significant jump suggests that the existence of an epidemic is unlikely. Conversely, from the police statistics in England and Wales an epidemic does appear to have occurred, but this is more likely to be attributable to recent definitional changes and increased confidence among victims to report incidents rather than a real rise in hate crimes.

In making the case for repealing hate crime laws, Jacobs and Potter (1998: 153) conclude that:

> Certainly, crime is a problem ... today. But the crime problem is not synonymous with the prejudice problem; indeed, there is very little overlap between the two. With the important exception of crime against women, most crime is intraracial and intragroup. Hard core ideologically driven hate crimes are fortunately rare. Teasing out the bias that exists in a wider range of context-specific crimes that may occur between members of different groups serves no useful purpose. To the contrary, it is likely to be divisive, conflict-generating, and socially and politically counterproductive.

While these views may seem fairly persuasive, Jacobs and Potter's provocative stance has been counter-attacked from a number of quarters. Their dismissal of the consequences and impacts of hate crime has raised concerns, particularly in the light of emerging literature supporting the claims of proponents of legislation (see Chapter 4). McLaughlin (2002) suggests also that Jacobs and Potter under-represent the struggle undertaken by minority and advocacy groups in order to have their plight taken seriously by the majority society, and that their definition of advocacy groups as deliberately and inherently antagonistic and divisive is critically flawed. Furthermore, he points out that much of the media coverage of hate crimes has traditionally been significantly less extensive and influential than Jacobs and Potter claim. Nevertheless, the views expressed by Jacobs and Potter have rightly sparked important theoretical and moral debates and raised important issues that have to be considered. The points that underpin their case, as McLaughlin suggests, deserve close attention and serious consideration, and remind us that legislating against hate is far from straightforward.

Barbara Perry (2002) also notes the importance of Jacobs and Potter's scepticism. However, she too is critical of their views. Perry takes particular issue with the claim that hate crime laws are socially divisive. Rather, she suggests, it is hate crimes that are, and always have been, socially divisive, and not the legislation. Perry argues that because hate crime is embedded in wider social structures (see Chapter 5), legislation is not the cause of intergroup hostility. Rather, the enactment of legislation is just one of many ways of responding to the manifestation of long existing antagonisms.

Thus far in this chapter we have outlined the case for hate legislation, and also discussed the range of counter-arguments put forward by critics. Yet despite these concerns, hate crime laws exist in one form or another in many countries around the world. It would seem reasonable to suggest then that the case *for* legislation outweighs the case *against*. While the views we have examined thus far have been largely theoretical, hate crime legislation in both the US and Britain has also been subjected to numerous legal challenges based on a number of different issues. So, if opponents of hate crime laws are by and large correct in their views, then we might reasonably expect challenges to legislation to have been successful in one way or another. The reality, however, is that for the most part they have not, and hate crime laws have survived almost every legal challenge brought against them. In the next section we shall examine the details of some of the key legal challenges that have established the boundaries of hate crime legislation, starting once again with those mounted in the US before moving onto Britain.

Challenges to hate crime legislation in the US

In the US, challenges to hate crime legislation have focused largely on issues of constitutionality, or to be more precise, *un*constitutionality. The simplified argument is that if generic criminal laws already cover the offences committed by hate offenders, then the recriminalisation and/ or sentencing enhancements added to those already existing offences effectively adds extra punishment for the offender's *beliefs* or *opinions* which society (or perhaps more specifically, legislators) have deemed to be unacceptable. Therefore, it could be argued as suggested above, that hate crime laws simply punish an offender's thoughts, which, critics point out, is a restriction on the right to free thought and free speech, in addition to being difficult to prove in court.

Numerous challenges have been brought before the US courts in the past ten years or so. An examination of all of these, significant as they may be, is beyond the scope of this book. Those readers particularly interested in these cases should see Streissguth (2003) for a comprehensive account of each case. For our purposes we shall restrict ourselves to an examination of three key cases that have been ruled upon by America's highest court, the Supreme Court, and have effectively set the boundaries for hate crime legislation across America.

Chaplinsky v. New Hampshire (1942)[1]

Although this case predates the modern legislation that we have focused upon thus far, the ruling of the Supreme Court justices in this case has had a significant impact on the development of hate crime legislation in the US.

The case centred on a Jehovah's Witness by the name of Walter Chaplinsky. Chaplinsky was distributing religious material on the streets of Rochester, New Hampshire, as he was freely entitled to do under the First Amendment of the US Constitution. He was subsequently arrested by the City Marshal when his activities were perceived to be posing a threat to public order in the locality. Upon arrest, Chaplinsky verbally abused the Marshal and was ultimately convicted for that verbal abuse in a public place under state law in a municipal court. The New Hampshire Supreme Court later rejected Chaplinsky's appeal that the law under which he was convicted was unconstitutional because it infringed upon his right to free speech and religious worship. The court found that spoken words that amounted to 'fighting words' were not protected by the constitution, and the conviction was upheld.

Two years after the original conviction the Supreme Court also rejected Chaplinsky's appeal. The court determined that aggressive 'fighting words' were not protected by the First Amendment, particularly because such words were likely to cause retaliatory action on the part of the abused, and therefore also disturbances of the peace. The implications of this ruling have been significant for the development and prosecution of hate crime legislation because it effectively meant that offenders who used racist or other defamatory language could no longer claim freedom of speech and therefore constitutional protection for their outbursts, and also that such language could be used as evidence of the perpetrator's intent or motive, or as a crime in itself (Streissguth, 2003).

R.A.V. v. City of St Paul, Minnesota (1992)[2]

The second key judgment by the Supreme Court that concerns us effectively struck down the hate crime legislation of the city of St Paul,

Minnesota, and in so doing delineated some of the boundaries for all hate crime legislation across the US.

The case concerned the alleged burning of a cross on the front lawn of a black family by Robert A. Viktora. Viktora was charged under St Paul's Bias Motivated Crime Ordinance which prohibited *the display of a symbol which one knows or has reason to know arouses anger, alarm, or resentment in others on the basis of race, color, creed, religion or gender.* At trial the charge was dismissed on the basis that the ordinance was 'substantially overbroad and impermissibly content-based'. However, the State Supreme Court later reversed the decision concluding that the ordinance was neither overbroad nor content-based.

This conclusion was based firstly upon the view that the phrase *arouses anger, alarm or resentment in others* had in previous state cases been limited to 'fighting words' as defined in *Chaplinsky* v. *New Hampshire*, and therefore could not be held to be overbroad. Secondly, the court held that the ordinance was not impermissibly content-based because it was 'narrowly tailored to serve a compelling governmental interest in protecting the community against bias motivated threats to public safety and order'.

On appeal, however, and in something of a blow to hate legislators, the US Supreme Court overturned the state Supreme Court's decision and declared the St Paul's ordinance invalid under the First Amendment. The Supreme Court decided that 'the ordinance unconstitutionally prohibits speech on the basis of the subjects the speech addresses'. In other words, while 'fighting words' may be regulated against on the basis of their *proscribable content*, the government is not at liberty to legislate against them on the basis of *non-proscribable content*. Put more simply, speech cannot be regulated just because the words contain a message that the government disapproves of. While actions can be legislated against, the message that those actions contain cannot.

The St Paul's ordinance was therefore unconstitutional because it placed special restrictions on those who expressed views on the basis of race, colour, creed, religion or gender, while at the same time allowing views to be expressed on other subjects. In other words, because St Paul had not criminalised *all* fighting words, the statute isolated certain words based on their content or viewpoint, thereby violating the First Amendment (ADL, 2004). In this sense then, abusive language towards blacks, for example, was not permissible under the law, while hate speech towards gays and lesbians was because this category of people was not included in the state-determined list of disfavoured subjects.

Furthermore, the Supreme Court found that the 'message' that the ordinance sent to the public that group hatred would not be tolerated did not justify the *selective* silencing of speech on the basis of its content. Finally, the court argued that the ordinance's content discrimination is not justified on the grounds that the ordinance is narrowly tailored to serve a compelling state interest in ensuring the basic human rights of groups historically discriminated against, since an ordinance not limited to the favoured topics would have precisely the same beneficial effect.

Perhaps unsurprisingly, Streissguth (2003) describes *R.A.V.* v. *St Paul* as a landmark case in the history of hate crime legislation. In effect, while offences such as those contained in the test case (arson, vandalism, trespass, etc.) could be punished by law, they could no longer be punished for their racist *content*, and legislation outlawing racist messages, displays and so on were also held to be invalid (Streissguth, 2003). While opponents of hate crime laws argued that this outcome effectively meant that separate hate legislation was redundant and that 'ordinary' criminal law should be used across the board, the effect in reality was that state legislators across America had to revise or create their laws within the confines of the *R.A.V.* v. *St Paul* judgment. In other words, hate legislation cannot punish beliefs, and those that attempt to do so are likely to be struck down.

Wisconsin v. Mitchell (1993)[5]

The case of *Wisconsin* v. *Mitchell* represents arguably the most significant legal decision with regard to hate crime. On 7 October 1989 a group of young black men severely beat a young white boy in Kenosha, Wisconsin, leaving him in a coma for four days. The beating was ordered by one member of the group named Todd Mitchell who allegedly said to the rest of the group: 'You all want to fuck somebody up? There goes a white boy; go get him.'

Mitchell was subsequently convicted for aggravated battery and the usual maximum sentence of two years imprisonment was increased to a maximum of seven years because the jury found that Mitchell had intentionally selected his victim on the basis of his race. Mitchell subsequently appealed the conviction on the basis that the sentence enhancement was unconstitutional under the First Amendment. The appeal was initially rejected by the Wisconsin Court of Appeals, but later reversed by the Wisconsin Supreme Court.

The State Supreme Court held that the legislation was indeed unconstitutional because it punished the reasoning behind the offender's selection of the victim and therefore punished the offender's mental and thought process, which was not permitted under *R.A.V.* v. *St Paul*.

In other words the law could not punish the offender's motivation simply because the thoughts behind that motivation were deemed to be offensive or abhorrent by government.

In a hugely significant decision the US Supreme Court reversed the decision of the Wisconsin Supreme Court and in doing so upheld the legality of applying enhanced sentences to hate crimes. Effectively, the US Supreme Court decided that the Wisconsin statute punished the *action* of the crime and *not* the thought processes behind it. In other words, the penalty enhancement punished the actions that arose from the offender's prejudice, rather than the prejudice itself.

The court also found that in deciding what sentence to impose on an offender, judges have traditionally considered a variety of factors in addition to bearing on guilt including the defendant's motive for committing the crime. Thus this is not a 'new' issue exclusive to hate crime; it is something that has always happened. Additionally, the court found that while the defendant's beliefs are not to be considered at sentencing, the admission of evidence relating to those beliefs should not be restricted in court.

Ultimately, the court decided that the Wisconsin legislation was qualitatively different to that that outlawed in *R.A.V.* v. *St Paul*. In this case, the law related to conduct that was *not* constitutionally protected, and not to speech or thought that was. The decision also reflected the issue of the greater individual and societal harm that hate crime produces, believing that the State's desire to redress these issues is sufficient to overshadow the debate surrounding officially designated offensive beliefs.

In addition, the court found that the Wisconsin statute had 'no chilling effect' on free speech and, significantly, that a defendant's previous statements or declarations *are* admissible as evidence of intent under the First Amendment.

The impact of this case has been hugely significant in the longevity of US hate crime laws. The US Supreme Court's decision to uphold Wisconsin's statute has legitimised the use of penalty enhancements for hate crimes across America, and has established a clear distinction between laws that punish hate *thought* (protected by *R.A.V.* v. *St Paul*) and laws that enhance punishment for hate *conduct* (unprotected by *Wisconsin* v. *Mitchell*). As such, Streissguth (2003) states that state supreme courts, citing this case as their precedent, have struck down almost every legal challenge brought against penalty enhancements for hate crimes.

Challenges to 'hate' legislation in Britain

In the previous section we examined some of the key legal challenges to hate crime legislation in the US. Clearly these challenges were brought on the belief that such laws were unconstitutional and unfairly regulated a person's beliefs and behaviours. In the UK there is no written Constitution to protect so the legal challenges to the provisions contained within the Crime and Disorder Act 1998 that we shall consider here are qualitatively different to those in the United States.

DPP v. Pal (2000)[4]

The first case of interest to us concerns an altercation between an Asian caretaker and an Asian youth. Having been told to leave a community centre by the caretaker of the premises an argument ensued in which the Asian youth pushed and kicked the caretaker and called him a 'white man's arse licker' and a 'brown Englishman'. The defendant was charged with racially aggravated common assault under section 29(1)(c) of the CDA 1998. However, while the assault was proved, the justices were unable to find that the offence was racially aggravated.

On appeal the prosecution argued that the offence came under section 28(1)(b) of the CDA 1998 which, it may be recalled from the previous chapter, states that the offence can be motivated in whole or in part by hostility towards a member of a racial group based on that person's membership of that group. The appeal, however, was rejected on the grounds that the defendant's hostility was not based on the caretaker being Asian and that the hostility was motivated by the caretaker's conduct and not his race. The decision rested upon the actual words used by the defendant that in the opinion of the court did not demonstrate hostility towards the Asian race, but hostility towards Asians working with white people, which does not fall within the requirements of the CDA 1998.

Nevertheless, while the finer points of the case resulted in its collapse, the assumption was made throughout that it is perfectly possible for a person to racially abuse a person of the same or similar race or ethnic group. Essentially then, the provisions of the CDA 1998 apply to *intra*-racial hostility as well as *inter*-racial hostility.

CPS v. Weeks (2000)[5]

The case of *CPS* v. *Weeks* dealt with the issue of what is and what is not racially abusive under certain circumstances in law. The case involved the chance meeting of two men in a car park, one of whom owed money to the other for building services rendered. In the ensuing argument the man who was owed money called the other 'a black bastard' and made threatening comments to him, and advised bystanders not to use his services. The defendant was charged with causing harassment, alarm or distress by using threatening, abusive or insulting words in a racially abusive manner under section 4(a) of the Public Order Act 1986 and section 31 of the CDA 1998.

In court the defendant claimed that his comments were not intended to be racist and were motivated solely by the victim's refusal to pay for the work that had been done and not by racism. The defendant was ultimately acquitted because in the opinion of the magistrates the Crown could not prove beyond reasonable doubt that he intended to cause the victim harassment, alarm or distress nor could they prove the defendant's awareness that his words might have been threatening, abusive or insulting.

At appeal the prosecution claimed that the magistrates were wrong to acquit given the explicit language used. However, the appeal was rejected and the verdict allowed to stand on the grounds that the absence of proof of awareness on the part of the defendant was immaterial, and that the way the defendant's language was used was a matter for the magistrates to decide based upon the facts of the case. Consequently the magistrates were free to find that the required intent for a conviction had not been present in this instance. Thus the motivating factor for the seemingly racist language used by the defendant was held to be the victim's refusal to pay, and thus the racist nature of the words was of little legal consequence.

Simply, then, this case effectively means that courts can determine what is racially abusive and what is not, depending on the circumstances of the case.

R v. White (2001)[6]

The case of *R v. White* further established the principle set in *DPP v. Pal* (2000) by confirming that Britain's 'hate' legislation refers to intra-racial hostility in addition to inter-racial hostility. The case involved a confrontation between a black bus conductress and a black passenger after the passenger was confronted on suspicion of theft from another passenger. In the course of the argument the passenger called the conductress 'a stupid African bitch' and on arrest called her 'an African c**t'.

The defendant was convicted under section 31 of the CDA 1998 for causing racially aggravated fear or provocation of violence. On appeal the defendant claimed firstly that the hostility expressed was not based on the victim's membership of a racial group because 'African' is not a single group but instead refers to numerous racial groups, and secondly that the necessary hostility could not be legally met because he was of the same racial group as his victim.

The appeal was rejected and the conviction upheld. The basis of this decision relates to the legal *intention* for the term 'race' to be as broad as possible and to avoid technicalities in its interpretation. In this sense, then, the court argued that the term 'African' in this case should be understood in its common sense meaning as would more likely than not be applied by the lay population of England and Wales. It was held to be reasonable to assume that to most people the term 'African' would mean a certain category of people with common characteristics and features, rather than for example many individual groups with subtle differences, as is technically the case. The outcome of this case is that it is legally possible to be racist towards members of one's own racial or ethnic group.

DPP v. McFarlane (2002)[7]

The case of *DPP* v. *McFarlane* raises similar questions as those considered by *DPP* v. *Pal*, but there are some subtle but significant differences.

In a dispute over a disabled parking space a white man who wanted the space for his father who was disabled racially abused the able-bodied black complainant who had parked in the space. In abusing the complainant, the defendant used the phrases 'wog', 'jungle bunny' and 'black bastard' and was charged with racially aggravated threatening behaviour under sections 31(1)(a) and (4) of the CDA 1998 and section 4 of the Public Order Act 1986. In court the district judge concluded that the phrases used, while clearly racist, were motivated by the taking of the parking space and not by hostility against the victim's racial group. As such the case was dismissed.

However, on appeal the case was sent back to the district judge with an instruction to convict the defendant of the full offences charged because in this case it was determined that other people's conduct was not a mitigating factor for the use of racist language. The public order offence had been proved, as had the use of racist language thereby satisfying the requirements of both Acts under which the charges had been originally brought.

In other words, the judge in this case had misunderstood the concept behind *DPP* v. *Pal*. In that particular case both parties were of Asian origin and the offence was not motivated by hostility towards the victim's racial background but motivated by hostility towards the victim's association with white people. In the present case the parties were of different racial groups but the hostility was based on the victim's membership of a racial group, thereby meeting the requirements of section 31(1)(a) of the CDA 1998.

DPP v. Woods (2002)[2]

Again, this case considers subtle differences to *DPP v. Pal*, although here the reasoning is much more straightforward to understand and sets some of the boundaries relating to when abuse is racially aggravated.

The case involved a black door supervisor who, having refused entry to licensed premises to a group of drunken young men, was subsequently assaulted and called a 'black bastard'. The defendant was charged with racially aggravated common assault under section 29(1)(c) of the CDA 1998. Despite admitting common assault, the defendant was found not guilty of racially aggravated assault on the premise that it was the refusal to allow entry that had caused the outburst, and that the victim didn't regard the comments as racially offensive either.

The prosecution appealed and the appeal was upheld and sent back to the magistrates with instruction to convict. In this case the opinion of the victim was deemed to be irrelevant as was the excuse that failure to gain entry to the premises was the motivating factor behind the abuse and not the defendant's prejudice. Here the magistrates had ignored the wording of section 28(3)(b) of the CDA 1998 which states that it is immaterial whether or not the offender's hostility is *also* based on any factor other than racial hostility. In other words, it was irrelevant if the hostility was based on failure to gain entry; the offence was still racially aggravated.

Concluding comments

This chapter has examined the arguments and counter-arguments in the debate surrounding the very existence of hate crime laws. For critics, hate crime legislation creates more problems than it solves and offers nothing of positive value to existing criminal law. On the other hand, for proponents specific laws 'must be seen as an important part of the ongoing process of identifying and articulating the values, sensibilities and ground rules of vibrant, multicultural societies, including the public recognition and affirmation of the right to be different' (McLaughlin, 2002: 497).

The very fact that hate crime laws have survived legal challenges as to their scope and legitimacy suggests that the case *for* legislation outweighs the case *against*. In his consideration of the debate, Rob White (2002: 502) concludes that:

> In the end ... the main thing to be learned from the debates over the use and appropriateness of the criminal law in dealing with hate crime is that the choices we make ought to be dictated by strategic objectives. Action should be guided by consideration of which measures, at any point in time, will best raise consciousness of the issues in the most productive way, and which will best serve to defend and extend the rights, legitimacy and safety of people subjected to hate crime. We should be under no illusion that legal reform is necessarily the sole answer, or that the proliferation of hate crime laws will actually solve the problem.

The principle behind hate crime laws is important in the process of responding to hatred and bigotry within society. It is, however, the way that this principle is unfolding in practice that is often cause for concern. A recent example of these concerns can be found in the debate surrounding the provisions in the Serious Organised Crime and Police Bill 2005. In February 2005 the government changed the wording of the Bill from *incitement to religious hatred* to *hatred against persons on racial or religious grounds* following pressure from performers and writers who argued that the proposed legislation would impose restrictions on free speech. Despite the change in wording, concerns still exist that the Act will impose such restrictions.

The creation of legislation to combat hatred is fraught with moral and practical difficulties, and this chapter has illustrated many of these. Nevertheless, regardless of the moral debate, hate crime legislation is on the statute books in a number of countries and has survived numerous legal challenges in both the US and the UK. This of course means that the law has to be enforced, and it is the issue of law enforcement to which we now turn.

Notes

1 *Chaplinsky* v. *New Hampshire* (1942) 315 US 568.
2 *R.A.V.* v. *St Paul, Minnesota* (1992) 505 US 377.
3 *Wisconsin* v. *Mitchell* (1993) 508 US 476.
4 *DPP* v. *Pal* (2000) crim. LR 756.
5 *CPS* v. *Weeks* (2000) co/3957/99.

and would try to help with the transition.

It was not all Palau wanted, but Nakamura judged it sufficient to meet the OEK demands. This was a major decision. Nakamura's changed position, he said, was based on the need to support the majority of the people of Palau. He called for a Compact ratification plebiscite. Only a majority vote was needed. That would be easy. If the vote were held, the struggle would be over: the Compact would be approved.

The Ibedul and Ms. Ngirmang sued again, arguing that the assurances by the United States required by Palauan law were not sufficient. The Palau Supreme Court dismissed the case on the grounds that this issue was a political one to be decided by the Palau president. The opponents had gained only delay. The ratification vote was moved back to November 9, 1993. To non-legal observers, the Palau Supreme Court decision seemed only one more in the endless stream of decisions for and against the government. But for the first time Palauan courts had deferred to elected Palauan officials and utilized a technical, legal doctrine to help the government to ratify the Compact rather than to block the Compact. A new approach was in the air.

The momentum built. Nakamura worked out a settlement of the IPSECO debt with the five banks. Palau agreed to pay $20 million over five years, less than half of what the banks had wanted. Palau had gambled for power and had won.

A month before the final Compact ratification vote, Nakamura called together the former presidents of Palau, Etpison and Remengesau, to urge passage of the Compact. To their credit, Etpison and Remengesau were willing to support their successor.

The unity declaration reflected a change in Palau. Some consensus building was essential. The new Palauan leadership seemed to realize this. The Compact had to be ratified and the struggle put behind them.

On November 14, 1993, 68 percent of the people of Palau voted to approve the Compact. That week, Kathleen Salii, Lazarus Salii's daughter, became the second Palauan woman member of the attorney general's office. Nakamura sent her a special congratulatory note.

On January 20, 1994, de Lugo announced that he would retire from the Congress at the end of the year. Miller's accession to power and de Lugo's departure meant Farrow must depart as well. "I am worried about Palau. Truly worried," Farrow said to me at lunch. I believed him. His was an imperialistic hand, but he cared about Palau. Now he couldn't follow through. There was no money for him, and time had run out.

Was the struggle finally over? To cynics the Compact battle was one more variation of a continuing theme: the struggle for power among the Ibedul, the Reklai, and their various allies going back to the nineteenth century. They saw little change.

But there was change.

De Lugo and Farrow visited Palau in the spring of 1994. To Nakamura's embarrassment and disappointment, de Lugo gave a speech urging the continued need to seek out the corruption of the past and to demand from the United States the fulfillment of all its trusteeship responsibilities before Palau permitted the United States to end the trusteeship and Palau gained its independence. He was asking them to reopen the negotiations. De Lugo had misread the mood in Palau. The Compact struggle, if it brought any lessons at all, demonstrated the immense cost to Palau of its intense, uncompromising island politics. The wounds had almost healed. The Palau leadership had moved beyond its Compact struggle. Independence was a done deal.

Not quite. In the summer of 1994, Isabella Sumang, Rafaela's daughter, who had testified before Senator Johnston in 1987, filed new lawsuits both inside and outside Palau (in the Northern Marianas and Hawaii) to stop the declaration by the United States and Palau that the trusteeship was ended. She argued that the vote was not counted correctly and that the Compact had not complied with federal environmental protection legislation.

Nevertheless, Nakamura announced that October 1, 1994, would be Palau's first Independence Day. It was a bold gamble. The president was publicly pressuring the plaintiffs and the courts to support him. Palau's Compact record did not augur well for this kind of public statement. Neither did the timing. It would take a miracle to win all of the three lawsuits within three months.

Notes

1. Page 199. *At the end of 1990*. Professor Roger Clark asked to testify before the Security Council—presumably in opposition to the termination—but his petition was turned down. *Washington Pacific Report*, Jan. 1, 1991, p. 3.

2. Page 199. *The State Department leaked a cable*. J. Williams, "Palau Pushed Gently Toward Change," *Pacific Islands Monthly*, June 1991, p. 50.

3. Page 200. *Before his indictment, Ngiraked circulated*. "F. Whaley, "Compact Petition Submitted," *Pacific Daily News*, April 16, 1992.

4. Page 200. *He delayed the vote*. Gibbons v. Etpison, Civ. A. Nos. 285-92 and 287-92; Order Granting Preliminary Injunction (July 9, 1992, Trial Division, Supreme Court of Palau). Subsequently, on August 7, 1992, the OEK passed RPPL 3-76 calling for a constitutional amendment on November 4, 1992, and setting out procedures for voting on the amendment. The Supreme Court subsequently decided against the plaintiff on October 8, 1992.

5. Page 201. *His Japanese father had been required*. The text is based on a discussion by the author with President Nakamura and his brother. Senator Sugiyama's father had a slightly different experience. When the United States ordered all Japanese, regardless of their marital status, out of Micronesia after the war, Sugiyama's father, in order to preserve his family's unity, took everyone back to Japan with him. He immediately started petitioning General MacArthur for

permission to return to Palau. After a year, permission was granted. But in 1947, Sugiyama was forced to return to Japan. He returned to Japan alone. For the next ten years he tried in vain to gain reentry into Palau to join his family. Not until the late 1960s and early 1970s did the United States allow Japanese fathers to return to Micronesia. This was too late for the Sugiyama family. Sugiyama's father had died in 1958, a heartbroken man. W. Pesch, "Nan'yo Life," *Pacific Daily News*, Islander Magazine, Sept. 26, 1993, p. 9.

6. Page 201. For the details of the 1992 elections, I am indebted to Professor Don Shuster of the University of Guam.

7. Page 202. *A new generation would decide.* F. Whaley, "Committee Meets with U.S. to Discuss Status," *Pacific Daily News*, Feb. 4, 1993), p. 3.

8. Page 202. *The Advisory Review Committee recommended ratification.* Advisory Review Committee, *Final Report, Compact of Free Association*, March 19, 1993.

9. Page 202. *The United States would treat a nuclear accident.* Letter from President Nakamura to Honorable Peter Sugiyama, President of the Senate, and Honorable Surangel Whipps, Speaker of the House, May 12, 1993, p. 9.

10. Page 203. *The Palau Supreme Court dismissed the case. Gibbons v. Etpison*, Civ. A. No. 435-92, Memorandum Decision, Trial Division, Supreme Court of Palau, July 2, 1993.

11. Page 203. *Settlement of the IPSECO debt.* "The Overview of 1993," *Tia Belau*, Dec. 31, 1993, p. 7.

12. Page 203. *Nakamura called together.* "Leaders United Behind Compact." *Palau Gazette*, Oct. 5, 1993, p. 1. The statement of the former president and Vice President Oiterong is set out in the *Palau Gazette*, Oct. 3, 1993, p. 5.

13. Page 203. *On November 14, 1993.* President's State of the Republic Address, *Palau Gazette*, April 29, 1994, p. 3.

14. Page 203. *Kathleen Salii, Lazarus Salii's daughter.* "Salii as New Assistant AG," *Palau Gazette*. Nov. 18, 1993, p. 7.

15. Page 203. *De Lugo and Farrow visited Palau.* "Congressman de Lugo Visits Palau," *Palau Gazette*, April 29, 1994, p. 1.

24

Commemoration of the Battle of Peleliu; The Special Palauan Conference

The fiftieth anniversary of the battle of Peleliu approached. But what of that brutal battle was there worth remembering? The American veterans were not sure. E. B. Sledge, whose book, *With the Old Breed at Peleliu and Okinawa*, was a powerful retelling of the pain of the combat of Peleliu, wrote a long, bitter letter denouncing the efforts to commemorate that battle. There was nothing worth commemorating. All the killing had been for no purpose. Why stir up once more the pain of that battlefield? He would not come to Peleliu.

A couple of weeks later Sledge wrote again. He apologized for the angry tone of his previous letter. He understood the well-meaning intent of the organizers and why, perhaps, some would wish to return. But he could not. The organizers wrote back to Sledge, thanking him for his frankness. They described what they hoped to accomplish and how carefully the commemoration was being planned. If he should change his mind, they would welcome him. Sledge wrote again, his third letter softer yet. He wished them well but he could not return to Peleliu.

No Palauan was on Peleliu at the time of the battle. They had been evacuated to Babeldaob by the Japanese military. Discussions of the battle never mentioned them. Indeed, until the commemoration day ceremonies, none of the American military men had ever met a Palauan. One of the by-products of the fiftieth commemoration ceremonies was the encounters with the curious children of Peleliu and the welcoming adults of Koror.

In the stateside literature on Palau, the Palauan view of the war was rarely noted. The Palau National Museum convened a three-day conference from September 6 to 9, 1994, entitled "The War in Palau: Fifty Years of Change," to provide that perspective, to examine the Palauan experience through World War II and the changes that followed it. It was the first time Palau convened a major conference at which Palauans produced the majority of the papers. The pain of the war on Babeldaob for Palauans was sketched in detail, together with the growth and pride in the changes in Palau since then, particularly its major institution, the Palau Community College.

With respect to the battle of Peleliu itself, Palau was neutral. Many of Palau's leading political figures, David Ramarui, Alfonso Oiterong, and former President Etpison, had been pressed into service, in non-combatant roles, with the Japanese. "The Palauans never had enemies; the Americans and Japanese were at war with each other," Etpison said, summing up the Palauan view. "And to this day, we still have no enemies. We are still good friends with both of them." As a result of President Nakamura's background —a Palauan mother and Japanese father—he retained an extremely positive view toward all of the war's combatants. The war, he felt, made his family stronger, and the Japanese and U.S. people gained a new understanding.

To the Americans returning to Peleliu, two hundred veterans and their wives, there was no neutrality. A few regarded the Japanese veterans, like themselves, as mutual combatants in a painful war. But most remembered the Japanese atrocities: the shooting of the wounded and the disfigurement of the dead. They could not forgive, not here on the battlefield where their friends had died.

American veteran groups had resisted Japanese participation in the commemoration day ceremonies. The Palau organizers, perhaps aware of U.S. attitudes, never officially invited the Japanese veterans. Nevertheless, about seven Japanese veterans and their relatives did come—about forty Japanese in all—and walked the battlefield during these commemoration days. They stayed apart, searching and finding The Pocket, the Japanese command center that had held out the longest, and one cave where some Japanese had stayed and survived for as many as two years after the war. Once in a while, by chance, a Japanese and an American would meet. The Japanese would hold out his hand and the American, tentatively, somewhat reluctantly, would take it. Some hoped the commemoration would serve as a reconciliation of old enemies, but that was not to be. On this battlefield during these days, the Americans were reconciling themselves to the death of their friends and to their own survival. To ask more was to ask too much.

The American veterans, now old, some infirm, and their wives walked along Orange and White Beaches, recalling where they and their comrades had invaded, pointing out where a pillbox or a cave had been. They would reach down, tear away the dense jungle growth of fifty years, and, invariably find it. Then they spoke of the battle, of the death of men who had fought with them and of their own survival. Many wives said their husbands had never talked of this before. The veterans would break down, and the tears would come. After the breakdown and tears, they turned and said, "I'm glad I came."

On Orange Beach, Major Everett Pope, one of the surviving congressional

Medal of Honor winners, walked with General Raymond Davis, who had also fought on Peleliu and later received a Congressional Medal of Honor for service in Korea. Pope had led a platoon of 250 men up Walt's Ridge. He had taken the ridge and held it. Only he and eight men had survived. Pope unfolded a portion of the top secret battle map that he had preserved for fifty years. He and Davis bent over it and pointed to various hills that they remembered, and ridges where they had fought, recalling the men who had died. After they walked back and forth over the dense jungle many times, they finally stopped. Pope refolded the map and gave it to Karen Whisenhunt, one of the organizers of the commemoration, and said: "I don't need this anymore. You keep it for the museum."

The ceremonies climaxed with a memorial service on Bloody Nose Ridge. The veterans and their wives climbed slowly up the former battlefield. Father Dennis O'Brien, who had also fought with the Old Breed fifty years ago, gave the invocation and benediction, blessing those who had died and those who had survived to pray there that day.

Twenty-one guns sounded. Some of the demons of Peleliu were laid to rest.

Notes

1. Pages 207-208. *The Palau National Museum convened*. The official name of the Palau National Museum is the Belau National Museum. In order not to confuse the reader, I have changed the spelling in the text. In all of the documents relating to the conference, the island is spelled as Palau.

2. Page 208. *Many of Palau's leading political figures*. D. Shuster, "David Ramarui and Alfonso Oiterong: Men of Dedication, Men of Integrity" (Paper presented at the Palau National Museum Conference, "The War in Palau: Fifty Years of Change," Sept.6-9, 1994.

3. Page 209. *The ceremonies climaxed*. 50th Anniversary Committee of the ROP, "All Gave Some, Some Gave All," *Commemoration of the 50th Anniversary of the Battle of Peleliu World War II* (Sept. 12-15, 1994).

25

Resolution of the Lawsuits

Although President Nakamura publicly proclaimed plans for the October 1 Independence Day celebrations, the lawsuits remained. They might frustrate Palau, as they had many times before.

The case brought in the Northern Mariana Islands was rapidly dismissed by the federal court. The court said that it was a local suit which should have been brought in Palau. One down.

In Palau, the plaintiffs, headed by Isabella Sumang, the daughter of Raphaela Sumang, appealed their case to the Supreme Court, filing their notice on September 6. The next day the Palau attorney general filed for an expedited schedule for brief and oral argument. The only reason for the expedited schedule—unstated—was that the president had already announced October 1 as the day for independence celebrations. Without waiting or even asking plaintiffs for their views, the Palau Supreme Court agreed to the expedited procedure. The Supreme Court once more was deferring to the Palau president. The pressure on the women plaintiffs grew. This time they gave in. They decided not to continue with the case. Two down.

Only the Hawaii case remained. In that case, the plaintiff, Isabella Sumang again, argued that the National Environmental Policy Act applied to the Compact and the analysis required by that act had not been performed. The Hawaii court is liberal, very supportive of the rights of native peoples. If the Hawaii District Court saw this as native people being trampled upon by the U.S. military, perhaps it would hold up the Compact.

Only two weeks remained before October 1. If the district court did nothing, the Independence Day celebrations would be a fiasco. Plaintiffs announced that Anne Simon, who had argued the *Gibbons v. Salii* case as far back as 1986 and who had argued against me in 1987 and 1988, was being brought back as counsel on the Hawaii case. It looked like a serious challenge, with a long, drawn-out battle in view. And then, surprising everyone, on September 19, with time counting down, Anne Simon agreed to withdraw the lawsuit. Further, the women agreed to bring no more lawsuits prior to October 1.

The miracle had occurred. The lawsuits had all been won with nine days still to go.

Notes

1. Page 211. *Two down. Wong and Tabalual v. Nakamura*, Civ. App. No. 7-94, App. Div. Sup. Ct. of Palau, Aug. 9, 1994.

2. Page 212. *On September 19, with time counting down. Sumang v. Babbitt*, Stipulation and Order for Dismissal of Specified Claims, Civ. No. 1 94-00140 HMF, Sept. 21, 1994.

26

Independence Day

The independence holiday weekend celebrations began with the water: motorboat racing under the Koror-Babeldoab bridge on Friday morning.

On the bridge, the Palauan flag, light pale blue for the sea with a yellow circle for the moon, symbolizing the calm and peacefulness of island life, flew from the light posts and the spokes of the bridge. On the bridge, a throng of Palauans—men and women dressed in colored tee shirts—looked down, waiting for the motorboats to appear. In the water, spectator boats waited as well, their decks covered to shield the sun. For a moment, it looked like a Renoir painting. Then, as the motorboats powered along the water and then under the bridge, the crowd on the bridge dashed from one side to the other. All cars halted as the crowd danced from side to side to the sound and sight of the plumes of the waves.

That night at a giant island buffet at the Palau Pacific Resort, the Palauans celebrated their unity. Vice President Tommy Remengesau, Jr., welcomed all past and present opponents and proponents of the Compact: Remeliik, "the father of our country"; Salii, "the architect of free association"; our "friends in the U.S. Congress, Congressman Ron de Lugo and Senator Bennett Johnson"; Ta Belau, "which helped to improve the Compact"; and the traditional leaders "who help to uphold our heritage." Above the broad beach and vast sea, very quiet, the calm of the dark ocean and bright moon did, indeed, reflect the peacefulness in the colors of the pale blue Palauan flags that fluttered everywhere in the light breeze.

Saturday morning, independence day, began with a parade that was a curious mixture of simple, local fare, the somewhat bizarre, and the foreign. North of the Asahi Stadium where the ceremonies were to be held and where the marchers were to come, the groups assembled: There were students, some in simple tee shirts, some more elaborate in matching colors, and some costumed in red loincloths and yellow sashes for the native war dance. Japanese Airlines, waiting for the Palau airport to be expanded so that it could fly in jumbo jets, produced a large decorative float, while the local Philippine Chamber of Commerce, wary of Palauan nativism, arranged for a dramatic native dance.

But it was not the marchers themselves who were particularly special. It was the people of Palau crowded along the side of the road, standing in the doorways and on balconies above the stores and homes along the parade route. Palauan style had always been cool: the facial expression without emotion, easily interpreted as hostile, although perhaps only cautious or insecure. Whatever the facial expression was intended to denote, it set foreigners back and kept them at arm's length.

But on this day that expression was gone. On this day the Palauans, all of them, were welcoming, excited, joyous. Outsiders were warmly greeted. Those, like me, who were known at a distance by many were suddenly greeted by many more. The celebrations opened up the people of Palau and showed that beneath their detachment could be, and indeed was, a pent-up welcoming soul.

At the baseball stadium, the festive mood continued. High in the sky, spreading across the entire outfield from one side of the stadium to the other, were blue and yellow balloons mimicking the Palauan colors. Surrounding them were flags of the international community: the Palauan flag surrounded by the U.N. flag on one side and the U.S. flag on the other. Along the two base lines, from home to first and home to third, were bright blue tents with the names of the sixteen Palauan states emblazoned in gold on the front. Most people sat inside the tents, protected from the hot sun.

The delegations from the sixty countries and island areas were announced one at a time and then escorted, to accompanying applause from the rear of the stadium, to the dignitaries' platform, which had been constructed behind home plate. Rekewis Paulus O. Sked of the Palau Society of Historians rose to the microphone on the platform and chanted in Palauan. Suddenly he stopped. From the stadium, strong and clearly eager, came the response. He continued, chanting a few more lines, and then stopped again, waiting for the audience response. Again, even stronger, it came. And so the pattern repeated until the chant ended. For the moment, the celebrations were for Palauans only, as they chanted their tradition and their joy.

Then, in the center of the ball field, next to the large flagpole which stood empty, the conch shell was blown seven times, the traditional call gathering the people together for a momentous occasion, reminding all of this distinctive island national tradition. At 1:01 p.m. on Saturday, October 1, the time chosen to correspond with 12:01 in the States, the three flags, the U.N. flag, the Palauan flag, and the U.S. flag, were lowered. The large Palauan flag was carried from the flagpole on the perimeter of the ballfield to the center, and then it alone was gradually raised. As it was hoisted, the Palauans in the tents and the foreigners on the platform began to applaud.

People ran forward, jostling one another to take pictures. The flag continued up the pole, halted about one quarter of the way up, and seemed to wait for the audience or for the wind. The wind rose and the flag responded, the blue field expanding in the wind so one could see the yellow moon. To the rising applause, as the Palauan national anthem began to play, the flag continued its ascent.

On the dignitaries' platform where the Palauans sat there were tears. President Nakamura turned to see his wife crying. He burst into tears himself and turned to embrace his wife, the first time he had ever embraced her in public.

But there were those who would not be embraced. The judges who had played such an intrusive role in Palauan life, Judges Sutton and Hefner in Saipan, Judge King in Hawaii, and Judge O'Brien in the Philippines, did not return for the ceremonies. No one from the U.S. Congress attended, neither staff nor members. And within Palau the Ibedul granted an interview to say this day would endanger the lands of Palau.

I talked to Tina Salii. The celebrations were not for her. She could not come, she said. But she was proud of the fact that her daughter—Kate, now a member of the attorney general's office, and Blanche—were both members of the Independence Day committee. They would attend and enjoy this day. Yvette, the third daughter, had flown over specially to participate in the ceremonies. Tina was pleased at that. But she repeated, "I cannot come." Carlos Salii articulated the reason. It was unjust. President Nakamura had fought the Compact throughout his political career and now on this day, as its champion, he would receive Palau's glory. Six years had gone by, but he could not remember Lazarus Salii's suicide without tears. Carlos Salii knew life could be unfair and politics even more unfair. He understood that, but he could not reconcile himself to it. He would not attend.

However, Nakamura and Remengesau had tried to be fair. Salii was mentioned in all the Independence Day programs and in all of their speeches, and both his contribution and his effort were recognized. They could have done much less.

Ambassador John Negroponte, heading the U.S. delegation, contrasted Palau independence with the independence of other countries: "Many nations in the '60s gained their independence only after violence and bloodshed. Indeed, the U.S. had gained its independence only after violent revolution. Palau's independence has come peacefully."

He was wrong, of course. Palau, too had suffered the agonies of an independence struggle. The fight had torn apart this small island. Bedor Bins and Lazarus Salii had died in the course of that struggle.

The people of Palau had been forced to look inward to soften their intense combative politics of old. They had fought to channel the strife within their own budding democracy and to embrace the opponents within their midst. And they had succeeded.

Freedom is a hard-won thing. Independence had not been given to the people of Palau. They had earned it.

Notes

1. Page 215. *However, Nakamura and Remengesau had tried.* See official Independence Day Program, Republic of Palau, October 1, 1994, p. 11; and Presidential Independence Day Address, Office of the President, October 1, 1994.

Bibliographic Essay

R. C. Kiste, "Micronesia," in Miles Jackson, ed., *Pacific Island Studies: A Survey of the Literature* (Westport, CT: Greenwood Press, 1986), is a good bibliographic essay. See also Goetzfridt and Wuerch, *Micronesia 1975-1987: A Social Science Bibliography* (Westport, CT: Greenwood Press, 1989).

F. Bunge and M. Cooke, *Oceania: A Regional Study* (Washington, D.C.: Foreign Area Studies, American University Press, 1984), is relatively current and allows one to get the names, places, and dates right. It is an excellent place to begin. L. Motteler, *Pacific Island Names: A Map and Name Guide to the Pacific* (Honolulu: Bishop Museum, 1986), sets out the geographic area clearly. Excellent and finely detailed maps of the trust territory, showing the various atolls in the district, with population figures and geographica' distances indicated, are also found in *Maps of Micronesia* (Saipan: Office of the High Commissioner, n.d.). M. Thyssen, *The Palau Islands* (Koror, 1988), has good maps and color of the flora and fauna of the Palau Islands. See also Palau National Museum, *Republic of Palau* (n.d.).

The best anthropological study of the Pacific, including Micronesia, is John Terrell, *Prehistory in the Pacific Islands* (Cambridge: Cambridge U. Press, 1986). The peopling of the Pacific has been a continuing issue. See "Peopling of the Pacific," in O. H. K. Spate, *Paradise Found and Lost*, Vol. III of *Pacific since Magellan* (Canberra: Australian National University Press, 1988). An excellent review article on the subject is P. S. Bellwood, "The Peopling of the Pacific," 243 *Scientific American* 2 (Nov. 1980). The issue grew more contentious after Andrew Sharp put forward the thesis that the dispersion of the population primarily resulted from accidental voyages. See A. Sharp, *Ancient Voyages in the Pacific*, (New York: Penguin Books, 1957). For an elaboration of the debate and limitations on Sharp's thesis, see J. Golson, *Polynesian Navigation: A Symposium on Andrew Sharp's Theory of Accidental Voyages*, (Sydney: A. H. and A. W. Reed, 1972).

Our knowledge of traditional islander navigation is now quite sophisticated. See D. Lewis, *We the Navigators: The Ancient Art of Land Finding in the Pacific*. (Wellington: A. H. and A. W. Reed, 1972), and T. Gladwin, *East Is a Big Bird: Navigation and Logic on Peluwat Atoll* (Cambridge: Harvard University Press, 1970).

The romance of the sea and its place in Micronesian life is caught in K. Brower, *With Their Islands around Them* (New York: Holt, Reinhart & Winston, 1974), and K. Brower, *A Song for Satawal* (New York: Harper & Row, 1983). See also R. E. Johannes, *Words of the Lagoon: Fishing and Marine Lore in the Palau District of Micronesia* (Berkeley: University of California Press, 1981).

The most famous Micronesian artist, Charlie Gibbons, a primitivist, resided in Palau and depicted in lovely colors the customs and festivals of Palau. See Hera Ware Owen, ed., *Charlie Gibbons, Retrospective Exhibition Catalog* (Saipan, 1980). Ms. Owen's brief introductory essays on Micronesian art and on Gibbons are very well done.

Micronesian archaeology, after long being moribund, has been revitalized since 1977. Davidson, "Archaeology in Micronesia since 1965: Past Achievements and Future Prospects," a paper prepared for the University of Guam's Micronesian Archaeology Conference in 1987, reviews the field and appends a useful bibliography. See also W. Morgan, *Prehistoric Archaeology in Micronesia* (Austin: University of Texas Press, 1988).

For the archeology of the Palau Islands, see George Gumerman, David Snyder, and W. Bruce Masse, *An Archaeological Reconnaissance in the Palau Archipelago, Western Caroline Islands, Micronesia*, Center for Archaeological Investigations Research Paper No. 23, (Carbondale, IL: Southern Illinois University 1981); and David Snyder and Brian Butler, *Archaeological and Historical Preservation in Palau: The Micronesian Resources Project* (Saipan, CNMI: Micronesian Endowment for Historic Preservation, U.S. Park Service, Division of Cultural Affairs, Republic of Palau, 1990). See also Douglas Osborne, *The Archeology of the Palau Islands: An Intensive Survey* (Honolulu: Bishop Museum Press, 1966).

The suicide of Salii and the surrounding controversy has generated book-length commentaries. Fred Kluge, *The Edge of Paradise* (New York: Random House, 1990), is a charming memoir that was very favorably reviewed in the States. Kluge, who knew Salii in 1970s when he was in the islands and kept up intermittent contact, upon hearing of Salii's death, revisited Micronesia, meeting many of the key political figures in Micronesia and Palau, and finally, Salii's family. The book's theme is that somehow the early promise of Micronesia has not been fulfilled. In Micronesia the book was less well received, perhaps because of that judgment.

The left continued its advocacy approach to Palau. Sue Rabbitt Roff's *Overreaching In Paradise: U.S. Policy in Palau Since 1945* (AK: Denali Press, 1991), is a very selective, one-sided telling of the tale, omitting, for example, any mention of Salii's death or any of the testimony before the Senate Energy Subcommittee except that of Gabriela Ngirmang. Bob Aldridge and Ched Myers, in *Resisting the Serpent: Palau's Struggle for Self-Determination* (Baltimore, MD: Fortkamp Publishing Co., 1990), write in a similar vein. They seem to me too casual with the facts and excessively editorial even by advocacy journalism standards. David Robie, *Blood on Their Banner: Nationalist Struggles in the South Pacific* (Leichhardt, NSW: Pluto Press Australia, 1989), has a brief chapter on Palau.

The academic legal/political scholarship in the field is small and very doctrinaire in its opposition to the Compact. See, e.g., Roger S. Clark, "Self-Determination and Free Association: Should the United Nations Terminate the Pacific Islands Trust?," 21 *Harvard International Law Journal* 1 (Winter 1980); J. Hinck, "The Republic of

Palau and the United States: Self-Determination Becomes the Price of Free Association," 78 *California Law Review* 915 (1990); Richard Parmentier, "The Rhetoric of Free Association and Palau's Political Struggle," 3 *The Contemporary Pacific* 146 (1991); and the various articles by Donald Shuster: "The Politics of Free Association and the Politics of Violence: An Essay on Recent Palauan Political History." Paper prepared for presentation at the Pacific Islands Political Studies Association Conference, May 23-25, 1988; "The Last Trusteeship: Island of Opportunists: A Personal View on the Republic of Palau." Paper prepared for presentation to the Guam Association of Social Workers, March 30, 1989; and "The Salii Presidency: Triumph to Suicide. A Personal View." Paper prepared for presentation at the Pacific Islands Political Studies Association Conference, Dec. 16-18, 1989. But see L. McKibben, "The Political Relationship between the United States and Pacific Island Entities: The Path to Self-Government in the Northern Mariana Islands, Palau and Guam," 32 *Harvard International Law Journal* 257 (1990).

The anthropological literature on Palau is much more extensive than elsewhere in Micronesia. The best studies, and very good indeed, are Richard Parmentier's *The Sacred Remains: Myth, History and Polity in Belau* (Chicago, IL: University of Chicago Press, 1987), and Mary McCutcheon's doctoral dissertation, *Resource Exploitation and the Tenure of Land and Sea in Palau* (Tucson, AZ: University of Arizona, 1981). Others are of less recent vintage. Robert McKnight's doctoral dissertation, *Competition in Palau* (Columbus, OH: Ohio State University, 1960), and Roland Force, *Leadership and Cultural Change in Palau* (1960), initiated the theme of excessive competitiveness in Palau. See also Roland Force and Maryanne Force, *Just One House: A Description and Analysis of Kinship in the Palau Islands* (Honolulu: Bishop Museum Press, Bulletin 235, 1972), and D. R. Smith, *Palauan Social Structure* (N.J.: Rutgers, 1982). A bit earlier is H. G. Barnett's *Being a Palauan* (New York: Holt, Rinehart & Winston, 1960); John Useem's *Coordinated Investigation of Micronesian Anthropology Report No. 21* (Washington, D.C.: Pacific Science Board, 1949); and A. J. Vidich's *Coordinated Investigation of Micronesian Anthropology Report No. 23* (Washington, D.C.: Pacific Science Board, 1949).

Academics generally explain Palau's nationalism and aggressiveness as related to competing forces of traditional clans and elected political officials. See, e.g., L. Gerston, "A Tale of Two Cultures: The Conflict between Traditional and Modern Intrusions in Palau," a paper presented at the Pacific Islands Political Studies Association (Dec. 16-18, 1989). A similar theme is Palau's nationalism versus colonialism. Frank Quimby, *Culture and Colonialization: Facts of Palauan Nationalism* (Alexandria, VA: Asian-Pacific Themes, 1988).

The role of women in the Pacific has not been the subject of extensive investigation. Karen Nero, "The Hidden Pain: Drunkenness and Domestic Violence in Palau," 13 *Pacific Studies* 63 (1990), opens up one important aspect of the issue in the Palauan context. On women's traditional roles in Micronesian society, see Francis X. Hezel, "The Dilemmas of Development: The Effects of Modernization of Three Areas of Island Life," *Journal of Pacific Society* (April 1987).

The first encounter between Palau and the West appears to have been in the course of Sir Francis Drake's round-the-world voyage in 1579. W. A. Lessa, *Drake's Island of Thieves: Ethnological Sleuthing* (Honolulu: University of Hawaii Press, 1975), discusses that somewhat controversial thesis in detail. The subsequent Spanish explorations are dealt with comprehensively in O. H. K. Spate, *The Spanish Lake,*

Vol. 1. of the three-volume series, *The Pacific since Magellan* (Canberra: Australian National University Press, 1979). The German involvement in the Pacific is explored in A. Knoll, and L. Gann, eds., *Germans in the Tropics: Essays on German Colonial History* (Westport, CT: Greenwood Press, 1987).

George Keate, *An Account of the Pelew Islands...From the Journals and Communications of Captain Henry Wilson, 1783* (London: G. Nichol, 1788), begins the Western contact literature. D. J. Peacock, *Lee Boo of Belau: A Prince in London* (Honolulu: University of Hawaii Press, 1987), makes as much as one can of what little is known of Lee Boo and his English sojourn. Spate places Lee Boo's sojourn within the "noble savage" literature, particularly the visits of the Tahitians: Omai in London and Aotourou in Paris. O. H. K. Spate, *Paradise Lost and Found*, Vol.3, *The Pacific since Magellan* (Canberra: Australian National University Press, 1988).

Horace Holden, *A Narrative of the Shipwreck, Captivity and Sufferings of Horace Holden and Benj. H. Nute* (Boston, MA: Russell, Shattuck & Co., 1836; reprinted Fairfield, WA: Ye Galleon Press, 1938). The Holden narrative was retold in Horace Lyman, "Recollections of Horace Holden," 3 *Oregon Historical Quarterly* 164 (1902) and as historical fiction by a captain of a destroyer escort that happened to light on Tobi, the small island where Holden was held captive: J. C. Meredith, *The Tattooed Man* (New York: Duell, Sloan & Pierce, 1958). See also L. W. Browning, "The Cruise of the U.S. Sloop-of-War *Vincennes*," (United Service, Nov. 1885). Captain Barnard's account has been recently published in Kenneth Martin, ed., *Naked and a Prisoner: Captain Edward C. Barnard's Narrative of Shipwreck in Palau 1832-1833* (Sharon, MA: Kendall Whaling Museum, 1980).

The German perspective is found in the classic works of Augustin Kramer and J. S. Kubary. They are available in English translations from Yale University Press, as is the German administration record. Their key works are: A. Kramer, "Studienreise nach den Zentral-und Westkarolinen, in *Mitteilungen aus den Deutschen Schutzgebieten* (1908) 21:169-86; and J. S. Kubary, "Die Palau-Inseln in der Sudsee" in *Journal des Museum Godeffroy* (1873) 1:177-238. The third of the German giants, Karl Semper, has been translated and published by the Micronesian Area Research Center in Guam. Karl Semper, *The Palau Islands in the Pacific Ocean*, trans. by Mark Berg (Guam: Micronesian Area Research Center, University of Guam, 1982). The work was originally published in German as *Die Palau-Inseln im Stillen Ocean* (Leipzig: F. Brockhaus, 1873).

In addition to Spate, the early Micronesian explorations are clearly and carefully set forth in Francis X. Hezel, *The First Taint of Civilization: A History of the Caroline and Marshall Islands in Pre-Colonial Days, 1521-1885*, Pacific Islands Monograph Series No. 1 (Honolulu: University of Hawaii Press, 1983).

There is little in English on the Japanese role in Micronesia. Mark R. Peattie, *Nan'yo: The Rise and Fall of the Japanese in Micronesia*, 1885-1945 (Honolulu: University of Hawaii Press, 1985), is an excellent, recent treatment. See also Tadao Yanaihara, *Pacific Islands Under Japanese Mandate* (New York: Oxford University Press, 1940). Two Americans who were allowed to visit wrote books on their observations: P. Clyde, *Japan's Pacific Mandate* (New York, MacMillan, 1935) (reissued by Kennikat Press, Inc., 1967); and Willard Price, *Pacific Adventure* (New York: John Day in association with Reynd and Hitchcock; reissued with changes as *Japan's Islands of Mystery* (New York: John Day, 1944). After the war, Price returned again, writing *America's Paradise Lost* (New York: John Day, 1966). To my knowledge, this is the only comparison of United States and Japanese rule in Micronesia made by an eyewitness.

For the general outline of the war against Japan, placing the battle for Peleliu and Angaur in perspective, see Ronald Spector, *Eagle Against the Sun* (New York: Free Press, 1985). For the description of the battle, I have relied most heavily on *George Garland* and Truman Strobridge, *Western Pacific Operations: History of U.S. Marine Corps Operations in World War II, Vol. 4* (Washington, D.C.: Historical Branch, U. S. Marine Corps., 1971); Bill Ross, *Peleliu: Tragic Triumph* (New York: Random House, 1991); Harry Gailey, *Peleliu 1944* (Annapolis, MD: Nautical and Aviation Publishing Co., 1983); and E. B. Sledge, *With the Old Breed at Peleliu and Okinawa* (Novato, CA: Presidio Press, 1981). This last is a superbly written description of the battle from the point of view of the fighting man. William Manchester, *in Goodbye Darkness: A Memoir of the Pacific War* (Boston, MA: Little, Brown, 1979), looks back on the battle as both a combatant and a historian. James Hallas, in *Devil's Anvil: The Assault on Peleliu* (Westport, CT: Praeger, 1994), discusses the battle giving more emphasis to the army's role. Mark Peattie, *Nan'yo: The Rise and Fall of the Japanese in Micronesia, 1885-1945* (Honolulu: University of Hawaii Press, 1985), discusses the battle in brief compass from the Japanese perspective.

An important history of Palau because it was produced by the islanders themselves is Palau Community Action Agency, *A History of Palau*, 3 Vols. (Koror, 1977). The official history, very detailed, of the U.S. military governance of the trust territory up to 1957 is Dorothy Richard, *U.S. Naval Administration of the Trust Territory of the Pacific Islands*, 3 Vols. (Washington, D.C.: GPO, 1957).

The best single volumes on the trusteeship period, though gradually losing their currency, are David Nevin, *The American Touch in Micronesia* (New York: Norton, 1977); Harold F. Nufur, *Micronesia under American Rule: An Evaluation of the Strategic Trusteeship (1947-77)* (Hicksville, NY: Exposition Press, 1978); and D. Hughes and S. Langenfelter, eds., *Political Development in Micronesia* (Columbus, OH: Ohio State Univ. Press, 1974).

Donald McHenry, *Micronesia: Trust Betrayed* (Washington, D.C.: Carnegie Endowment for International Peace, 1975), tells the story of the U.S. governance with great passion and clarity. Although not to be read as a sole source, it is essential for an understanding of the issues.

For the discussion of the U.S. testing in the Marshall Islands, I have relied primarily on J. Weisgall, *Operation Crossroads: The Atomic Tests at Bikini Atoll* (Annapolis, MD: Naval Institute Press, 1994); Alcalay, "Maelstrom in the Marshall Islands: The Social Impact of Nuclear Weapons Testing," in Catherine Lutz, ed., *Micronesia as Strategic Colony: The Impact of U.S. Policy on Micronesian Health and Culture* (Cambridge, MA: Cultural Survival, 1984); and Giff Johnson, *Collision Course at Kwajelein: Marshall Islanders in the Shadow of the Bomb* (Honolulu: Pacific Concerns Resource Centre, 1984). See also Jane Dibblin, *Day of Two Suns: U.S. Nuclear Testing and the Pacific Islanders* (London: Virago, 1988). A brief history of the relocation of the Bikinians is found in Robert Kiste, "Identity and Relocation: The Bikini Case," in 26 *Pacific Viewpoint* 116 (1985).

Straightforward, useful historical accounts of recent political events in the various districts of the trust territory and in Guam are found in various chapters in *Politics of Micronesia* (Suva: Institute of Pacific Studies, University of the South Pacific,

1983).

Francis X. Hezel, *The Catholic Church in Micronesia* (Chuuk, ECI: Micronesian Seminar, 1991), presents a very sympathetic description of the growth of the Catholic church in the various islands of Micronesia, including Palau. See also John Garrett, *Footsteps in the Sea: Christianity in Oceania to World War II* (Suva: University of the South Pacific, Suva, 1992).

The role of education in the proselytization process is discussed in Donald Topping, "Identity and Literacy: The Power of the Written Word," 12 *Pacific Perspective* 41 (1985). Aiavao, "Who Is Playing Naked Now? Religion and Samoa Culture," 12 *Pacific Perspective* 8 (1985), is an important, troubling response by an islander to the impact of Western religion on island societies.

For an account of the first Palau plebiscite, in addition to the other Micronesia plebiscites, from detached observers, see Austin Ranney and Howard Penniman, *Democracy in the Islands: The Micronesian Plebiscites of 1983*, (Washington, D.C.: American Enterprise Institute, 1985).

The U.N. reports include: On the December 1, 1986, plebiscite, *Report of the United Nations Visiting Mission to Observe the Plebiscite in Palau, Trust Territory of the Pacific Islands, February 1983*, 50 U.N. TCOR Supp. (No. 3) at 38, U.N. Doc. T/1851 (1983); and on the June 30, 1987, plebiscite, *Report of the United Nations Visiting Mission to Observe the Plebiscite in Palau, Trust Territory of the Pacific Islands, December 1986*, 54 U.N. TCOR Supp. (No. 1) at 13-14, U.N. Doc. T/1906 (1987). See also International League for Human Rights, *Report of the International Observer Mission on Palau Referendum, December 1986* (May 1987).

The military issue is omnipresent and controversial in the trust territory. The case for the strategic importance of the islands is set forth in James H. Webb, Jr., *Micronesia and U.S. Pacific Strategy: A Blueprint for the 1980s* (New York: Praeger, 1974), and William Roger Louis, ed., *National Security and International Trusteeship in the Pacific* (Annapolis, MD: U.S. Naval Institute, 1942). For a case against the islands' military importance, see Donald McHenry, *Micronesia: Trust Betrayed* (Washington, D.C.; Carnegie Endowment for International Peace, 1976), and, more generally challenging the nuclear buildup in Micronesia and elsewhere in the Pacific, see Hayes, Zarisky and Bello, *American Lake: Nuclear Peril in the Pacific* (NY: Viking Penguin, 1986). I don't know of any detailed analysis since the breakup of the Soviet Union.

Henry Schwalbenberg's memoranda published by the Micronesian Seminar in Chuuk discuss the Palau Compact and the U.S. military options very clearly and are still illuminating: H. Schwalbenberg, "Nuclear Weapons and the Compact: How Safe and How Moral," (Chuuk, Micronesia Seminar, Feb. 1982); "American Military Needs in Micronesia: Valid Perceptions or Unnecessary Contingencies?" (Chuuk: Micronesia Seminar, Oct. 1982); and "After Palau's Plebiscite What Comes Next?" (Chuuk, Micronesia Seminar, April 1983). The economic issues of the Compact, together with good economic data on the Japanese and German periods, are found in The Micronesia Seminar, *Past Achievements and Future Possibilities* (Chuuk,

Hezel's most recent volume tells the colonization-decolonization story of Micronesia basically through 1981. It is a useful supplement to the books noted. On the whole, his treatment of the United States period is less detailed than the earlier Guam and Japanese periods of governance. Francis X. Hezel, *Strangers in Their Own*

Land: A Century of Colonial Rule in the Caroline and Marshall Islands, Pacific Islands Monograph Series No. 13 (Honolulu: University of Hawaii Press, 1995).Micronesia Seminar, 1984).

For a review of Palau's economy and capital needs at present, see Palau Office of Planning and Statistics, *Republic of Palau: First National Development Plan 1987-1991* (Koror, 1987); Palau Ministry of Resources and Development, *Capital Improvement Project: Continuous Funding Plan for Fiscal Years 1993-1996* (Koror, 1992); and *Economic Development Plan (1995-1999)* (2 vols.) (Koror, 1994). See also Commission on Future Palau/U.S. Relations, *Report to the Third OEK and the President of Palau* (Koror, June 1989).

On the serious health problems (suicide, drugs and alcohol abuse) in the islands, see F. Hezel, D. Rubinstein, & H. White, eds., *Culture, Youth and Suicide in the Pacific: Papers from an East-West Center Conference* (Honolulu: University of Hawaii Press, 1985). Donald H. Rubinstein, "Suicide in Micronesia and Samoa: A Critique of Explanations," in 15 *Pacific Studies* 51 (1992), points out the uniqueness of the Palau situation.

My own book—Arnold Leibowitz, *Defining Status: A Comprehensive Analysis of U.S. Territorial Relations* (The Netherlands: Martinus Nijhoff, 1989)—contains a very detailed discussion of the Covenant and Compact negotiations with the Northern Mariana Islands, the Marshall Islands, the Federated States of Micronesia and Palau.

The Subcommittee on Public Lands and National Parks of the House Committee on Interior and Insular Affairs held a series of hearings on various aspects of the Compact: Compact of Free Association: Hearings before the Subcommittee on Public Lands and National Parks of the House Committee on Interior and Insular Affairs, 89th Cong., 2nd sess., U. S. Serial Set No. 98-56, Parts I-VIII, 1984. Other congressional committees held hearings and prepared reports as well. See, e.g., *U.S. Senate, To Approve the Compact of Free Association. Hearings before the Committee on Energy and Natural Resources on S. J. Res. 286, A Resolution to Approve the Compact of Free Association and for Other Purposes*, S. Hearings 1067, 98th Cong., 2nd sess., May 24, 1984; House of Representatives, *Micronesia Compact of Free Association: A Review of H.J. 620. Hearings before the House Committee on Foreign Affairs*, 98th Cong., 2nd sess., Sept. 18, 1984. See also, e.g., U. S. Senate, Committee on Energy and Natural Resources, *Report Approving the Compact of Free Association*, S. Rep. 626, 98th Cong., 2nd sess., Sept. 20, 1984; House of Representatives, *Compact of Free Association. Hearings before the Subcommittee on Public Lands of the Committee on Interior and Insular Affairs*, U.S. Serial Set No. 99-9, Parts I-III, 99th Cong., 1st sess., 1985; *U. S. Senate, Compact of Free Association. Hearings before the Committee on Finance, Senate Hearings 182*, 99th Cong., 1st sess., July 29, 1985; and *House of Representatives, Micronesian Compact. Hearings before the Subcommittee on Immigration, Refugees, and International Law of the Committee on the Judiciary*, U.S. Serial Set No. 99-11, 99th Cong., 1st sess., July 18, 1985.

With respect to Palau, key hearings were held before the House Foreign Affairs Committee reviewing the changes that had been made in the Compact to accommodate Lazarus Salii: House of Representatives, *The Compact of Free Association Between the United States and Palau, Hearings and Markup before the Committee on Foreign Affairs and its Subcommittee on Asian and Pacific Affairs on H.J. Res. 626*, 99th Cong., 2nd sess., May 8, 21, June 5, 1986. See also U.S. Senate, *Compact of Free Association, Hearings before the Committee on Energy and Natural*

Resources on S.J. Res. 325, 99th Cong., 2nd sess., May 9, 1986.

The hearings looking into the intimidation and violence in connection with the ratification of the Compact were:

> House of Representatives, *Palau, Oversight Hearings before the Subcommittee on Insular and International Affairs of the Committee on Interior and Insular Affairs, Part I,* 100th Cong., 1st sess., July 23, 1987.

> U.S. Senate, *Compact of Free Association, Hearings before the Committee on Energy and Natural Resources on S. J. Res. 231,* 100th Cong., 2nd sess., January 28, 1988.

> House of Representatives, *Developments Regarding the Compact of Free Association between the United States and Palau. Hearings and Markup before the Subcommittees on Human Rights and International Organizations, and on Asian and Pacific Affairs of the Committee on Foreign Affairs on H.J. Res. 479,* 100th Cong., 2nd sess., December 17, 1987 and March 31, 1988.

After the tumult and shouting died, the House Interior and Insular Affairs Committee held two Oversight Hearings. Neither of them was printed.

> House of Representatives, *Implementation of the Compact of 1985, Oversight Hearings before the Subcommittee on Insular and International Affairs of the Committee on Interior and Insular Affairs,* 100th Cong., 1st sess., July 18, 1989.

> House of Representatives, *Future Political Status of Palau, Oversight Hearings Before the Subcomm. on Insular and International Affairs of the Committee on Interior and Insular Affairs,* 100th Cong., 2nd sess., May 2, 1991.

The issue of the deepwater port can be seen in U.S. Senate, *Palau Deepwater Port, Hearings before the Committee on Energy and Natural Resources,* 95th Cong., 1st sess., March 24, 1977.

The examination by the General Accounting Office of the Salii administration is found in two reports: GAO, *U.S. Trust Territory: Issues Associated with Palau's Transition to Self-Government* (GAO/NSIAD 89-182), July 1989, and the accompanying *Supplement* (GAO/NSIAD 89-182S).

The pre-1986 Compact cases discussed in the text are as follows: *Gibbons v. Salii,* 1 ROP Intrm. 333 (Palau Sup. Ct. App. Div. 335, 1986), and *Gibbons v. Remeliik,* Civ. No. 67-83 (Palau Tr. Div., Aug. 1983). See also, *Koshiba v. Remeliik,* Civ. Act. No. 17, 83 (Palau Tr. Div., Jan. 1983).

The post-1986 Compact cases are *Merep v. Salii,* Civ. A. 139-87 (ROP Sup. Ct. Tr Div., 1987); *Inabo v. Rep. of Palau,* Civ. A. 125-87 (Palau Sup. Ct. Tr. Div., 1987); *Ngirmang v. Salii,* Civ. A. No. 161-87 (Palau Sup. Ct. Tr. Div., 1987); *Fritz v. Salii,* Civ. A. No. 161-87 (Palau Sup. Ct. Tr. Div., 1988); and *Fritz v. Salii,* Civ. Appeal No. 8-88 (Palau Sup. Ct. App. Div. 1988). After the Salii administration, the key Compact cases are *Gibbons v. Etpison,* Civ. A. Nos. 285-92 and 287-92 (consolidated), Order Granting Preliminary Injunction (July 9, 1992),and Trial Decision (October 8, 1992) (Palau Sup. Ct. Tr. Div. 1992); *Gibbons v. Etpison,* Civ. A. No. 435-92, Memorandum Decision (Palau Sup. Ct. Tr. Div. 1993); and *Wong v. Nakamura* and *Sumang v. Nakamura,* Civ. A. No. 2-94, Decision and Order (Palau Sup. Ct. Tr. Div., Mar. 25, 1994), Judgment (Palau Sup. Ct. Tr. Div. July 22, 1994).

The IPSECO cases are as follows:

Morgan Guaranty Trust Company of N.Y. v. Republic of Palau, 639 F.Supp.706 (S.D.N.Y. 1986).

Morgan Guaranty Trust Company of N.Y. v. Republic of Palau, 657 F.Supp.1475 (S.D.N.Y. 1987).

Morgan Guaranty Trust Company of N.Y. v. Republic of Palau, 680 F.Supp. 99 (S.D.N.Y. 1988).

Morgan Guaranty Trust Company of N.Y. v. Republic of Palau, 693 F.Supp. 1479 (S.D.N.Y. 1988).

Morgan Guaranty Trust Company of N.Y. v. Republic of Palau, 702 F.Supp. 60 (S.D.N.Y. 1988).

Morgan Guaranty Trust Company of N.Y. v. Republic of Palau, 924 F.2d 1237 (2nd Cir. 1991).

Morgan Guaranty Trust Company of N.Y. v. Republic of Palau, 767 F.Supp. 561 (S.D. N.Y. 1991).

Morgan Guaranty Trust Company of N.Y. v. Republic of Palau, 971 F.2d 917 (2nd. Cir. 1992).

Index

About the Author

ARNOLD H. LEIBOWITZ has written extensively about the territories, Commonwealths, and Freely Associated States of the United States, and has represented almost all of them before the Federal government since 1964, when he was General Counsel of the U.S. Commission of the Status of Puerto Rico. His book, *Defining Status: A Comprehensive Analysis of U.S. Territorial Relations*, is the leading reference work in the field, having been cited by the U.S. Supreme Court and a number of lower courts. He represented the Trusteeship of Palau from 1986 to 1988.

6 *R* v. *White* (2001) CA ECWA [2001] 1 WLR 1352.
7 *DPP* v. *McFarlane* (2002) EWHC Admin 485.
8 *DPP* v. *Woods* (2002) EWHC 85 Admin.

Chapter 9

Policing hate crime in New York and Philadelphia

As an academic my interest in hate crime has emerged from a specific interest in the policing of hate crime both in this country and in the United States. In late 1999, as a postgraduate student, I was invited by London's Metropolitan Police Service to undertake a small-scale research project to assess the unfolding of new policies and practices for policing hate crime following the publication of the Stephen Lawrence Inquiry. The research subsequently expanded and continues to date. While my original focus was on the Metropolitan Police, in the summer of 2003 I began a comparative study of the policing of hate crime in New York and Philadelphia to see how policing practices in this field differed among the three cities. My interest in New York as a comparison with London, and Philadelphia as a comparison with both, arose primarily from my own curiosity in relation to some basic numbers which I have placed in Table 9.1 (Hall, 2004).

Table 9.1 illustrates approximate figures for a small number of comparable variables. Of particular interest are the figures for London and New York. The two cities have a similar population, both of which are extremely diverse in their make-up. Broadly, while London and New York are comparable on a range of demographic criteria, the size of the hate crime 'problem' in the two cities and their respective approaches to policing hate crimes are hugely different.

Both cities have the largest police forces in their respective countries, yet the approximate number of police officers dedicated to hate crime investigation differs significantly between the two. In London, as we shall see later in the next chapter, there are 32 dedicated hate crime units, while in New York there is just one. Both work to proscriptive policies that state what action is required of the police in every hate

Table 9.1 Comparative data for London, New York and Philadelphia

	London	New York	Philadelphia
Population (millions)	7.5	8	1.5
Area (sq. miles)	620	309	129
Boroughs/precincts	32	5/74	23
No. of police officers	25,550	39,110	6,600
Central hate crime unit	Yes	Yes	Yes
Local hate crime units	Yes	No	No
Uniformed officers responsible for			
initial investigation	Yes	Yes	Yes
Minimum standards for investigation	Yes	Yes	Yes
Hate crime investigators	300	20	5
Diverse community	Yes	Yes	Yes
History of police–minority group			
tension/significant cases	Yes	Yes	Yes
Partnership approach to combating			
hate crime	Yes	Yes	Yes
No. of recorded hate crimes in 2001	20,628	484	c.100

crime investigation ('minimum standards'), yet the number of recorded hate crimes is vastly different. The figure listed in Table 9.1 for London (20,628) is for racist offences only. The figure for New York (484) includes hate crimes based on race, colour, national origin, ancestry, gender, religion, religious practice, age, disability and sexual orientation.

It was this significant difference in recorded hate crimes between the two cities that fuelled my interest in the different ways in which hate crime is socially constructed and policed in different jurisdictions. In this regard Philadelphia also provides a useful comparison with London and New York. The city and its police force are considerably smaller, as is the number of recorded hate crimes and officers dedicated to investigating them. Yet they too have a dedicated hate crimes unit, minimum standards for investigation that should be adhered to, and work in partnership with other agencies. Crucially, in each of the cities the hate crime investigators are rarely, if ever, the first to respond to a potential hate crime, and all three cities have a history of police-community tension.

Simply, the three cities provided a valuable comparison of the policing of hate crime in major cities on both sides of the Atlantic. While Table 9.1 shows many similarities, the way in which hate crime is policed in fact varies greatly. As such, the next three chapters will predominantly draw upon my own ethnographic research into the policing of hate crime in the three cities. This chapter will focus on New York and Philadelphia, and will outline the policing policies and practices in both cities. This will provide the necessary context for a comparison and examination of the practices adopted in London, which shall be the focus of the next chapter. Chapter 11 will then critique the different police responses, identify common and specific problems and challenges, and offer suggestions for improving police performance.

Policing hate crime in New York City

The New York City Police Department's Hate Crime Task Force (HCTF) was originally established in 1980 as the Bias Incident Investigation Unit for the purpose of monitoring crimes based on race, religion or ethnicity, and was the first dedicated hate crimes investigation unit of any city police force in the US. In 1985, the role was expanded to include sexual orientation and in 1993 was further expanded to include physical disabilities. In 2000, the Hate Crimes Act was signed into law and the definition of a bias or hate incident was expanded to include gender, age and the category of sexual orientation to include the lesbian, gay, bisexual and transgender (LGBT) community. In 2002, the unit was redesignated the Hate Crime Task Force.

In addition to the investigation of hate crimes, the HCTF provides support to victims following an offence, produces statistical data on hate crime patterns and trends to identify problems or potential problems in the city, liaises closely with prosecutors and advocacy groups, provides training assistance for officers working in the various precincts and provides an educative role in the community.

At the time of the study in the summer of 2003 the HCTF comprised approximately 20 detectives, and was structured thus, with the commanding officer, his deputy and a lieutenant in management and supervisory positions, and the detectives divided into small teams of approximately five officers under a sergeant (see Figure 9.1).

The hate crime 'problem' in New York

In 2001 there were 484 confirmed hate crimes across the five boroughs of New York (Manhattan, Queens, the Bronx, Brooklyn and Staten Island), representing a 4 per cent increase in the number of hate crimes from the preceding year (see Figure 9.2).

Of these 484 hate crimes, 118 cases were determined to be directly related to the terrorist attack on the World Trade Center in lower

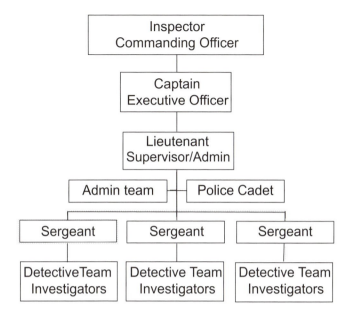

Figure 9.1 The organisation of the NYPD Hate Crime Task Force.

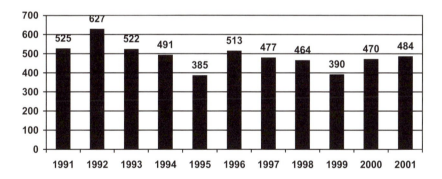

Figure 9.2 Recorded hate crimes in New York by year (NYPD, 2002)

Manhattan on 11 September 2001. These offences fit neatly into the 'retaliatory' category proposed by Levin, McDevitt and Bennett that was discussed in Chapter 5. Of these retaliatory attacks, 85 were 'anti-ethnic' and 33 'anti-religion' or 'anti-other', reflecting a 286 per cent increase in anti-ethnic incidents and a 58 per cent increase in anti-religion/other. Without the attacks on 11 September the recorded number of hate crimes would have shown a 22 per cent decrease on 2000.

153

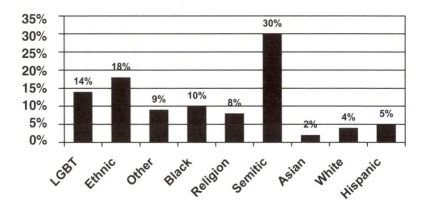

Figure 9.3 Hate crime victimology in New York in 2001 (NYPD, 2002).

Overall, 2001 saw a decrease in anti-Semitic (<26 per cent), anti-black, anti-white and anti-sexual orientation cases. Nevertheless, anti-Semitic hate crimes still accounted for the largest number of recorded hate crimes in New York in 2001, followed by anti-ethnic crimes and offences against the LGBT community (Figure 9.3).

There was also a drop in felony crimes (<15 per cent) but a rise in less serious misdemeanour crimes (>7 per cent). Across the city hate crimes decreased in all boroughs except Manhattan North (>39 per cent) Manhattan South (>34 per cent) and the Bronx (>10 per cent), and there were no discernible patterns in hate crime other than those related to 11 September. Figure 9.4 shows that in 2001 there were 66 hate crime felonies, of which 40 were assaults. The remaining 26 felonies were

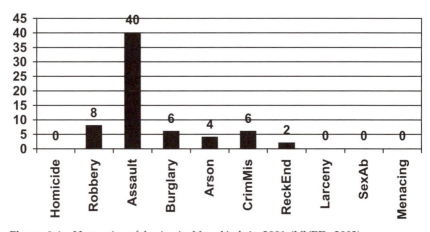

Figure 9.4 Hate crime felonies in New York in 2001 (NYPD, 2002).

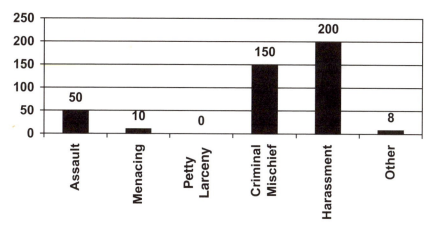

Figure 9.5   Hate crime misdemeanours in New York in 2001 (NYPD, 2002).

spread relatively evenly between robbery, burglary, arson and criminal mischief, with the remaining two crimes of reckless endangerment. There were no recorded hate motivated murders (the deaths on 11 September were classified as acts of war, not hate-motivated murders) and no hate-motivated sexual offences.

Of the 40 assaults, 35 per cent were against members of the LGBT community, 25 per cent were anti-ethnic and 18 per cent anti-Hispanic, with assaults against whites, blacks, Asians and 'others' making up the rest. In 16 per cent of the assaults the perpetrator used a knife (14 per cent) or a gun (2 per cent) with physical force alone used in 23 per cent of cases and a baseball bat used in 5 per cent of the cases. The remainder of the assault weapons were classified as 'other' which indicates support for McDevitt, Levin and Bennett's (2002) findings (see Chapter 5) that the majority of hate offenders will use whatever 'weapons' happen to be at hand at the time. Figure 9.4 therefore indicates that the vast majority of recorded hate crimes in New York are accounted for not by serious felony offences, but by less serious misdemeanour crimes, and this is reflected in the figures contained in Figure 9.5.

Figure 9.5 shows that the majority of hate crimes in New York in 2001 were crimes of harassment, followed respectively by less serious acts of criminal mischief and minor assaults. This lends support to the views expressed in Chapter 4 that hate crimes are frequently 'low-level' offences rather than more serious crimes, and while we should not forget the disproportionate impact of these 'lesser' offences, the low-level nature of many hate crimes can nevertheless have important implications for the policing of hate crime in general, and we shall discuss these in detail in Chapter 11.

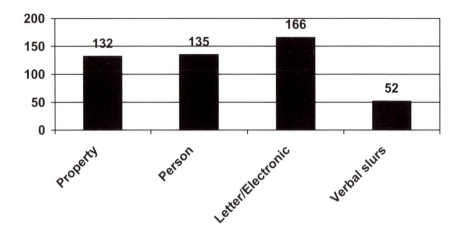

Figure 9.6   Hate crimes by type in New York in 2001 (NYPD, 2002).

The types of hate crime recorded by the NYPD in 2001 are seen in Figure 9.6. The majority of hate crimes were committed by way of malicious communication, either by letter or by e-mail. Crimes against the person came second, closely followed by crimes against property and, finally, verbal slurs. In other words, of all the hate crimes recorded by the police in New York, a little under three-quarters involved no 'physical' crime against the victim.

Policing hate crime in New York: policy and practice

The New York City Police Department's Patrol Guide (2000) procedure number 207–10 outlines the NYPD's policy for responding to bias-motivated incidents. For policing purposes, as we noted in Chapter 1, a bias incident is defined as:

... any offence or unlawful act that is motivated in whole or in part by a person's, a group's, or a place's identification with a particular race, religion, ethnicity, sexual orientation or disability as determined by the Commanding Officer, Bias Incident Investigation Unit. Disability [is defined as] the possession by a person of any of the following: a physical, medical, mental or psychological impairment or a history or record of such impairment. This includes the sustaining by a person of any injury or damage to any system of the body including muscular, sensory, respiratory, speech, heart, reproductive, digestive, blood, immunity (i.e. AIDS) and skin. Also included among those who have a disability are recovering alcoholics, and former abusers of drugs and other substances who currently are not abusing alcohol, drugs, or other substances. (NYPD, 2000: 1)

The proscriptive policy makes it quite clear that the HCTF is rarely, if ever, the first to respond to an incidence of hate crime. As with the majority of crimes it is a uniformed officer responding to a call for assistance who invariably is the first to come across a hate crime. The Patrol Guide states that when a patrol officer is despatched to the scene of a possible hate crime they are required to determine if the incident is motivated by bias or prejudice. Where they suspect that a bias incident has occurred they are required to request a patrol supervisor to respond to the incident.

In addition to responding to the immediate needs of the situation, the patrol supervisor is required to request the commanding officer or duty captain of the precinct in which the incident has taken place to respond if they believe the incident may be motivated by bias. The commanding officer or duty captain is then required to determine if an incident is bias-motivated and if so refer the incident to the HCTF for further investigation.

Where an incident is determined at the precinct level not to be a possible hate crime, the commanding officer or duty captain is required to notify the precinct detective squad, the Operations Unit and the HCTF of the decision. A detective squad officer will then conduct an investigation and is required to send a copy of the complaint report and the complaint follow-up report to the HCTF within ten days of the incident.

However, if the occurrence is referred to the HCTF as a possible bias incident then the commanding officer or duty captain in that precinct is still required to initially respond to the immediate needs of the situation. They are also required to request detective squad personnel to conduct an immediate investigation and confer with the HCTF detectives. The detective squad officer is required to forward a copy of the complaint report and complaint follow-up report to the commanding officer of the HCTF within ten days. The commanding officer or duty captain in the precinct then has to obtain a bias incident log number from the Operations Unit and forward an 'unusual occurrence report' to the Chief of Detectives and the HCTF, and to forward copies of the report to the Deputy Commissioner of Community Affairs, the precinct commanding officer and the Police Service Area/Transit District commanding officer. Finally, he or she is required to direct the crime prevention officer, where appropriate, to contact and advise the complainant about measures to take to prevent future victimisation.

The detective squad member is then responsible for conducting the investigation unless they are relieved by the HCTF, which is solely responsible for determining whether or not an incident is a hate crime. The personnel of the HCTF are therefore required to evaluate the incident in question and make a determination about whether to assume complete control of the investigation, to participate jointly with precinct detective squad personnel or to allow the precinct detectives to take full responsibility for the investigation.

Whatever path is chosen, the HCTF is required to visit and interview the victims of bias incidents upon the completion of an investigation. Once an investigation is complete and as far as possible all the facts of the case have been obtained, then and only then is a determination made by the commanding officer of the HCTF to label an incident a 'hate crime', and it is the results of these determinations that appear in the recorded hate crime statistics.

Deciding what is and what is not a 'hate crime'

While the decision to officially label an incident as a 'hate crime' can only be taken by the commanding officer of the HCTF, in reality this decision is taken at a number of different stages of the policing process. In many respects the most important decision is taken by the initial responding officer, upon whose decision the rest of the process is largely dependent. If he or she decides that an incident is not bias-related and determines that the response of the patrol supervisor is not required then others will not have the opportunity to determine differently. The same principle also applies to the decisions of the patrol supervisor, and to a lesser extent to the commanding officer or duty captain if he or she determines that an incident is not bias-motivated and fails to notify the HCTF. In other words, the decision-making process presents a number of opportunities for possible hate crimes to be 'filtered out' of the system and never to come to the attention of the HCTF. Because of this, being able to accurately determine what is and what is not a hate crime in relation to the law is crucial.

While the decision-making of more senior officers is frequently based on experience and common sense (Hall, 2004), written criteria and guidance are provided to NYPD officers from a number of sources, most notably the NYPD themselves, the Anti-Defamation League and the International Association of Chiefs of Police.

In assisting officers to determine the likelihood of an offence being bias-motivated, the HCTF (undated) states that the following criteria and questions should be considered:

1. The motivation of the perpetrator.
2. The absence of any motive.
3. The perception of the victim.
4. The display of offensive symbols, words or acts.
5. The date and time of occurrence (corresponding to a holiday of significance, i.e. Hanukkah, Martin Luther King Day, Chinese New Year, etc.).
6. A common sense view of the circumstances surrounding the incident (considering the totality of circumstances):
   a. The group involved in the attack.
   b. The manner and means of the attack.
   c. Any similar incidents in the same area or against the same victim.
7. What statements, if any, were made by the perpetrator.

Questions to be asked:

1. Is the victim the only member or one of a few members of the targeted group in the neighbourhood?
2. Are the victim and perpetrator from different racial, religious, ethnic, or sexual groups?
3. Has the victim recently moved to the area?
4. If multiple incidents have occurred in a short time period, are all the victims of the same group?
5. Has the victim been involved in a recent public activity that would make him/her a target?
6. What was the modus operandi? Is it similar to other documented incidents?
7. Has the victim been the subject of past incidents of a similar nature?
8. Has there been recent news coverage of events of a similar nature?
9. Is there an ongoing neighbourhood problem that may have spurred the event?
10. Could the act be related to some neighbourhood conflict involving area juveniles?
11. Was any hate literature distributed by or found in the possession of the perpetrator?

12. Did the incident occur, in whole or in part, because of racial, religious, ethnic, or sexual orientation difference between the victim and the perpetrator, or did it occur for other reasons?
13. Are the perpetrators juveniles or adults, and if juveniles, do they understand the meaning (to the community at large and to the victim) of the symbols used?
14. Were the real intentions of the responsible person motivated either in whole or in part by bias against the victim's race, religion, ethnicity, or sexual orientation, or was the motivation based on something other than bias, e.g. a childish prank, unrelated vandalism, etc.?

Note: If after applying the criteria listed and asking the appropriate questions, substantial doubt exists as to whether or not the incident is bias motivated or not, the incident should be classified as bias motivated for investigative and statistical purposes.

Remember: The mere mention of a bias remark does not necessarily make an incident bias motivated, just as the absence of a bias remark does not make an incident non-bias. A common-sense approach should be applied and the totality of the circumstances should be reviewed before any decision is made.

Source: NYPD (undated cited in Hall, forthcoming)

In their research of the NYPD's Bias Incident Investigation Unit (BIIU, before the change of name), Jacobs and Potter (1998) are critical of these criteria and questions. They suggest that they are so broad that practically any intergroup offence could plausibly be labelled as a hate crime. In particular they question why the second of the criteria – the absence of any motive – should support an inference of bias motivation. They also ask how much weight should be afforded to the victim's perception, who might be particularly sensitive to any negative encounter with a member of another group and who themselves may, for example, be racist or homophobic. Indeed this has important implications for the situation in England and Wales where the view of the victim cannot be questioned when a possible hate crime is reported. This is an issue to which I shall return. Despite Jacobs and Potter's criticisms, it should be remembered, however, that these criteria and questions are simply there to *assist* officers in making a judgment about bias motivation and that *evidence* must be present to support and justify any decision that is taken. Jacobs and Potter do not acknowledge this latter point.

Nevertheless, despite the importance attached to the decision-making of patrol officers and the guidance provided to assist them in making an accurate decision (regardless of the alleged limitations), there is evidence to suggest that the hate element of crimes is sometimes missed by police officers, be it deliberately or unwittingly. For example, on 19 September 2003 two patrol officers working in the borough of Staten Island were suspended from duty (and later dismissed) for failing to recognise the racist nature of a victim's complaint and for trying to discourage the victim and her friends from reporting a racist incident (for which there were later eleven arrests). The supervising officer was also suspended and subjected to disciplinary action. While the severity of the penalties may act as a deterrent against misclassification, it is impossible to know how many similar incidents never come to attention. Thus, while every stage of the decision-making process is crucial, it is this initial decision that is perhaps the most important but also arguably the weakest link in the whole process.

Further problems arise when the offence is not wholly motivated but instead is motivated 'in part' by an offender's bias. Determining the extent to which bias was a contributory factor to the commission of the offence, and to what extent the requirements of the law are met in terms of mounting a successful bias crime prosecution, presents a particular challenge to the police. It is here that a consideration of the totality of the offence characteristics becomes especially necessary.

In addition to inaccurate decisions, the length of the decision-making process is also potentially problematic, given that a hate crime may not come to the attention of the HCTF ('the experts') until the various stages of investigation described above have been undertaken. In some cases, as the Patrol Guide suggests, this may take up to ten days, although the time taken during the period of my research was never more than about 36 hours at most (Hall, 2004). Nevertheless, any significant delay may make the HCTF's investigation more difficult, particularly if the precinct detective squad adopt a 'hands off' approach to an incident and decide to leave the investigation for the HCTF.

On the other hand, of course, where accurate decisions are made they serve several important purposes. Firstly, because non-hate crimes are weeded out, those who are arguably in most need of assistance from the HCTF come to the fore and are afforded the appropriate response. By identifying the causal factors of an incident (based on a thorough investigation of the evidence), false and inaccurate allegations made by complainants can be more readily identified and responded to appropriately. As we shall see, this is in stark contrast to the situation sometimes found in England and Wales. Second, and related to the first, is the fact that because the law is used as a key reference point in the decision-making process, the specialist services of the HCTF are focused on the victims of hate 'crimes' as opposed to hate 'incidents' and therefore the finite resources of the Task Force can be more appropriately allocated to those in greatest need of them. Again, this is also in stark contrast to the situation sometimes found in England and Wales.

In addition to these practical issues, the political importance attached to the decision to label a hate crime should not be underestimated. Jacobs and Potter point out that given the politically sensitive nature of the decision to label a hate crime it was necessary to establish a Bias Review Panel in 1987, consisting of several senior ranking NYPD officers, to determine whether a case initially labelled as a hate crime should remain so. In this respect the labelling decision is subject to a form of 'quality assurance' for its accuracy and, just as importantly, to meet the concerns of outsiders that labelling decisions are primarily weighted towards the self-serving interests of the police department through the non-labelling of incidents as hate crimes. Because of the sensitive nature of hate crimes the HCTF is also subject to intense scrutiny from the media, political pressure and community interest, thus adding to the pressure to apply the hate crime label appropriately.

Police performance

Following their study of the BIIU, Jacobs and Potter (1998) were critical of the performance of the NYPD in terms of their ability to solve hate crimes (remembering that the HCTF shares responsibility for the policing of hate crimes with the rest of the police department). In 1994 arrests were made in approximately a quarter of all reported hate crimes. For property crimes the arrest rate was significantly lower, at approximately 10 per cent (Jacobs and Potter, 1998). In 2001, the arrest rate was much the same. Figure 9.7 shows the case closings for hate crimes in New York in 2001, and illustrates that in the vast majority of hate incidents an arrest is not made.

Jacobs and Potter suggest that the low clear-up rate for hate crimes can be attributed to a number of factors, most notably the greater propensity for offenders to be strangers to their victims and the propensity for offenders to act in groups. They also attribute the low clear-up rate to wider police hostility or indifference towards hate crime victims, resulting in a lack of commitment to an investigation. Throughout my own study of the HCTF the commitment towards victims shown by the unit's detectives was for the most part unquestionable, although the commitment of other officers is more difficult to ascertain, and the example of the Staten Island incident in 2003 (above) illustrates the point that Jacobs and Potter are making.

I will further examine the inherent difficulties in policing hate crime in Chapter 11, where I shall argue, as a number of other academics have, that the nature and characteristics of hate crime effectively mean that the clear-up rate is a relatively meaningless measure of police performance. It is therefore important in my opinion to measure 'success' in other ways. The 'success' of the HCTF (or any other aspect of policing hate crimes) might be better measured against the numbers of hate crimes reported by victims, where depending on the circumstances an increase may signify an increase in trust in the police, or where a decrease may perhaps suggest success in deterring hate crimes. Victim satisfaction with the police response, as indicated by qualitative and quantitative surveys, is of significant importance in assessing the 'success' of the police and is of far greater informational value than clear-up rates.

It may also be possible to further measure 'success' against the educative role undertaken by the unit, or the strength of the message conveyed to the public that hate crimes will not be tolerated and the suffering of victims will be treated seriously. We might also consider: the ability of the unit to respond proactively to a perceived threat or tension in a community; the collecting and collating of hate-related intelligence; the training of other police officers to respond appropriately to hate crimes; the ability of the unit to liaise with advocacy groups and 'build bridges' between minority communities and the police; or similarly

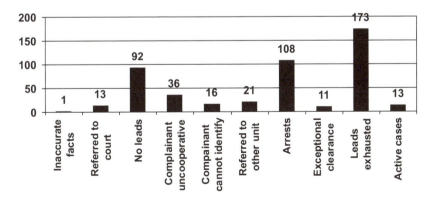

Figure 9.7   Case closings in New York in 2001 (NYPD, 2002).

their ability to act as a conduit between the victim and the 'ordinary' police whom the victim may not trust. All of these represent significant functions undertaken by the HCTF, which are not measurable simply by considering clear-up rates, yet the importance of which should not be underestimated.

Policing hatred in Philadelphia

Philadelphia, in the state of Pennsylvania, is by far the smallest of the three police departments in the study. It has a population of approximately 1.5 million that is policed by around 6,600 officers. Despite its size, Philadelphia nevertheless shares a number of important features with New York and London (see Table 9.1) yet it polices hate crime very differently, making it ideal for a comparative study.

The Philadelphia Police Department (PPD) (1999: 1) states that:

It is the policy of the Philadelphia Police Department to ensure that rights guaranteed by federal, state and local law are protected for all citizens regardless of their actual or perceived race, ethnicity, gender, sex, sexual orientation, age, disability, religion. When such rights are infringed upon by violence, threats or other harassment, the Department will be vigilant in its efforts to rapidly and decisively identify perpetrators, arrest them, and bring them before the court. All acts of violence or threats, including bias-related incidents, will be viewed as serious, and the investigations will be given priority attention. Such acts generate fear and concern among victims and result in loss of public confidence.

The PPD recognises hate crime as any incident that is committed against a person or property which is motivated by malicious intention because of a person's actual or perceived race, ethnicity, religion, national origin, gender, sex or sexual orientation. However, the state law under which hate crimes are prosecuted in Philadelphia (Ethnic Intimidation 2710 PCC) is considerably narrower in its scope, and this is reflected in its title. The law recognises offences committed with malicious intent and motivated by hatred on the basis of race, religion or national origin, but not gender, sex or sexual orientation. Nevertheless, it is the policy of the PPD to investigate these as hate crimes.

The Conflict Prevention Resolution Unit (CPRU)

Just as in New York, the PPD has a central 'hate crimes' unit. This was established in 1986 with the goal of enhancing the police department's ability to render assistance to those who had been victimised because of their race, colour, national origin, religion or sexual orientation. However, the role of this unit is significantly different to that in New York, both in terms of its size and the functions it performs. At the time of the study the unit consisted of just five detectives, with eight seconded indefinitely to other units.

Rather than assume responsibility for the investigation of reported hate crimes in the city, the CPRU performs more of a 'consultative' role for the police department. Except for exceptional circumstances where the police commissioner may direct the CPRU to assume full responsibility for an investigation, the unit acts in a secondary capacity to assist the Detective Division of Occurrence with the investigation of bias incidents. Throughout the course of an investigation the CPRU works in partnership with detectives and other law enforcement officers to ensure that evidence is properly processed, interviews are properly conducted and the required paperwork is completed. The unit also performs an important liaison function between the police and victims and community groups throughout an investigation. The investigation of hate crimes is therefore not the main responsibility of the CPRU, but it performs a number of other important functions.

Central among these is the CPRU's role as the PPD's liaison with the various advocacy and community groups, federal and state agencies, social services and community-response agencies, all of whom have an interest in responding to hate incidents and community tensions in the city. The CPRU also acts as the PPD's central repository for hate incident investigations, and is therefore responsible for 'keeping an eye on things' and submitting weekly reports to the commissioner, monthly reports of ongoing investigative activity to the PPD's Research and Development Unit, and annual reports to federal and state agencies.

In addition to their role in specific investigations and data collation, the CPRU also works in partnership with schools and community groups to develop awareness and prevention programmes to address hate and prejudice. The unit's officers also meet with local residents, neighbourhood groups and community leaders to appraise them of ongoing police activity, to allay or respond to any community concerns, to determine if victims are receiving an appropriate service from the police, and to provide practical advice about preventing hate-related incidents. In this way the CPRU is able to 'keep its finger on the pulse' in relation to community fears or tensions.

Finally, the CPRU is a member of the Philadelphia Inter-agency Task Force which comprises various agencies with an interest in responding to hate crimes in the city. In this way the CPRU is able to contribute to information sharing and the development of investigative and intervention strategies. Similarly, the CPRU also has a community outreach programme and holds quarterly meetings with local community groups.

Police procedure

The process by which a potential hate crime is identified, labelled and responded to is shorter than is the case in New York, but no less subjective. Directive 83/139 of October 1999 sets out the police response to a reported incident. The directive states that when a responding officer suspects the incident may be motivated by bias, they are required to request the presence of a supervisor and take appropriate immediate action to respond to the incident. The officer is then required to confer with the supervisor to determine the cause of the incident, and the supervisor will then make the determination as to whether the incident meets the definition of a bias incident or the Ethnic Intimidation law. At this stage the CPRU can be used as a resource for consultation or assistance in making the decision. Once this is done the incident is passed, together with the relevant paperwork, to the Detective Division for investigation.

Just as in New York, the PPD contains within its directive a list of factors to consider when making a determination about an incident. In recognising that motivation is subjective, the PPD (1999: 2) encourages officers to consider the following:

1. The offender and victim were of different racial, religious, color, ethnic origin or sexual orientation group.
2. Bias-related oral comments, written statements or gestures were made by the offender, which indicate his/her bias.
3. Bias-related drawings, markings, symbols, or graffiti were left at the crime scene.
4. Several incidents have occurred in the same locality, at or about the same time, and the victims are all of the same racial, religious, color, national origin or sexual orientation group.
5. The offender was previously involved in a similar hate crime or is a member of a hate group.
6. Offender has hate inspired tattoos, literature, or is dressed in regalia representing a hate group.

What is particularly interesting about the PPD's directive, however, is a note that is included within the document that states that:

> It is important to recognise that most incidents between different individuals or groups are NOT the result of hostility based on one of the above mentioned affiliations. Simply because two combatants are of different racial groups, for example, does not mean that ethnic intimidation has occurred. Additionally, individuals of the same religion, ethnic, or racial groups can also be involved in bias incidents. (PPD, 1999: 3)

The note makes it perfectly clear that incidents that occur between members of different groups are usually not motivated by hate or bias, and that such an assumption should not be made. Rather, there needs to be more substantial evidence before an incident can be labelled as a hate crime. As we shall see over the course of the next two chapters, this is a situation that is vastly different to that found in England and Wales and is a significant factor in determining the number of hate crimes recorded by the police.

Concluding comments

In this chapter I have outlined the policies and procedures for policing hate crimes in New York and Philadelphia. The main purpose of the chapter was not to critique these, although I have alluded to some areas of concern, but rather to provide a context within which to compare the policing of hate crimes in London which will form the focus of the next chapter. As we shall see, the way in which hate is responded to in this country is significantly different to the United States, and after I have outlined these policies and procedures it will be possible to offer a critique of the policing of hate crimes in both countries, and to identify the various problems and challenges associated with doing so.

Chapter 10

Policing hate crime in London

The most striking differences between New York and London are the number of hate offences recorded by the police, and the number of police officers (and specialist units) dedicated to the investigation of hate crimes. In this chapter I shall explore the policing of hate crime in London, drawing again from my own ongoing research. Rather than presenting a critique, this chapter will be predominantly descriptive of the policing approach to hate crimes adopted in London over the past five years or so. This will allow for a comparison with the approaches of New York and Philadelphia that were discussed in the last chapter, and provide the context for a critique in the next chapter.

Any discussion of the policing of hate crime in London (or indeed anywhere else in this country) would be incomplete, however, without first making reference to the Stephen Lawrence Inquiry. The murder of Stephen Lawrence and the subsequent public inquiry in 1999 served as a catalyst to raise the issues of hate, crime and policing to unprecedented levels in this country, and brought about significant changes to the way that hatred is policed in England and Wales. It is therefore important to begin our consideration here.

Stephen Lawrence, Sir William Macpherson and the Metropolitan Police Service

The events of the evening of 22 April 1993 are well documented. At approximately 22:30, 18-year-old Stephen Lawrence and his friend Duwayne Brooks were subjected to an unprovoked racist attack by five white youths in Well Hall Road, Eltham, South-east London.

Stephen Lawrence was stabbed twice during the attack and died shortly afterwards. The Metropolitan Police Service (MPS) investigation that followed has been the subject of fierce controversy. Following a complaint by Stephen's parents about the Met's handling of the case and two unsatisfactory internal PCA investigations, a public inquiry was set up by the then Home Secretary Jack Straw in July 1997.

The Lawrence Inquiry is by no means the first report to critically examine the issues of race and policing. However, Sir William Macpherson's report into matters arising from the murder of Stephen Lawrence is undoubtedly 'the most radical official statement on race, policing and criminal justice ever produced in this country' (McLaughlin, 1999: 13). Furthermore, the inquiry offered the first public opportunity to re-examine issues of policing and race since the Scarman Report into the Brixton disorders in 1981.

The Stephen Lawrence Inquiry

The Stephen Lawrence Inquiry was divided into two parts. Part One was concerned with the matters arising from the death of Stephen Lawrence and Part Two with the lessons to be learned for the investigation and prosecution of racially motivated crimes.

The findings from Part One of the Inquiry have received unprecedented publicity. It is clear that there were fundamental errors made during the investigation of Stephen Lawrence's murder. The Inquiry concluded that the investigation was 'marred by a combination of professional incompetence, institutional racism and a failure of leadership by senior officers' (Macpherson, 1999: 46.1).

Specific areas of criticism included the lack of direction and organisation of the initial response, the provision of first aid, command and control at the scene of the murder, family liaison and victim support, the actions and inaction of senior investigating officers, the surveillance operation, the handling of suspects and searches of their addresses, the management of informants, and issues relating to policy and records. Furthermore, the Inquiry was highly critical of the internal reviews that failed to expose these inadequacies. However, the Inquiry rejected suggestions that collusion and corruption affected the murder investigation.

Nevertheless, evidence that emerged during Part One of the Inquiry highlighted widespread racial insensitivity and negative racial stereotyping on the part of the police. Thus an issue of central concern is that of institutional racism that has been identified within the Metropolitan Police Service. The Inquiry defined this as:

169

... the collective failure of an organisation to provide an appropriate and professional service to people because of their colour, culture, or ethnic origin. It can be seen or detected in processes, attitudes and behaviour which amount to discrimination through unwitting prejudice, ignorance, thoughtlessness and racist stereotyping which disadvantages minority ethnic people. (Macpherson, 1999: 6.34)

The Stephen Lawrence case clearly demonstrates that the manifestation of racism within police culture at an institutional level can have serious implications for the proper investigation of racist incidents.

While Part One of the Inquiry examined issues closely connected to the investigation into the murder of Stephen Lawrence, Part Two examined many of the wider issues concerning policing and race. Unsurprisingly, the Inquiry uncovered evidence that highlighted the lack of trust that exists between the police and the minority ethnic communities. Significantly, this lack of trust was found to be greater in the Metropolitan Police Service area than anywhere else in the country.

Opinions aired at the public meetings held during Part Two of the Inquiry clearly showed that minority communities believe that the police discriminate against them. They widely believe that junior police officers discriminate against them in practice at the operational level, and that officers support each other in such discrimination. Indeed, Younge (2000) suggests that the Inquiry:

provided evidence that there is a persistent and consistent propensity to shove ethnic minorities to the bottom of every available pile and not only leave them there but blame them for being there as well. (2000: 2)

The Inquiry found that distrust and dissatisfaction with the police and other agencies in the investigation of racist incidents had led to a disinclination to report. It was widely felt that the Police Service lacked the commitment to take effective action against racist crimes and regularly ignored and belittled such incidents, and did not or would not realise the impact of less serious, non-crime incidents upon the minority ethnic communities.

The Inquiry suggested, therefore, that:

... their [the ethnic minority communities'] collective experience was of senior officers adopting fine policies and using fine words, but of indifference on the ground at junior officer level. The actions or inactions of officers in relation to racist incidents were clearly a potent factor in damaging public confidence in the Police Service. (1999: 45.12)

The Inquiry also expressed concerns relating to the disproportionate use of 'stop and search', the number of ethnic minority deaths in custody, the widely misunderstood operational definition of a racist incident, the need for a multi-agency approach to combat racism and the system for making complaints against the police.

Following the evidence presented to Part Two of the Inquiry, Macpherson concluded that:

The message is uncompromising. A new atmosphere of mutual confidence and trust must be created. The onus to begin the process which will create that new atmosphere lies firmly and clearly with the police. The Police Services must examine every aspect of their policies and practices to assess whether the outcome of their actions create or sustain patterns of discrimination. The provision of policing services to a diverse public must be appropriate and professional in every case. Every individual must be treated with respect. 'Colour-blind' policing must be outlawed. The police must deliver a service which recognises the different experiences, perceptions and needs of a diverse society. (Macpherson, 1999: 45.24)

This view is reflected in the 70 recommendations made by the Inquiry team, including a new Ministerial Priority for all Police Services:

… to increase trust and confidence in policing among minority ethnic communities. (1999: Recommendation 1)

Policing hate crime: the police response to Macpherson

The Stephen Lawrence Inquiry was highly critical of the Metropolitan Police Service's policy and practice in relation to ethnic minority groups and racist incidents. Responding to these issues, providing an effective police service that is responsive to the diverse population of London, and achieving the new Ministerial Priority presented the MPS with arguably the most fundamental challenge in its history. The extent of this challenge was recognised at the highest level and the

MPS acknowledged that significant changes needed to be made to their operational approach in terms of defining standards for investigations, training, senior management oversight and the demonstration of fair practice.

As such, the Service has undertaken a 'substantial programme of change'. The 'Diversity Strategy' is aimed at rebuilding public confidence, and improving the quality of the MPS's performance in relation to racially motivated crime and the service provided to victims (MPS, 1999a). Furthermore, a number of the initiatives contained within the Diversity Strategy are directly aimed at challenging institutional racism within the Service. The MPS believes that by impacting upon the way the Service operates day to day, the organisational culture will change.

The Stephen Lawrence Inquiry expressed concern over the ACPO definition of racially motivated crime, as indeed had Her Majesty's Inspector of Constabulary two years earlier (HMIC, 1997). The concern centred on evidence suggesting that the ACPO definition was not universally understood nor accepted across the Service, and that widely differing interpretations by officers often resulted in problems in its application. In the case of Stephen Lawrence, the Inquiry concluded that a lack of appreciation or willingness to accept that racism was a motivating factor in the murder had obscured and impeded the approach to the investigation.

The MPS accepts that failure to identify the racial element in crimes not only affects their ability to respond effectively but also impacts on ethnic minority victims' confidence in the police (MPS, 1998). As such, a clear and uncompromising definition of a racial incident has been accepted for operational use by the MPS. A racist incident, as recommended by the Macpherson Inquiry, is now defined as:

any incident which is perceived to be racist by the victim or any other person. (Recommendation 12)

In essence, this is the same as the previous ACPO definition – an incident has a racial element if anyone says it has. The important difference here is that the apparent priority given to the views of the police officer, and thus the element of discretion afforded to the police in the recording of such incidents by the old definition, is now removed. This new definition is plainly more victim oriented, and crimes and non-crimes reported as racially motivated must now be recorded as such and investigated with equal commitment regardless of the perception of the reporting or investigating officer. Theoretically, it is now impossible for a police officer to refuse to accept that a reported incident is not racially motivated if that is the view held by the complainant or anyone else. This has significant both positive and negative implications for the investigation of racist crime, as will become evident in due course.

Policy on the recording of racial incidents was first introduced by the MPS more than 20 years ago and for the past 13 years the Service has been issuing instructions and guidance on responding to racial attacks and harassment. As McLaughlin (1999) suggests, there have been many efforts to reform relations between the MPS and black Londoners since the Scarman Report in 1981. However, evidence from Part One of the Stephen Lawrence Inquiry demonstrated the significant gulf that existed between policy and practice in the Metropolitan Police Service, and suggested that many of the much-lauded post-Scarman race and community policing initiatives were either ineffective or never implemented (McLaughlin, 1999).

Since 1993 (incidentally the year that Stephen Lawrence was murdered) somewhat more visible efforts have been made by the Met to turn policy intent into operational action. As a part of this developmental process, the MPS area has been divided into a number of geographical commands and specialist crime investigation units have been established on each command. This restructuring has taken place to allow operational decision-making (and accountability for those decisions) to be closely linked to those who implement such decisions. Thus a significant amount of discretion on the implementation of policy relating to racially motivated crime has been afforded to each of the 33 Operational Command Units (OCUs). The reasoning behind this discretion is that (at least theoretically) policy can be adapted to suit specific local circumstances, demographics and crime patterns.

The Stephen Lawrence Inquiry, however, expressed concern in relation to this situation. In particular there was evidence to suggest that this discretion had led to policy being disregarded in some areas and that there was often a lack of clarity in lines of command. The response of the Metropolitan Police Service has been to develop and impose a corporate template upon OCUs in relation to the way racially motivated crimes are dealt with. All OCUs are now required to maintain Community Safety Units (CSUs) with specific responsibility for dealing with racially motivated crime and other 'hate' offences, including domestic violence. This requirement has been accompanied by the imposition of corporate standards for the investigation of such crimes and the care of victims and witnesses to which all OCUs must adhere (MPS, 1998).

The Stephen Lawrence Inquiry left little doubt that there was an urgent need for significantly improved quality control and management oversight within the MPS and the Service's response was to establish the Racial and Violent Crime Task Force (now the Diversity Directorate). The role of the Task Force has been to set and implement an agenda for reform that will lead to a greatly enhanced police response to racist crime. The 'quality' strategy is based upon the improvement of operating standards, training and management oversight and accountability. As such, the terms of reference for the Directorate are:

- To provide oversight for the Metropolitan Police Service of all racial and violent crime. This includes a mandate to monitor cases, to review appropriate cases and to deliver improvements;
- To set and develop operating standards for investigation, victim care, the use of intelligence and community safety units;
- To ensure that appropriate training is developed and delivered.

(MPS, 1998: 1)

As suggested above, the Stephen Lawrence Inquiry has demonstrated a significant gap between policy and practice within the MPS and has highlighted 'the wretched state of the management and supervisory systems of the Metropolitan Police in the early 1990s' (McLaughlin, 1999: 14). Herein lies the reason behind the first of the Directorate's terms of reference. The Service has recognised the need for senior management to oversee and constantly monitor the MPS's response to racist crime (both locally and Service-wide) and to adopt an effective interventionist approach to ensure that the gap between policy and practice is bridged. The Directorate therefore provides an oversight through the monitoring of racist incidents, area trends and police performance in relation to these incidents, in addition to conducting 'victim satisfaction' surveys and 'dip sampling' of cases.

Significantly, the Directorate's objectives and practices are not developed in a 'police vacuum'. The MPS expressed its desire to involve the wider community in its activities and as such a Lay Advisory Group (LAG) and other working groups have been established to advise, guide, review and develop the Met's approach to racist crime. At the time of its establishment in February 1999, the Lay Advisory Group had 50 members drawn from a wide range of backgrounds and of which 80 per cent were from visible ethnic minorities. Crucially, the LAG have a mandate to operate independently of police management and to directly and constructively challenge police policy and practice.

In light of the findings of Part One of the Stephen Lawrence Inquiry, the reasons behind the second of the terms of reference are clear. The establishment of specialist Community Safety Units (CSUs) across all OCUs has already been noted above but their importance within the MPS's process of change with regard to racist crime cannot be understated. Indeed, establishing and supporting the Community Safety Units is, at least in theory, the core business of the Racial and Violent Crime Task Force (Hall, 1999, 2002a).

The need for specific training of police officers was also made clear by Part One of the Stephen Lawrence Inquiry. Given the culture and predominantly white ethnicity of the police, improving officers' understanding of (and attitudes towards) cultural diversity is crucial in addressing racism. HM Inspector of Constabulary (1999) shares this view. Following a thematic inspection into the race relations of a number of forces across the country (including the MPS), HMIC concluded that:

> training can significantly influence the way in which forces can impact upon and improve their organisational culture, individual attitudes and behaviour and should be seen by chief officers as a long-term investment. [However] HM Inspector was drawn to the disappointing conclusion that training in general awareness of varying cultural issues, the investigation of crime with a racial element, the prudent use of discretion including stop and search powers, and addressing inappropriate behaviour has been marginalised (HMIC, 1999: 8)

Clearly, this situation needs to be addressed across all police services, and in more recent years progress has been made in this area.

The response of the MPS has been to introduce a Service-wide training programme for both police and civilian staff, and to provide resources and support for local training on racial incidents and community and race relations (CRR) issues. Indeed, this process began prior to the commencement of the Stephen Lawrence Inquiry with a locally tailored pilot training programme in Lambeth involving significant input from local ethnic minority groups. The apparent success of the pilot scheme resulted in its application across other boroughs, including Greenwich, Tower Hamlets and Hounslow in the first instance, with all Boroughs having now followed suit.

Furthermore, National Police Training in association with ACPO and the Police Federation has drawn up Minimum Effective Training Levels (METLs) with regard to CRR and equal opportunities. These nationally agreed standards of competency are now effective in all recruit, probationer, detective and management training. Additional training is also provided for senior investigating officers in the management of 'critical incidents', and a four-week training course on Hate Crime and Domestic Violence is provided for CSU staff. To ensure that improvements in training standards are consistently delivered to the required standard the MPS has established a Diversity Training Support Unit to coordinate the delivery of training and to ensure that CRR issues are included in all future training programmes in any area of policing.

The Met's Diversity Strategy is therefore designed to challenge police policy, practice and behaviour that has (either intentionally or unintentionally) racist consequences and to change the way the Service operates to better meet the needs of ethnic minorities in London. The issues outlined above are those that are most likely to have a direct impact upon victims of hate crime and the way the police respond. Other policies are now in place regarding the recruitment and advancement of minority ethnic officers, and quality control measures now exist to promote fair practice in the use of police powers including covert integrity testing for officers whose behaviour gives cause for concern.

The Stephen Lawrence Inquiry clearly identified a legacy of fundamental problems relating to the MPS's policy and practice with regard to incidents motivated by racism, and called the police and others to account for their actions in the Lawrence case. Individual, cultural and institutional racism within the police service has at least been acknowledged, as have the consequences in terms of the failure to deliver either a quality of service or equality of service (Bowling, 1999). The next step, as Bowling (1999) suggests, is to address these issues and in doing so provide an effective service to, and equal protection of, a diverse population.

The 'post-Lawrence' environment has offered a significant window of opportunity for the MPS and indeed all other forces to address these issues and to deliver real change in their policies and practices. All of the changes outlined in this section are important in addressing the complex issue of hatred and the Diversity Strategy as a whole represents a significant change in the way that the MPS operates with regard to hate crime.

Refocusing the police response to hate crime

In essence, two significant interrelated issues emerged from the Lawrence Inquiry. The first was the inescapable need for the MPS to re-establish trust and confidence in policing among minority ethnic communities and the second was the equally inescapable need for a major revision of the way in which racist crime (and other hate crime) investigations are conducted and victims are treated.

While the re-establishment of trust will inevitably be a slow and ongoing process, the MPS has revised and outlined its position with regard to the way hate incidents should be dealt with by its officers. Community Safety Units (CSUs) responsible for the local implementation of these initiatives have been established in every London borough. A total of 32 Community Safety Units exist across the MPS area to offer support and protection to victims of hate crime and domestic violence. These have now replaced the MPS's previously existing Racial Incidents, Domestic Violence and Vulnerable Persons Units.

Every case (and every victim) of hate crime is unique. As a consequence of the particular impact of race/hate crime on both victims and the wider community, the Metropolitan Police Service now recognises that victims of such crimes will often require a different and *appropriate* level of support and of service. The Community Safety Units have been established to deliver improved standards of service and investigation with the intention of:

... reducing these crimes using a variety of tools including intelligence and a proactive approach that targets perpetrators and supports victims, especially those who are repeatedly victimised. (Metropolitan Police Service, 1999e: 2)

In light of this approach, two central aims have been identified for the CSUs:

To investigate, identify and prosecute perpetrators to the satisfaction of the victim and community.

And where a criminal prosecution of a perpetrator is not feasible:

To identify and pursue alternative courses of action (where appropriate with/by partner agencies).

It is stressed, however, that these objectives are not mutually exclusive and consideration should always be given to pursuing both objectives simultaneously where appropriate. Therefore the investigative approach adopted by the Community Safety Units extends, in theory at least, beyond traditional 'reactive' policing methods and encourages the proactive application of a range of intelligence tools to construct practical victim-centred solutions. An outline of the Met's proposals for effectively combating hate crime will be the subject of the following sections of the chapter.

Intelligence initiatives

In the past the role of the police in relation to racist (hate) incidents has been largely reactive. Sibbitt (1997) suggests that this has contributed significantly to the erosion of trust and confidence in policing that is evident among minority ethnic communities. Despite an increase over the years in the amount of intelligence collected on criminals in general, Sibbitt (1997) stated that there had been no coordination of intelligence or general information on the suspects of racist incidents.

Sibbitt (1997) also found that the police appeared to put little effort into identifying suspects (and indeed had little incentive to do so), suggesting that the officers did not treat such incidents seriously or did not perceive incidents such as low-level harassment to be a 'police problem'. Consequently, few suspects were identified by the police resulting in a notable absence of any action being taken against perpetrators.

In the context of Stephen Lawrence's murder, the Inquiry concluded that the investigation was hindered by such a lack of criminal intelligence. The Racial Incidents Unit (RIU) concerned held little useful information about possible suspects, and none in relation to the five prime suspects. The reason for this was that RIUs only held information relating to suspects involved in racially motivated crimes, and no such identifiable crimes had been committed by the five suspects prior to the murder of Stephen Lawrence.

The Inquiry found that more general information about criminal activities was available from the Local Intelligence Officer than from the RIU. Disturbingly, however, the Inquiry also found that during the course of the murder investigation both of these sources of intelligence were in fact available in the same office but a lack of cooperation and co-ordination had prevented any exchange of potentially vital information about potential suspects.

The value of criminal intelligence is clear. Regardless of any efforts made by the MPS their resources (and the resources of partner agencies) to combat hate crime are inevitably finite. Therefore, in order to provide the most effective service to victims, it is important that these limited resources are focused efficiently to where they are most needed and to where the most significant results are likely.

The Stephen Lawrence Inquiry stated that:

It is most important that intelligence on violent and racist individuals should be collected, so that those investigating crimes have ready access to information which may lead them to the perpetrators of such crimes. (1999: 35.13)

Therefore one of the most significant of the MPS's proposals for the investigation of racist crime involves a shift from the aforementioned predominantly reactive response to one that incorporates a strong proactive element, drawing upon the principles of intelligence-led policing. This shift has been aided by the Crime and Disorder Act 1998, section 115 of which makes it lawful for responsible authorities, their cooperating partners and persons acting on their behalf to exchange relevant information where this will support the implementation of an effective strategy to reduce crime and disorder.

Central to the MPS's revised approach to racist crime has been the development and use of four intelligence initiatives.

The Strategic and Tactical Intelligence Cell
The development of the Strategic and Tactical Intelligence Cell is perhaps the most significant initiative, representing the first integrated intelligence system in the MPS. Operating at force level, this corporate database aims to provide the Racial and Violent Crime Task Force and therefore the MPS with a clearer and more focused picture of racist and violent crime in the capital. This is achieved by retrieving intelligence and crime reports from every divisional/area computer database within the MPS simultaneously.

Through the use of a number of analytical processes (including the identification of crime trends and patterns, victim and offender profiles, geographical 'hotspotting' of crime locations, and identifying the scale and nature of offences) actionable information is available to assist the MPS in the identification and arrest of offenders, the disruption of suspects, and the prevention and detection of racist crimes, with the underlying aim of increasing victims' confidence in the Service.

The information collected by and contained within the intelligence cell is drawn from a wide variety of both internal and external sources. For example, internal sources of information include crime records (CRIS System), the CRIMINT (Criminal Intelligence) system, other MPS and specialist databases and the Police National Computer. External sources of intelligence might include local authorities, agencies and departments, victim support schemes, local representative and monitoring groups, industry and business, schools and colleges, CRE and various other 'open sources'.

Collating and analysing this data has enabled the Racial and Violent Crime Task Force to provide a number of intelligence packages to teams of detectives which has subsequently enabled specifically targeted operations against the perpetrators of hate crimes to be undertaken throughout London. Furthermore, the dissemination of this researched intelligence to the local level has resulted in the identification of 'prominent nominals' (suspected perpetrators known to be or likely to be active in a local area) facilitating targeted plans for action.

Proactive tools
The MPS Policing Plan now encourages the use of proactive initiatives against racist crimes and their perpetrators. Indeed, proactive initiatives (such as surveillance and video recording of suspects) against individuals or in areas with a high number of racist incidents can be highly effective. These principles, which have been successfully used by the MPS in past operations against street robbery and burglary, have been modified to target perpetrators of racial harassment. Local Intelligence Units and Community Safety Units are able to employ 'CRIMINT' software to build and 'map' intelligence on individuals suspected of committing racist crimes.

This software is instrumental in the application of a number of proactive tools. Intelligence and information contained within the CRIMINT system can be used to inform covert policing tactics including undercover and decoy operations, the deployment of informants, the use of physical and technical surveillance and so on. Furthermore, the system can be used adopt an intelligence-led approach to identifying offenders by facilitating crime-pattern analysis to inform police patrolling and to initiate operations, by identifying 'perpetrator communities' and 'problem families', by identifying vulnerable individuals/areas and by raising the profile of offenders among officers.

Community intelligence
HMIC defines community intelligence as:

... local information, direct or indirect, that when assessed provides intelligence on the quality of life experienced by individuals and groups, that informs both strategic and operational perspectives in the policing of local communities. (1999: 47)

Community intelligence therefore involves the gathering and analysis of information to enable trends to be identified and informed decisions to be taken in relation to factors affecting community tensions and local quality of life issues.

At OCU level information on problems and issues affecting their respective local communities is entered into the CRIMINT system by officers throughout the course of their normal duties. Community intelligence held on CRIMINT may be drawn from a variety of different sources and will include information on the following categories (MPS, 1999d):

- *Significant events or incidents which may affect or indicate community tension* – including public events (demonstrations, meetings, etc.), deaths in police custody, religious festivals, extremist activity and so on.
- *Officer safety information* – including a suspect's predicted/known response to the police (violence, resistance, carrying/use of offensive weapons against police, etc.).
- *Incidents of inter-group rivalry* – including rivalry between or within ethnic/religious groups.
- *Any other incident which may indicate or cause changes in community tension* – including police raids in sensitive areas/premises, threats to community safety, repeated incidents of serious anti-social behaviour, enhanced media interest in local problems.

The careful collation and analysis of the information contained within the community intelligence system provide OCUs with the potential to identify the issues that damage the quality of life for those living in the local community and allow for pre-emptive measures to be taken.

Open source intelligence
Intelligence from open sources is defined as:

… publicly available information appearing in print or elec-tronic form. Whatever form it takes, open source involves no information that is classified at its origin; is subject to proprietary constraints (other than copyright); is the product of sensitive contacts; or is acquired through clandestine or covert means. (MPS, 1999d: 41)

As such, useful open source information may emerge from sources such as television, radio and the media. It may also emerge from the Internet, commercial databases, CD ROMs, or through more 'grey' areas such as conference proceedings, company reports, telephone directories and so on. Racial equality councils, local authorities, monitoring, campaign and political groups and local forums may also be sources of open intelligence that can be disseminated and acted upon without fear of compromise to the originator or the need for confidentiality.

Supporting communities and preventing hate crime

The second of the primary aims for the Community Safety Units ('where a criminal prosecution of a perpetrator is not feasible, to identify and pursue alternative courses of action where appropriate with/by partner agencies') demonstrates the MPS's acceptance of the fact that they cannot effectively tackle racist crime by working alone. Given the nature of racist crime, the MPS acknowledges the fact that there are many incidents where the involvement of the police may be minimal but where the scope for alternative courses of action against perpetrators is considerable.

It is crucial, therefore, that the police are successful in forging effective and cooperative partnerships, both internally and externally, with parties with different roles but with the shared goal of eradicating hate crime in the local community. Indeed, the formation of such partnerships is a statutory requirement of the Crime and Disorder Act 1998.

The MPS (1999d) states that key partners and what might be achieved from working in partnership will generally include the following:

- *Race equality councils/monitoring groups* – to establish information-sharing protocols, to share policy information, to discuss scope for inputs to police training in race issues, to develop multi-agency race hate panels for determining suitable courses of action in individual cases, to encourage reporting, and so on.

- *Local authority housing and community landlords* – to agree zero tolerance approaches towards offenders, to share information in relation to eviction or anti-social behaviour orders, to ensure action against racist graffiti and other environmental factors which may have an impact on racist crime, to address target hardening where necessary, and so on.

- *Education authorities* – to encourage reporting of racist incidents in schools and colleges, to promote anti-racism to youth, to design diversionary programmes and identify racist trends, and so on.

- *Youth offending groups (including the Probation Service, Social Services)* – to develop positive action/work with young offenders and those at risk of becoming offenders.

- *Others* – including local businesses and at risk groups (e.g. shopkeepers), religious groups and charities, Crime Concern, Victim Support and any other local groups with whom there is scope for sharing information and promoting anti-racism.

(MPS, 1999d: 65)

Through the development of such partnerships and the formation of a local multi-agency working group consisting of representatives of the key partners, the implementation of a local crime reduction strategy becomes possible. The options for the prevention of racist crime that subsequently become available through the pooling of resources and dissemination of ideas/information are divided into three categories by the MPS (1999d).

Victim-based prevention

Victim-based prevention involves identifying common victim traits and strategies that can enable action by victims and potential victims so as to reduce their risk of victimisation, but without the imposition of lifestyle constraints that would in themselves constitute a form of victimisation.

Crime prevention methods within this category might include the provision of English language courses, mobile phones and phone help-lines, and the establishment of local support networks to reduce the feelings of isolation that many hate crime victims experience. In terms of preventing/tempering racist attacks on the home, options might include the provision of fireproof letterboxes, fire extinguishers and smoke detectors, and other general target hardening measures and other aspects of 'security by design'.

Housing issues can also play a significant role in reducing the risk of victimisation, particularly as section 17 of the Crime and Disorder

183

Act 1998 requires crime prevention to form part of a local authority's housing allocation policy. Following the principles of defensible space (Newman, 1972) and crime prevention through environmental design (Jeffery, 1971), some properties will inevitably offer better protection for potential victims of racist crime and will therefore be more suitable for occupation by vulnerable tenants. Where this is the case, cooperation between relevant authorities (including housing associations) allowing the exchange of tenants would increase the degree of protection afforded to (potential) victims, or if necessary (as a last resort) move them away from the source of their victimisation.

Perpetrator-based prevention

This category contains options for action centred on the perpetrators of racist crimes. The most obvious of these is arrest and conviction and prosecutions for racist offences are now 'fast-tracked' by both the police and the CPS. However, numerous other options are available to the police and their partner agencies, and these are particularly important given the problems associated with successfully prosecuting hate crimes that we noted in Chapter 7. One such option is provided by the Crime and Disorder Act 1998 in the form of Anti-Social Behaviour Orders to cut down on persistent serious anti-social behaviour.

Other tools include the promotion of Crimestoppers to encourage reporting and the active acquisition of photographs and CCTV footage of active suspects/perpetrators with a view to briefing officers for preventative and investigative purposes.

Of course the ideal perpetrator-based prevention should focus on the young so as to intervene in the development of bias-motivated behaviour. Here, those involved in the education system may have a significant role to play (see Chapter 12), but the police and other agencies can have a significant impact by taking action against the corrupting influences that breed such behaviour in the young.

Once again, housing issues can play a pivotal role. As with victims, some properties may be more suitable for housing known perpetrators than others, depending on their architectural features and location. Furthermore, the use of strict tenancy agreements (including the possibility of eviction for racist behaviour, obtaining injunctions, possessing buildings and otherwise prohibiting behaviour under sections 144 and 152 of the Housing Act 1996) can help to control anti-social behaviour. Where offenders are moved, established information-sharing protocols between agencies will allow for housing providers to undertake preventative and supportive measures in anticipation of further offending, and also allow the police to keep track of perpetrators.

Finally, other perpetrator-based initiatives might include the use of publicity through the media highlighting inter-agency successes, the 'naming and shaming' of convicted offenders, and the publicising of anti-hate crime operations. The tasking of informants and overt intelligence gathering (letting offenders know they are known to the authorities) are also available options.

Offence-based prevention

The MPS state that:

> Offence-based pre-emptive prevention revolves around identifying prevalent race/hate offences and taking steps to change the environment or conditions surrounding them to effect prevention. (MPS, 1999d: 78)

Options in this category also draw heavily on the principles of defensible space (Newman, 1972) and environmental design. Incorporating crime prevention measures into environmental planning as required by section 17 of the Crime and Disorder Act 1998 (such as increasing natural/technical surveillance and improving lighting) can help to make the commission of hate crime more difficult for the offender thereby increasing the chances of detection and potentially reducing the fear of crime.

Other measures might include targeted patrols in problem areas, professional witness schemes, CCTV installation and the promotion of Anti-hate (through various organised events or activities) in co-operation with community groups.

The partnership approach, together with the increased emphasis on proactivity and the use of intelligence, represents a significant change in the way that the MPS approaches the investigation of incidents of hate crime. While these changes in policy are relevant to every MPS officer, the emphasis for change rests largely with the borough-based Community Safety Units which have been established to lead the MPS's response in relation to hate crime.

The role of Community Safety Units

The MPS has made a commitment to deliver an enhanced service to victims of hate crime. This is to be achieved by investigating, identifying and prosecuting perpetrators to the satisfaction of the victim and the community and, where a criminal prosecution is not possible, by identifying and pursuing alternative courses of action with partner agencies. The responsibility for delivering the changes outlined in this chapter lies predominantly with the MPS's Community Safety Units. The role of the Community Safety Units and the officers therein was set by the Racial and Violent Crime Task Force and delivered through 'Special Notice 7/99 Minimum Investigative Standards for Community Safety Units' (MPS, 1999e) and, latterly, the revised Minimum Standards for Investigation of July 2000. These notices set out the responsibilities of MPS officers ranging from the initial investigator through to the Borough Commander in relation to the investigation and supervision of racist (and other 'hate') crimes. However, given the focus of this chapter, only those relating directly to the CSUs will be discussed here.

There are 32 Community Safety Units in London, one for every borough. All reported incidents of hate crime (racist, homophobic and so on) and domestic violence are allocated via computer to the relevant CSU by the Crime Management Unit (CMU). Once allocated to the CSU, crimes are re-allocated to a member of the CSU staff for investigation. Special Notice 7/99, and latterly the Minimum Standards of 2000, states that in all cases the first task for the investigating officer is to undertake a risk assessment of the potential for the reported situation to develop into a 'critical incident' and to act accordingly. A 'critical incident' is defined as:

> ... any incident where an individual is believed to be seriously endangered; the confidence of that person, their family and/or community cannot be assumed; and a early response by the police is critical to safeguard that person's interests and subsequent enquiries. (MPS, 1999e: 9)

With regard to supporting victims the CSUs have a number of responsibilities and procedures to follow. The investigating officer from the CSU is firstly required to contact the victim within 24 hours of receiving the complaint. This is to advise the victim that the complaint will be investigated thoroughly by the police and to advise them of any progress made. The call is also essential for establishing what further assistance is required, for checking details of the crime report and for arranging a personal visit to see the victim at the earliest opportunity. Depending on the circumstances of the case in hand and where appropriate, the CSU officer investigating the case will arrange for the victim to be seen by those providing specialist support (for example, scene examiners, the FME, the crime prevention officer, local authority officers and other relevant agencies with whom the CSU is in partnership). Each decision is documented on the Crime Report Information System (CRIS). In addition, for incidents involving attacks against property, the CSU officer in liaison with the crime prevention officer will conduct a home security survey to assess the possibility of providing target-hardening measures.

The MPS (2000c) has also published a CSU 'Hate Crime Victim Charter' in a number of languages that outlines the standard of service that victims can expect to receive from the Unit and also offers advice and information about procedures and available options for further support. It is the responsibility of the CSU officer to ensure that a copy of this charter is sent to every hate crime victim within five working days. The investigating officer is bound by the charter to undertake the following actions, where appropriate, in *every* reported case:

- To deal promptly and sensitively with the investigation;
- To make extensive local enquiries to trace any witnesses;
- To take statements from victims and other witnesses as appropriate;
- To take appropriate action in accordance with the wishes of the victim;
- To arrest the suspect if there is sufficient evidence and a power of arrest exists;
- To make use of interpreting services as appropriate;
- To obtain any forensic evidence that may be available;
- To provide mobile phones for emergency use if the situation demands;
- To consider the use of surveillance cameras, professional witnesses and increased uniformed patrols in appropriate cases;
- To regularly update the victim with progress of the investigation;
- To provide advice on court procedures, dates of hearing and results as appropriate;
- To give advice on applying for compensation from the Criminal Injuries Compensation Board where appropriate;

- To contact Victim Support unless instructed otherwise by the victim;
- To provide the victim with details of other relevant agencies who can offer assistance.

Where the crime is relevant to the victim's home the officer will undertake a home security survey that could, depending on the circumstances of the case, result in the free provision of door and window locks, a fireproof letterbox and a personal attack alarm.

With regard to the investigative duties of the CSU, Special Notice 7/99 stated that a key role of the initial CSU response is to review the quality of the initial investigation and to identify gaps in the evidence collection and victim support. Where such gaps are identified the CSU officers are responsible for addressing any shortcomings as a matter of priority. Subject to the victim's consent, details of the incident should then be shared with other agencies as identified above so that additional and appropriate support can be provided.

The investigating officer should then adopt an intelligence-led approach to the investigation to gather further evidence, incorporating the expertise of the Divisional Intelligence Unit, CID, local beat officers, borough liaison officers, and so on. Where suspects are arrested for hate crimes they become the responsibility of the CSU. The MPS now adheres to a positive prosecution policy in relation to hate crimes and this states that where sufficient evidence exists a suspect should be charged with the offence. The MPS also states that mitigating factors are unlikely to affect a decision to prosecute and as such the authority of the crime manager must be sought in order *not* to charge a suspect. In the event of a suspect being released from custody, the CSU officer is responsible for informing the victim before this occurs.

Where a suspect is charged with an offence and not held in custody, the CSU investigating officer is responsible for consulting with the Crown Prosecution Service to ensure that the accused is bailed to appear at the next weekday court sitting, thereby reducing the opportunity for victim/witness intimidation. In addition, the CSU officer is responsible for passing on the fears of the victim relating to the accused so that appropriate bail conditions can be sought. If bail is granted, the CSU officer must reconsider the risk assessment and offer appropriate support. Prior to any trial, the CSU officer is also responsible for obtaining a pre-trial statement from the victim detailing the evidence, background details and any psychological impact or trauma suffered so that this may be considered by the court during the course of the trial.

Where a prosecution has not taken place or has failed, Special Notice 7/99 states that:

CSU officers must demonstrate their ability to resolve hate ... crime imaginatively, by taking effective action in partnership within the wider context of the Crime and Disorder Act 1998. (MPS, 1999: 12)

The notice also states that where no person has been charged, it is the responsibility of the CSU investigating officer to inform the victim of any significant developments (such as the recovery of stolen property, results of lines of inquiry, any risks to safety and so on) and to discuss alternative options for action.

The activities of the CSU outlined above are under the immediate supervision of an officer of the rank of sergeant or above. The supervisor is responsible for ensuring that all these tasks are conducted satisfactorily and that the charter standards for investigation and victim care set for the CSUs are met.

Concluding comments

This chapter has outlined the MPS's post-Macpherson approach to combating hate crime. The information discussed here has been drawn largely from documentation published by the MPS in outlining their intentions for the future, and from my own ongoing research of CSUs since the publication of the Stephen Lawrence Inquiry.

While the issues discussed here have been police specific, many of the initiatives discussed will necessarily concern other criminal justice agencies involved in responding to hate crime, and in many cases they represent models of 'good practice' for tackling hate crime. Of course, providing victims with a high-quality service and winning the trust of minority communities will not be achieved by simply making promises. The MPS, and all other police services and criminal justice agencies, will be judged by their actions and service delivery in the real world, and the complexities and pressures of policing 'in the real world' mean that things do not always unfold as smoothly as intended. In the next chapter I shall offer a critique of the policing of hate crime per se, and examine the problems and challenges faced by the police in effectively responding to hate crime.

Chapter II

Policing hate crime: problems, challenges and solutions

In the last two chapters we have discussed different approaches to the policing of hate crime, many of which represent both recent developments and models of good practice in this area. However, hate crime poses rather a unique and complex challenge to the police, and the introduction of new approaches to combat it is not a guarantee that 'success' will be achieved. In this chapter I shall examine some of the key problems and challenges that the police face in their attempts to effectively respond to hate crime, and will offer some suggestions for overcoming these.

Over-policing and under-protecting?

One of the key barriers to the effective policing of hate crimes is the negative perception of the police held by many members of minority groups, and in particular the police action or inaction that has contributed to the formation of those perceptions. Simply, if the police do not have the trust and confidence of significant sections of the public then their ability to respond to those that are victimised is fundamentally constrained.

At the numerous public forums held around the country as a part of the inquiry into the murder of Stephen Lawrence (Macpherson, 1999), one theme of particular interest here consistently emerged. It was starkly apparent from the views expressed by members of the public that black people's experience of the police in England and Wales was overwhelmingly one of being 'over-policed' and 'under-protected'. It was clear that these views were not simply an angry response to the police handling of Stephen Lawrence's murder but are in fact deeply rooted in lived experience over a significant period of time.

The issue of the 'over-policing' of black people can be traced back over a significant period of time. Indeed, one of the first studies examining this issue conducted by Hunte in 1966 stated that 'it has been confirmed from reliable sources that sergeants and constables do leave stations with the express purpose of going "nigger hunting". That is to say, they do not get their orders from superiors to act in this way, but among themselves they decided to bring in a coloured person at all costs' (1966: 12).

Clearly Hunte's study is now dated but the theme of 'over-policing' has been reflected in numerous studies conducted by various researchers and organisations throughout the 1970s, 1980s and 1990s. Detailed accounts of these studies are available elsewhere (see, for example, Bowling and Phillips, 2002) but, briefly, concerns have been raised in relation to the excessive use of what are perceived to be oppressive police tactics and operations disproportionately targeted at black people. Particular research attention has been paid to the use of persistent and discriminatory stop and search, inappropriate police attitudes and behaviours towards black people, and arbitrary and violent arrests. Other studies have focused on issues such as repeated police harassment and abuse, coordinated and targeted patrols, the disproportionate involvement of black people as offenders in the criminal justice system and, to a lesser extent, black deaths while in police custody.

From a cursory overview of existing criminological literature it would appear that the concerns expressed at the public meetings for the Stephen Lawrence Inquiry are well founded and have deep historical roots.

With regard to the nature of the relationship that exists between the police and minority ethnic communities, extensive literature supported by survey evidence has consistently demonstrated a greater degree of dissatisfaction with the police among minority ethnic groups, particularly Afro-Caribbeans, as compared with whites. Indeed, Alibhai-Brown suggests that 'most black people in Britain do not trust the police and are suspicious and deeply apprehensive of the entire criminal justice system' (1999: 1). However, the results of a study undertaken by Bradley (1998), summarised in Table 11.1, indicate that negative attitudes towards the police exist across all ethnic minority groups and are not just confined to members of the black community.

Reiner (1992) suggests that these attitudes are the product of 'the catastrophic deterioration of relations with the black community' (1992:

191

Table 11.1   Perceptions of the police – ethnic social groups

Pakistani (young men)	Indian (older women)	Afro-Caribbean (young/mid-life women)	Afro-Caribbean (older men)
Based on direct personal experience they perceive the police:	Based on personal experience and that of close contacts, they perceive the police:	Based on many confrontations experienced, they have very negative views of the police and perceive that:	Overall, they regard the police approach and performance as disappointing:
• target them as different • base attitudes on negative and outdated stereotypes • lack social awareness and skills: especially on cultural and religious differences • fail to see opportunities for positive and effective influential role in the community	• lack apparent sympathy or concern • work on simplistic/ irrelevant stereotypes • are distant, based in cars, out of touch • need to have contact and understand the community more • their plea is to 'treat us with respect!'	• they can't be relied on • they target/ victimise young Afro-Caribbean young men • racism is rife in police force • police have little knowledge of ethnic communities • the complaints procedure cannot be trusted	• not proactive, just wait and react • not streetwise/ involved • poor compared to UK/ Caribbean in the past

Source: Bradley (1998: 8)

102) that can be traced back to the early 1970s. Reiner explains that at that time evidence of blacks being disproportionately involved in arrests for certain offences (particularly street crimes) was beginning to accumulate, and it became apparent that this situation was due in part to discrimination and racism embedded in police culture. Furthermore, as stated above, a number of studies demonstrated that the police disproportionately and overwhelmingly exercised their powers against blacks, particularly in respect of 'stop and search' (Willis, 1983) and the decision to prosecute (Landau, 1981).

Consequently, 'a vicious cycle of interaction developed between police stereotyping and black vulnerability to the situations that attract police attention' (Reiner, 1992: 102). This delicate situation was made even more acute by an emerging consciousness of being discriminated against that developed among black individuals who increasingly saw themselves as the targets of policing. This heightened self-consciousness permeated through the black community, and inevitably through other minority communities, resulting in the widespread lack of confidence in the police that is evident from the views expressed in Table 11.1.

A second crucial issue is that of the 'under-protection' of members of minority communities. Of particular concern are the perceptions held by ethnic minority groups relating to the police response to racist hate crimes. It is widely documented that minority victims 'perceive the police response as frequently inadequately sympathetic or effective' (Reiner, 1997: 1012). In their evidence to the Royal Commission on Criminal Procedure in 1979, the Institute of Race Relations submitted a report highlighting many concerns about the police response to such incidents. The report claimed that:

> Police officers have frequently failed to recognise the racial dimension of attacks; that there has often been a significant time delay in response to calls for assistance; an unwillingness to investigate or prosecute offenders; the provision of inadequate advice; and general hostility towards victims. (Holdaway, 1996: 58)

More recent evidence demonstrates that these concerns are as relevant today as they were in 1979, if not more so as communities have become more diverse (Holdaway, 1996; HMIC, 1999). In addition to surveying individuals for their experiences of victimisation, Bowling's empirical study of North Plaistow in London (Bowling, 1999) also examined victims' satisfaction with the police response. While satisfaction varied with the ethnic and gender characteristics of the victim, overall the study showed that fewer than one in ten respondents were very satisfied with the way the police handled the matter and less than half were very or fairly satisfied. Half were dissatisfied and one-fifth very dissatisfied. These figures concur with those of the British Crime Surveys that consistently indicate that victims of racial incidents are substantially less likely to be satisfied with the police service than victims of crime in general.

The North Plaistow study showed that the most common complaints among those who were dissatisfied with the police response were that the police did not do enough, that they failed to keep victims informed (90 per cent of respondents felt that the police should have kept them better informed) and that they did not seem interested. A number of respondents also felt that the police were prejudiced in the speed of their response to incidents, did not do enough to apprehend the offender, were disinterested and impolite, and made mistakes or handled matters badly. In only 6 per cent of cases was the victim informed about Victim Support, and again only 6 per cent felt the police were very sympathetic when dealing with the incident. Thirty-nine per cent of respondents were of the opinion that victims of racist incidents were treated fairly and equally compared with other people requesting services from the police (Bowling, 1999).

Perhaps the greatest concern, however, is that a report published by HM Inspector of Constabulary was able to conclude that the majority of forces visited appeared complacent about the existence of any problem in this area of policing (HMIC, 1999). The Metropolitan Police Service (1999d), however, has now acknowledged this problem. The MPS states that:

> Many victims of race/hate crime have little knowledge of the authorities that seek to serve them other than that they do not seem to get protection from them. They have had, within their collective experience, a number of hostile and prejudiced encounters with the police that lead them to view us [the police] at best as unsympathetic and at worst actively racist. (1999d: 90)

Clearly, the perceived attitude and response of the police have huge implications. Essentially, following the physical and psychological trauma of any hate attack, hostile, ineffective or insensitive policing is tantamount to secondary victimisation. This may leave the victim and the wider community feeling unprotected by those who are supposed to protect them and therefore increasingly vulnerable and isolated. If this is the case, and trust and confidence in the police is lost, then hate victims will stop turning to the police for assistance, even when they are subjected to ongoing violence and harassment (Human Rights Watch, 1997).

Evidently, a salient feature of the non-reporting of racist incidents is indeed the perception that is held by ethnic minority groups that the police are not interested in investigating such incidents (Fitzgerald and Hale, 1996). This situation is reflected in the huge differences in figures that are consistently found between official police records of racist incidents and national and local victim surveys (see Chapter 4). However, the non-reporting of hate incidents to the police is not just confined to ethnic minority groups. For example, numerous studies have revealed extremely low reporting rates for homophobic incidents (Blackbourn, 2004). Indeed, American research by Herek, Cogan and Gillis (2002) suggests that non-reporting of homophobic hate crimes may be as high as 90 per cent, primarily as a consequence of the fear of discrimination and mistreatment by the police and of fear of revealing their sexual orientation. In this country the police themselves have acknowledged this, and that hate crimes in general are significantly underreported (ACPO, 2000, 2005).

Hate crime as a process

In Chapter 4 we suggested that hate crime is best viewed as an ongoing process. Viewing hate crime in this way can help to further explain the negative views of the police that many members of minority groups hold. The underlying rationale is that there is a fundamental mismatch between the nature of hate crime and the requirements of the criminal justice system. With reference to racist victimisation, Ben Bowling (1999) argues that the problem is that while hate crime is best viewed as an ongoing *process*, the police and wider criminal justice system necessarily respond to *incidents*. Bowling suggests that racist victimisation does not occur in a moment, but rather it is ongoing, dynamic and is embedded in time, space and place, and must always be kept in context if it is to be understood and responded to effectively.

The contextual factors to which Bowling refers include historical patterns of xenophobia, the lived experience of the individuals and communities targeted, local population and power dynamics, the attitudes and behaviours of offenders and the 'perpetrator community', the wider issues of local, national and international discourses and practices of race and nation and, in particular, practices of racial exclusion. Victimisation therefore describes an ongoing and dynamic process that occurs over time and within specific social, political and historical contexts. Because of these dynamics, racist victimisation never occurs in a moment, and can never be meaningfully reduced to an isolated 'incident'.

In other words, an individual becomes a victim of hate crime through an ongoing process that necessarily occurs over a period of time and is influenced by many different factors. For Bowling, this presents a significant problem for the agencies of the criminal justice system. These agencies recognise and respond to incidents, which Bowling defines as a one-dimensional, narrowly restricted time-slice, within which only the actions of the immediate protagonists are of any relevance. In this sense, Bowling points to the fact that English criminal law understands crime only as a single event committed by an individual with criminal intent.

He suggests that when the process of racist victimisation is reduced to a series of isolated incidents they become describable and measurable but appear random and inexplicable to outsiders, and are impossible to properly understand because the lived experience of the victim is drained of any context. When hate crime is reduced to an 'incident', the ongoing process of fear and intimidation that was described in Chapter 4 becomes lost to outside view. Similarly, as we also noted in Chapter 4, many victims are subject to so many 'incidents' in a bout of victimisation that it often becomes impossible to identify where one ends and the next begins. One incident may appear minor and relatively meaningless, but the cumulative effect of the victimisation is often significant. What may appear to be a minor incident to an outsider may in fact just be the tip of the iceberg.

Bowling suggests that as the 'incident' is transformed from the world of the victim's experience into an object for policing it is placed in the context of the police organisational and cultural milieu, an environment that is usually antithetical to that of the victim. The net result of the process–incident contradiction, according to Bowling, is that while the police may feel that they have responded appropriately and effectively, the victims are frequently left with feelings of dissatisfaction, fear and a perception of being under-protected.

The hierarchy of police relevance

In addition to the process–incident contradiction, Bowling, citing research by Grimshaw and Jefferson (1987), argues that the existence of a 'hierarchy of police relevance' can also have an impact on the policing of racist hate crime. The underlying assumption here is that the dominant influence on the work of a police officer attending the scene of an incident is the legal structure. Bowling suggests therefore that the nature of the police response is determined by the attending officer's decisions about the relevance of the incident to the police. Where an incident is clearly defined in criminal law as 'police relevant' then the response of the police officers will be predictable and will reflect legal reality. On the other hand, where the incident is in some way legally ambiguous the outcome will be similarly so, and the actions of the police officer will be guided by operational common sense.

In other words, on attending an incident the police officer can decide his or her course of action from a range of available options from making an arrest or conducting an investigation to simply moving on to the next call for assistance, depending on the requirements of the law and the needs of the immediate situation. Where the incident is clearly a matter for the police and the law clearly requires them to undertake a certain action then their options are relatively limited (for example, to make an arrest, undertake an investigation or complete some paperwork). Conversely, where the matter becomes more ambiguous in terms of its relevance to the police the options available to the officer increase (for example, to take no further action, or to move on to the next call).

In this sense then there exists a hypothetical 'hierarchy of police relevance' that officers use, often subconsciously, that determines their response to any given incident. At the top of the hierarchy are what Bowling terms 'good crimes'. These are clear criminal offences with innocent, reliable and credible victims, perpetrators that are 'real' criminals, and that offer a clear opportunity of detection and arrest and a good result in terms of securing a conviction. Further down the hierarchy are 'rubbish' crimes, in which the 'quality' of the victim and perpetrator may be poor, where there is a much reduced chance of detection and arrest, or where there is an increased likelihood that the victim will withdraw the allegation at a later date. At the bottom end of the hierarchy are what Bowling terms 'disputes' or 'disturbances', which are frequently perceived to be legally ambiguous and of limited police relevance.

In his interviews with police officers Bowling (1999) found that with the exception of certain crimes (such as robbery, assault and theft) where the legal relevance to the police is clear, racist offences tend to be viewed as being at the lower end of the hierarchy of police relevance. Bowling found that the perpetrators of racist hate crimes were largely perceived by the police as being 'yobs' or 'hooligans', and that racist incidents were regarded as acts of 'yobbishness'. In this sense both the offence and the offender often fall into the category of 'rubbish', and receive less attention from the police than 'real' crimes. Similarly, Bowling's research highlighted the extent to which, from a police perspective, racist incidents routinely fall short of the criteria required to classify them as a 'good crime' and are regarded as 'disputes' or 'disturbances'. In other words, in all but the most serious crimes, racist incidents tend to appear at the lower end of the hierarchy of police relevance, and as such receive less police attention than crimes where the legal duty to respond is unambiguous. Crucially, Bowling's research illustrated that this placing of racist incidents in the hierarchy, most notably by rank and file officers, remained consistent despite changes in force policy and the force prioritisation of racist offences. In assuming that the majority of hate offences are simply minor incidents, the disproportionate impact that these can have on victims that we discussed in Chapter 4 is often not appreciated and overlooked by the police. The result of this clash of perceptions is that victims may feel that their victimisation is not taken seriously by the police.

The extent of police discretion and the rudimentary decision-making process, predominantly by rank and file officers, of course has important implications for the number of hate crimes that are ultimately recorded and investigated. The hierarchy of relevance indicates a historical propensity for racist incidents not to be recorded or treated appropriately, except where the offences are particularly serious. In turn this has helped to create a lack of trust in the police among minority groups that has subsequently led to a disinclination to report offences committed against them. This of course is crucial because if hate crimes are not reported to the police, then for the most part they cannot be responded to. However, the dynamics of this situation have been somewhat changed by the post-Macpherson definition in England and Wales where the element of police discretion has, theoretically at least, been removed.

The impact of definitional change

In an attempt to increase trust and confidence in the police, the current definition of hate crime used by police forces is deliberately broad and inclusive, designed to 'catch' as many offences as possible, restrict the decision-making of police officers and encourage better recording practices. There is evidence to suggest that there has been considerable success on each of these counts. Consider, for example, the statistics for racist incidents in England and Wales in recent years.

In the year following the adoption of Macpherson's definition, the number of racist incidents for all police force areas in England and Wales rose from 23,049 to 47,814. In London the number of racist *incidents* rose from 11,050 in 1998/99 to 23,346 in 1999/2000, while reported racist *offences* rose from 9,503 to 20,632. The number of people accused of racist incidents also rose from 1,554 to 3,280 (Grieve, 2004). In 2002 the number of racist incidents stood at 54,351, with considerable variation in numbers across individual police force areas. Dorset, for example, encountered just 69 incidents, while the Met recorded 16,711 incidents, itself a 19 per cent fall on the previous year. These figures underline the importance attached to definitions of hate crime, and how the size of the hate crime problem is socially constructed.

The debate

While the rationale behind the current definition is clear, and indeed was absolutely right for the immediate 'post-Macpherson' era, in my opinion the time has now come to revisit the definition and to engage in a debate about its merits six years on from its adoption. Clearly such a debate is highly sensitive and there will be much reluctance to engage in this given the nature of the subject. However, in my opinion it would be irresponsible not to at least consider this issue because the case for revising the definition is worthy of debate at this juncture.

The main concern relates to the volume of incidents and the subsequent impact on investigations. While this may not seem problematic for areas where the number of recorded racist crime is low, volume is a critical issue where recorded incidents are high. Consider, for example, the Metropolitan Police Service. At present there are approximately 300 officers working within Community Safety Units (after abstractions) across the 32 boroughs. If we take the 16,711 racist incidents and divided them between the CSU officers then each officer will be investigating 55.7 racist incidents per year. If we then add the other types of offences allocated to CSUs, such as homophobia, domestic violence, offences relating to faith, disability, age and so on, then the number of incidents to be investigated by each officer per year will be potentially very high.

Furthermore, each case has to be investigated to the minimum standards without exception and there is no latitude for prioritisation or discretion with regard to the individual merits of cases. In addition, all of this assumes even distribution of offences along geographical and temporal lines and the even distribution of officers across CSUs which, of course, is not the case meaning that the problem will be more acute in some areas than others and at different times than others. My own research, for example, has revealed some CSU officers in London with a caseload of up to 40 live investigations at any one time. Such a situation is clearly unsustainable in the long term and risks investigative errors and shortcomings in service provision to victims, and also the occupational health of the Service's officers. Indeed this mirrors the situation that Macpherson's definition was created to avoid.

A further unintended consequence of the current definition relates to the type of incident that is being reported, recorded and investigated.

In unquestioningly accepting the perception of victims (or any other person), there is evidence from my own research and the research of others that the situation is being abused in order to further personal or group interests, and to secure the services available to victims of hate crime. For example, Eugene McLaughlin states that:

There is evidence that police officers and white residents in certain neighbourhoods, as part of a backlash, are interpreting virtually any conflictual encounter with non-whites as a 'race-hate' act and reporting it as such. Hence, we are witnessing, through the mobilisation of white resentments, a determined effort to subvert the meaning and purpose of the new policy on racial incidents. (2002: 495)

The danger is that 'genuine' and deserving victims of hate crime are at worst being lost in the volume of crimes reported, or being potentially denied the services they need because police resources are being wasted by false reports over which the police have no discretionary control. In this sense, then, the situation created to ensure that victims receive the service they need may in fact be contributing to them not receiving those services because, of course, police resources are finite. The existence of this situation is neither in the police nor the victim's interests.

Furthermore, evidence from my own research in this area has indicated that rank and file police officers will report incidents as hate crimes even where it may not be clear that one has occurred simply to 'cover their backs' against possible sanctions for not accurately recording a hate crime. This clearly serves to increase the workload and intensify the pressure on hate crime investigators. Similarly, the creation of specialised investigative units has resulted in the perception among some rank and file officers that hate crimes 'are no longer their problem', and are content to pass on incidents that may be better dealt with there and then (Hall, 2002a). This can give victims the initial impression that the police are not interested, which as we have seen has been a key factor in the erosion of confidence in the police in the past.

Clearly, the current definitions in use are designed to remove the discretionary element from the police at the reporting and recording stage to help overcome some of the problems outlined in this chapter. Essentially, under these definitions, a crime is a hate crime if anyone perceives it to be so, not just if the investigating officer concludes that a hate motivated offence has occurred. The adoption of such definitions has many crucial implications for the police investigative process. In sum, there is evidence (Hall, 2002a, 2004) that there is now a propensity for officers to err on the side of caution and report incidents as hate crimes, whereas previously they may not have done so, which was Macpherson's intention. But this can cause an entirely new set of problems in terms of the ability of the police, and in particular those dedicated to investigating hate crimes, to respond to the high volume of incidents now being recorded. Ironically this can inevitably lead to officers contravening policy by prioritising offences further down the investigative process out of necessity forced by finite resources, and reintroduces the element of police discretion concerning the merits of individual cases that Macpherson's definition was intended to eliminate. The new definition may therefore have the same, albeit unintended, consequences as the previous one.

It concerns me, therefore, that an effective police response may be hindered by both the size of the problem and the amount of resources available to combat it. One of the issues that we may be forced to consider sooner rather than later, and one that may involve a controversial revision of Macpherson's recommendation, is whether to reintroduce an element of discretion back into the recording and investigative processes in order to better manage the hate crime problem in high volume areas. I have already suggested that I believe that the current situation is potentially unsustainable in some police force areas in the long term, so the need to address this issue will likely become increasingly pressing.

But if we are to introduce an element of subjective judgment about the qualitative merits of hate crime cases, just how and where will discretion be introduced, and by whom? In my opinion it would be equally irresponsible and indeed socially and politically unacceptable to revert back to the pre-Macpherson era by placing the discretion solely back in the hands of police officers. The failings of the Lawrence case demonstrate that this situation is not one that can be relied upon, and to revert back would in my opinion be a retrograde step for the police service and would damage already fragile police–community relations. The BBC's recent *Secret Policeman* documentary is evidence enough that such a move would be viewed with suspicion and mistrust. There is also the danger that the impact of non-crime incidents will also be potentially overlooked.

So we must look elsewhere. The situation in New York provides us with options. When the system works it is clear that 'genuine' victims receive the service designed for them and non-hate offences are 'weeded out' and appropriately assigned for investigation elsewhere. In this sense the NYPD's Hate Crimes Task Force investigates 'hate crimes' in the truest sense of the term, and their finite resources are not wasted on 'dubious' claims of victimisation. However, my own research has indicated that some victims 'slip through the net' as a consequence of the police decision-making process at various levels of the service prior to incidents reaching the Task Force. Although the penalties for the misclassification of hate crime are serious for officers, there is evidence that this occurs, although to what extent it is impossible to say. Such uncertainty would not be acceptable in the UK, particularly at this time.

There is of course no straightforward answer to this problem. There is a crucial need to overcome the historical problems that culminated in the Stephen Lawrence Inquiry and to improve the police response, but there is also the need to manage the size of the current hate crime problem so that an effective response can be properly and appropriately delivered to the victims of hate crime. However, while reintroducing some form of discretionary element is an important consideration, it is unlikely to be an attractive option. On the other hand, the issue of resourcing remains an ongoing problem for most police services. Alternative ways of improving the police response are therefore likely to be more palatable and desirable at the present time.

Improving the police response to hate crime

Before I begin this section of the chapter I would like to make two points that should be understood before reading further. The first concerns the various criticisms made of the police in relation to their response to hate crime, many of which I have outlined in this chapter. My point relates not to the criticisms themselves because they are often well founded, but to the use of the term 'the police'. 'The police' are an organisation made up of many thousands of individuals, but of the various criticisms made of 'the police', many imply a blanket condemnation. Within the organisation there will inevitably be officers whose behaviour will give cause for concern, but we should not forget that there are also a great many police officers with a genuine and unquestionable dedication to helping victims of hate crime and bringing the perpetrators to justice. This may be an obvious point to make, but it is one that I believe is often overlooked when we criticise 'the police'. There are many officers that I have met over the past six years in the course of my research both in this country and in the United States whose commitment to tackling hate crime is often underestimated, under-appreciated and largely unrecognised both by their organisation and by those looking in from the outside. This view is formed not just on the basis of my own perceptions from my research, but also more appropriately from the views of many victims of hate crime that I have spoken with in that time.

The second point is that many of the approaches to hate crime that I described in Chapters 9 and 10 represent, in theory if not always in practice, what I would consider to be models of good practice for responding to hate crime. The existence of specialist investigative units with officers dedicated to hate crime investigations, the use of proactive and intelligence tools, partnership approaches, community outreach, independent involvement, minimum standards and so on are all important developments in the policing of hate crime, and this should be borne in mind as we consider how we might improve the police response to hate crimes.

In his consideration of the policing of hate crimes, John Grieve (2004) has identified a number of key factors for achieving success. As the (now retired) Deputy Assistant Commissioner of the Metropolitan Police charged with leading the Met's response to the Stephen Lawrence Inquiry, many of the factors that Grieve identifies were implemented and have already been outlined in Chapter 10. Nevertheless it is worth considering some of these issues further.

For Grieve there are a number of positive activities that the police can undertake that when set within a human rights context can improve their response to hate crimes. In referring to the Met's Diversity Strategy (1999a), Grieve suggests that there are six strategic approaches for improving the policing of hate crime, which are placed under the headings of leadership, resolving problems and investigating and preventing crime through an inclusive approach, challenging processes and procedures, increasing the diversity of the workforce, training and a coordinated communications strategy. The related activities are identified as the investigation and prevention of hate crime, appreciating diversity, creating an organisation people want to work for and interacting with the public.

All of these represent what Grieve labels as 'key success factors' for the investigation and prevention of hate crimes. Leadership, he suggests, requires compliance with minimum standards for investigation, comparable satisfaction levels for those reporting hate crimes to those that are provided to all other victims, and the adequate resourcing of proactive intelligence-led operations against hate crimes and hate crime perpetrators. The inclusive problem-oriented investigation and prevention approach requires third-party reporting procedures and cooperation between the police and partner agencies to ensure effective information sharing. Challenging procedures and processes would include auditing activities and investigations under the Race Relations (Amendment) Act 2000, and testing hate crime investigations under 'best value' reviews.

Increasing the diversity of the workforce is a difficult but crucial challenge that has potentially invaluable benefits. For Grieve, it involves the creation of a group of police and non-police staff who are knowledgeable about a wide range of different interacting communities and the relevant issues that relate to the investigation of hate crime. In addition, immersive training is necessary, Grieve suggests, for leaders and investigating officers, and for everyone involved in critical incident management (a critical incident is defined as any event where the effectiveness of the police response is likely to have a significant impact on the confidence of the victim, their family and/or the community). Finally, a coordinated communications strategy would involve publicly promoting the activities of the police in taking action against hate crime, publicising prosecutions, prevention, best practice and so on.

Furthermore, Grieve underscores the importance of critical incident management, the role of family liaison and independent involvement in the development of effective practice in policing hate crimes. Critical incidents and practical street-level solutions, he suggests, are no longer just the concern of senior officers, but are now at the heart of responding to the challenges of contemporary policing, and in particular form the basis of tactical doctrine to respond effectively to hate crimes. Central to this is the role of family liaison officers (FLOs). These are investigators who are trained with specialist skills in relation to supporting victims and their families following an incident. In maintaining open dialogues with families, their support networks and their community, FLOs are also well placed to enable the flow of evidence and intelligence, thereby improving investigative opportunities (Grieve, 2004). Understanding, supporting and cooperating with families is therefore significant in the effective response to hate crimes, and families of victims should be viewed as partners in an investigation.

Independent involvement in policing, Grieve argues, is important because it ensures sensitivity to and early consideration of family and community concerns. He also suggests that it helps to avoid the kinds of misunderstandings of community concerns that have historically caused the police specific problems. Independent involvement also represents visible openness and accountability and can help to challenge the mindsets and assumptions held by the police that have often proved barriers to the effective policing of minority groups and hate crimes.

The underlying concern for Grieve is that the policing of hate crimes should be conducted in a human rights context. This is also reflected in recommendations for the improvement of policing of hate crimes made by American academic David Bayley (2002). Bayley argues that while the police cannot directly reduce hatred, they can significantly contribute to the creation of an environment that lessens the likelihood that hatred will result in interpersonal violence by acting in ways that create bonds of citizenship. Crucially, this can be brought about through existing policing practices as well as through specific initiatives. He suggests that the police can create 'bonds of citizenship' by being fair, effective and open in all their activities. For Bayley, fairness involves acting in accordance with internationally recognised standards of human rights; effectiveness means being responsive to the needs of both individuals and groups; and openness requires transparency and accountability in all aspects of policing activity.

Bayley suggests that when the human rights of everyone are protected, then diversity ceases to be a threat. In other words, if the police have both the willingness and the capacity to protect everyone equally then the hatreds that exist in a multicultural society may begin to be eased as perceived threats from 'outsiders' or 'others' are lessened. The effective protection of human rights can be achieved, he argues, in a number of ways. First, it important that officers in leadership positions demonstrate through word and action that the protection of human rights must permeate all aspects of policing. Second, effective systems of police discipline should be created to hold accountable those officers who violate human rights. Third, a simple, user-friendly complaints system should be in operation. Fourth, a code of police conduct should set standards for all policing activity, in particular to help officers to understand what values should be exemplified in any action they take. Finally, and similar to Grieve's notion of submersive learning, police training should be available for all officers and recruits that will allow them to see the world from multicultural points of view.

Protecting human rights is therefore crucial in the process of gaining the trust and confidence of minority communities who, as we have seen, are often suspicious and mistrustful of the police. If the police demonstrate fairness, then it follows that public alienation will begin to decrease and their willingness to assist the police will begin to increase (Bayley, 2002). As Grieve (2004) suggests, improving public confidence in policing will in turn improve reporting rates, intelligence flow and investigative opportunities.

Related to this is the issue of police effectiveness. Bayley suggests that public dissatisfaction, disaffection, alienation and suspicion of authority are fuelled by police inability to equally protect that public. Providing an effective, appropriate and equal service to all members of a diverse society is therefore crucial. As we have seen, the historical failure of the police in Britain to provide an appropriate service and protection for all was reflected in the opinions aired at the public meetings throughout the hearings for the Stephen Lawrence Inquiry.

Given this significance, Bayley makes several suggestions for improving the effectiveness of the police. Among these are calls for the creation of independent advisory boards and the assigning of patrol officers to particular geographical areas for a period of time to increase familiarity with the area and its residents. He also suggests the re-examination of the way in which the police receive requests for assistance to ensure they are accessible and 'user-friendly' to all, and recommends that supervising officers should contact individuals who solicited help from the police to establish their satisfaction with the service they received.

Finally, Bayley (2002) suggests that for fair and effective policing to realise its full potential, these qualities have to be demonstrated to the public. In other words, the police should demonstrate openness in their activities not only in terms of what they do, but also in what they achieve. To demonstrate fairness and effectiveness in policing, Bayley recommends that police services evaluate their operational strategies (either themselves or preferably through civilian review) to determine whether the desired results are being achieved, and that they also publish information concerning complaints about the police and the outcomes of those complaints. He also suggests that such complaints against the police should be independently investigated. Bayley further advocates civilian oversight and involvement in policing activity, including, for example, public 'ride-alongs' in police vehicles, visits to police facilities and involvement in police training. Such activities help to make the police more accessible and understandable to those who perhaps only see or hear negative accounts of their activities. Finally, Bayley advocates diverse recruitment into the police to reflect the community they serve, to demonstrate sensitivity to multicultural interests and to provide expertise about diverse communities.

In the conclusion to his work, Bayley makes two points that I would like to draw attention to. First, he suggests that the key to developing a police service that can be successful in responding to hatred and in meeting the needs of a multicultural society is the development of vocational pride in undertaking the task. My own research has indicated a perception among some police officers that hate crimes are 'griefy', problematic and troublesome to deal with because of many of the issues described in this chapter. This perception clearly needs to be addressed and challenged if 'vocational pride' is to be achieved.

The second point that Bayley (2002: 90) makes is interesting for its simplicity in what is clearly a complex issue. He concludes his article by saying:

> Let me propose, in conclusion, a simple test for whether the police are succeeding in their lonely mission of building citizenship among a diverse population. It is this: do parents, regardless of community, teach their children to go to the police for help when they are alone and away from home? If they do, citizenship is secure. If they do not, the police are failing.

Limitations to change: a cautionary note

Over the course of the last three chapters I have outlined different policing approaches to hate crime, examined the related problems and challenges that make the policing of hate crime a complex task, and considered various proposals for improving police effectiveness in this regard. Many of the recommendations put forward in this chapter have been implemented in one form or another in each of the three police services I have referred to, and have been introduced through various written policy documents. Furthermore, many of these developments and tactical approaches represent models of good practice and are advocated by ACPO in its *Guide to Identifying and Combating Hate Crime* (2000) and the revised and updated version entitled *Hate Crime: Delivering a Quality Service (Good Practice and Tactical Guidance)* published and distributed to police services in England, Wales and Northern Ireland in January 2005.

The problem, however, is that changes to proscriptive policy are not a guarantee that success will be achieved 'in the real world'. Indeed there is substantial historical evidence that suggests that the transformation of police policy into effective practice is a complex and vulnerable process, particularly in the field of police–community relations. Bowling (1999) suggests that during the 1980s and 1990s in Britain very little changed in policing practice despite numerous policy changes aimed at improving the police response to racist incidents. Part of the reason for this can be found in the problems that we have outlined already in this chapter.

Clearly, from the limited evidence presented here, there is a belief among minority groups based on experience that the police are either unable or unwilling to effectively investigate crimes against them and that their cases are not taken seriously. This situation is compounded by research evidence that historically points to widespread and discriminatory 'over-policing'. The extent to which such ineffective policing is the result of individual or institutional prejudice and discrimination, inadequate resources, poor policing at lower levels or bad management at upper levels, or a product of the nature of hate crime itself is difficult to determine and has been the subject of much debate (Human Rights Watch, 1997; Reiner, 1997).

A further explanation may also be found, however, in a theoretical model proposed by Grimshaw and Jefferson (1987) in their study of beat policing in which they examined the transformation of police policy into police practice. Although there is not the space here to examine their work in detail, Grimshaw and Jefferson (1987: 199) hypothesised that:

Policies involving operational and related tasks will be characterised by the values of operational common sense, and those involving administrative tasks will be characterised by rational scientific management values ... the 'success' of policy in influencing practice will be task related. Thus, the impact of those policies bearing on operational and related tasks where occupational common sense is to the fore will be less decisively calculable and more unpredictable in effect than those policies bearing on administrative tasks.

In other words, gaps between what is supposed to happen (policy) and what actually happens (practice) when responding to an incident are likely to appear where the actions of the police in any given situation are guided by operational common sense afforded to them through the opportunity to use their own discretion rather than being strictly guided by the requirements of law or management directives which restrict their discretion. It is largely for this reason that the discretion afforded to police officers in determining what is and what is not a hate crime has been removed by the definitions adopted in Britain following the Stephen Lawrence Inquiry. In the US, however, where police discretion in determining the bias element of an incident remains much greater than in this country, this issue may be more acute.

This is significant because, as Bowling (1999) has argued, the discretion afforded to police officers when responding to racist incidents has historically been problematic and has contributed to the failure of police policy to improve operational performance. He argues that despite force prioritisation of racist incidents throughout the 1980s and 1990s, for deep-rooted legal, organisational, structural and cultural reasons, operational practice remained largely unchanged throughout. The incident–process argument, the hierarchy of relevance, legal constraints, a lack of financial and legal resources, an occupational culture of prejudiced attitudes and discriminatory behaviour, the discretion afforded to the police when responding to an incident, community suspicion of the police and the nature of hate crime itself have, for Bowling, all contributed to the failure of the police to protect minority groups despite apparent improvements in policy. It is important, therefore, that new and innovative approaches to policing hate crime are regularly evaluated to ensure that the desired results are being achieved.

Concluding comments

In this chapter I have outlined some of the problems and challenges that the police face when responding to hate crime. I have also presented some suggestions for improving the police response, many of which have been implemented or are being implemented by police services, and in many cases these represent a significant change in the police approach to hate crime. However, while many of the policing strategies that have been implemented and discussed in the last three chapters are aimed at overcoming the problems discussed in this chapter, Grimshaw and Jefferson's model reminds us that changes in police policy are not a panacea for the policing of hatred, and we should not expect them to be so. Changing policy is one thing, but making those changes effective in practice is often quite another. We should remember too that prejudices are normal to the human condition so it should come as little surprise that they are also present in police officers and this will have a further bearing on the police response to hate crimes.

The size and nature of the task necessarily means that the policing of hatred is complex, and improving police performance in this regard cannot and will not happen overnight. But while the police do hold a key position in the fight against hate crime and their performance can undoubtedly be improved, the police cannot combat hatred by themselves, and we should not expect them to. The 'hate crime problem' is far bigger than the police organisation; it is a problem deeply rooted in society. Because of this the police are just a part, albeit a key part, of a much bigger picture. An effective response to hate crimes necessarily requires a more holistic approach that extends beyond policing and the wider criminal justice system, and it is to these issues that we now turn.

Chapter 12

Community responses to hate crime

The last decade of the twentieth century saw an increasing political and social concern with criminal behaviour motivated by racism, and latterly by religious intolerance. In response to a perceived rise in racially motivated offending across Europe and a general shift in social attitudes regarding the abhorrence of crimes motivated by bigotry, the UK followed a number of other European countries by introducing specific legislation to combat it. As we have seen, the 1998 Crime and Disorder Act, later amended by the Anti-terrorism, Crime and Security Act of 2001, contains provisions for additional penalties to be imposed by the courts to nine pre-existing offences where it can be proved that those offences were racially or religiously motivated either in whole or in part. In other words, not only is the offence punished but also the specific motivation behind it.

More recently, as we have also noted, the rather narrow focus on race has begun to widen to incorporate other aspects of diversity. The Criminal Justice Act 2003 allows for homophobic motivation and bias against disability to be taken into account by sentencers as aggravating factors in an offence, and the Serious Organised Crime and Police Bill before Parliament in 2005 proposes a new offence of *hatred against persons on racial or religious grounds*.

From the evidence presented in Chapter 3, crimes motivated by prejudice and bigotry are obviously nothing new. However, recent official recognition of these offences as a distinct category of criminal behaviour has effectively presented the criminal justice system with a 'new' category of offender. Hate offenders present something of a unique challenge to the criminal justice system in that the law is concerned with not only the crime, but also with the specific motivation behind their offending. It establishes a need to specifically recognise and address the underlying prejudice that informs that behaviour.

This chapter will explore the challenge that hate offenders present. It will be argued that the prison system and traditional community punishments are relatively ineffectual in challenging hate-motivated behaviour. Instead, it is argued that for most hate offenders, community sentences that simultaneously punish the crime and challenge the offender's erroneous belief systems offer better potential for effective intervention. In relation to the unique characteristics and dynamics that relate to hate offenders (outlined in Chapter 5), this chapter will outline some of the key limitations of traditional custodial and community sentences. The chapter will then examine recent developments in programmes designed for intervening in hate-motivated behaviour and argues that while innovative community sentences undoubtedly hold the greatest potential, they are not a panacea. The chapter will also briefly consider attempts to prevent hatred from outside the criminal justice system. It is concluded that the development of successful programmes of intervention and prevention is at best uncertain largely because of both the complex nature of hate and prejudice, and our relative lack of understanding of them.

A punitive approach to hatred

We saw in Chapter 7 that despite increasing recent interest in crimes motivated by hate, the term 'hate crime' does not specifically appear in any UK legislation and therefore does not officially exist as a distinct category of criminal behaviour in itself. Instead, specific legislation prohibits certain acts, which are already outlawed in other legislation, but allows for hate to be used as an aggravating factor that attracts heavier penalties upon conviction.

The increasingly punitive approach to hate crimes and hate offenders through the imposition of enhanced sanctions for those convicted of specific hate-motivated offences makes it increasingly likely that the prison service will become increasingly involved with hate offenders. It is therefore important to consider the role of the prison service in responding to hate offenders and its role in preventing future offending.

Imprisonment of hate offenders raises a difficult dilemma. On the one hand there is the need to protect the public from dangerous offenders, but on the other there is the need to effectively address the underlying causes of the hate crime (i.e. the offender's prejudice) in order to prevent future offending. Prison may achieve the former (at least for the duration of the offender's incapacitation), but it tends to fall short on the latter.

The problems associated with imprisonment as a response to hate offenders are threefold. Firstly, because the chances of being caught, convicted and ultimately sent to prison are remote for most hate offenders the deterrent value of prison is weak at best. Second, prisons are often divided along racial and ethnic lines, and are therefore 'hotbeds' for prejudice, intolerance and hate group activity and recruitment (Gerstenfeld, 2004). Third, simply punishing offenders is not enough. If future offending is to be prevented, then some form of rehabilitation that addresses the offender's prejudicial attitudes that caused the offence to occur in the first place is crucial. In an overcrowded prison system, where both effective rehabilitative programmes and the opportunities to implement them are relatively rare, it is unlikely prison will offer any effective solution beyond simply removing them from society for a period of time. Indeed, Levin and McDevitt (2002) argue that imprisonment may in fact be counterproductive because hate based views may be hardened while in prison thereby increasing the likelihood that they will be physically expressed following release.

The best hope, it would seem, lies in a dual approach whereby offenders are rightly punished for their crime, but also in which their underlying prejudices are challenged and addressed. Rehabilitating offenders, as well as punishing them, would appear to hold the key to preventing future offending. The question of course is how do we respond to hate as a prejudice and rehabilitate offenders?

Clearly, much will depend on the type of offender involved. If we refer back to the table of offender characteristics developed by McDevitt, Levin and Bennett (2002; see Chapter 5) we can get some clues about the likelihood of influencing, deterring or indeed preventing future offending. From the evidence presented in the table, those offenders who commit hate offences for the 'thrill' hold the best hope for success in challenging their behaviour. Where the offenders are characterised as 'defensive', 'retaliatory' or 'mission', the chances of success in this respect become increasingly uncertain as the perpetrator's 'commitment to bias' increases. Fortunately, those motivated by the thrill are more common than the other types. Still, if the prison system fails to effectively address the offending behaviour of those that are convicted, then we need to consider employing alternative sentences to imprisonment. Perhaps, then, community sentences offer better prospects.

Some degree of success, particularly for first-time offenders, has been achieved in the United States through probation and community service sentences. Levin and McDevitt refer in particular to sentences consisting of probation including some form of community service to a local minority group or minority group organisation. Based largely on contact theory (Allport, 1954), the intention here is that the offender will learn about the community they have targeted through contact with its members while at the same time returning something positive to that community by repairing some of the damage and harm caused. Such an approach, however, is not always straightforward. As Levin and McDevitt (2002: 201) suggest:

A major limitation of the community service sentencing approach is its lack of formal treatment programs. Having a location for the assignment of offenders is one thing; putting together an effective program to reduce hatred is quite another. Having an offender paint the exterior of a synagogue that he has defaced might return something to the community he has harmed, but it is questionable that this activity alone would teach the offender why what he did was wrong. To do that, he would need a program that effectively addressed his misconceptions.

Similarly, writing of probation practice with regard to racially motivated offenders in the UK, Dixon and Court (2003) acknowledge the limitations of existing practices. Given the unique nature of hate offending, they suggest that generalist offender programmes are relatively ineffective because they fail to adequately address the dynamic risk factors that are, as we have seen, inherently associated with hate as a motivation for crime. Similarly, Dixon and Court suggest that general cognitive behavioural programmes for hate offenders are ineffective because they fail to impact upon the emotional aspects of this type of criminal behaviour. Echoing Levin and McDevitt, Dixon and Court (2003: 150) argue that the complex psychological processes and the wide range of risk factors that underpin hate offending can only be effectively dealt with by developing interventions specifically tailored to hate offenders.

But what elements might such interventions contain? In light of the problems associated with the prison system and community sentences that fail to effectively tackle the offender's underlying prejudice, Levin and McDevitt (2002: 203) make a number of suggestions for the content of such offender programmes, stating that:

a model hate crime offender treatment or rehabilitation program must include the following elements: assessment, discussion of impact on victims, cultural awareness, restitution/community service, delineation of legal consequences, participation in a major cultural event, and aftercare.

For Levin and McDevitt each stage represents an important step in the rehabilitation of hate offenders. Based upon their offender typology, the assessment allows trained professionals to understand the type of offender they are dealing with, and the strength of their prejudicial attitudes. Such understanding will serve to guide the programme in the most suitable direction. Following the assessment, Levin and McDevitt point to the importance of explaining to the offender the harm they have caused to their victim. Many hate offenders see their victims as 'different', 'inferior' or 'inhuman' and reversing this dehumanisation process is an important aim.

Furthermore, Levin and McDevitt suggest that many hate offenders readily accept false and negative stereotypes of their victim's group. Thus it is important to identify and challenge these misconceptions while simultaneously promoting the benefits and values of diversity within the community. Attempting to deconstruct stereotypes and misconceptions about a group is a crucial element of increasing an offender's cultural awareness and understanding.

In addition, the sentence should contain a genuine reparative and restitutive element. It should be related to the community harmed, yet tailored to avoid resentment on the part of the perpetrator. In this sense then, involving the offender in a major cultural event within the victim's community can help the offender to see the victim as a human being thereby serving both a reparative purpose to the victim and their community and as an educative experience for the offender. In addition, the legal consequences of pursuing hate-motivated behaviour should be explained, particularly as many young hate offenders may be of the opinion that they can still 'get away with it', even if they are caught again.

A further suggested component of a rehabilitative programme involves 'aftercare' for the offender so that they can return to the programme to resolve any remaining issues if they feel they need to. Finally, Levin and McDevitt suggest, such offender programmes should be continuously evaluated and monitored, and amended as new and improved information about prejudice and hatred comes to light.

Such rehabilitative programmes may sound ambitious, possibly overly optimistic. There is little doubt that adopting such an approach for hardened hate offenders may be highly unsuitable. Nevertheless, for young, first-time or thrill offenders, a carefully designed and implemented programme containing these elements may prove to be of value. Therefore, while acknowledging that for hardened hate offenders the only realistic option may be incarceration, Levin and McDevitt (2002: 207) optimistically suggest that for other offenders:

> Intermediate sentences – less than prison but more than probation – are necessary for assuring that hate crimes are treated more seriously than ordinary offences. However, many hatemongers can be rehabilitated – if they are fortunate enough to benefit from a serious but humane and imaginative approach to criminality.

Questions remain, however, as to what form this 'humane and imaginative' approach should take in reality, and how realistic a proposition it really is. However, some clues in this regard may be found in the developments and debates that have taken place within the National Probation Service in recent years.

According to the National Probation Service (NPS) (2004), the aims of probation are to protect the public, to reduce reoffending, to properly punish offenders in the community, to ensure the offender's awareness of the effects of crime on victims and the public, and to rehabilitate offenders. To this end, the work of the NPS broadly involves assisting sentencers through pre-sentence reports following an offender's conviction, combining the continuous assessment and management of risk and dangerousness with the provision of expert supervision programmes designed to reduce reoffending, and the supervision of offenders sentenced to unpaid work in the community through community punishment orders (NPS, 2004). In the UK the Probation Service therefore occupies a unique position among criminal justice agencies in terms of working with hate offenders, and in particular race-hate offenders.

In 2000, following academic and professional criticism of the Probation Service's approach to racially motivated offenders (RMOs), the Probation Service's Accreditation Panel established a national sub-group to specifically identify and develop effective programmes of intervention with RMOs (Dixon, 2002). Having conducted a literature review in an attempt to establish 'what works', a theory manual was published in 2001 with the purpose of assisting practitioners and informing future programme development. Ultimately the Accreditation Panel concluded that no firm decision could be made regarding the most effective way to deal with RMOs and recommended that a range of different approaches be piloted and evaluated in an attempt to uncover effective interventions (Dixon, 2002).

On the basis of this recommendation, David Perry (2002) states that the National Probation Directorate identified three potential avenues to explore in relation to RMOs. The first is to test the impact of existing general offending behaviour programmes on RMOs. The justification for this approach is that in addition to the unique factors that influence hate offending, many RMOs also share similar criminogenic risk factors with other types of offenders, and therefore interventions that are already in place, if managed appropriately, may prove to be valuable with RMOs.

The second potential avenue for working with RMOs involves the development of a citizenship education module to be added to existing general programmes of intervention. Perry suggests that by developing an RMO's knowledge, skills and identity in the area of 'citizenship', the additional factors that specifically relate to racist offending may be challenged.

The third avenue involves the development of new programmes specifically for RMOs that draw upon existing knowledge about hate offenders and offending. David Perry argued that this option would only be pursued if the other two failed to work or when the dynamic risk factors alluded to above are conclusively identified. This approach mirrors that of the rehabilitative programme suggested by Levin and McDevitt but is also the most complex of the three approaches given that the potential factors that combine to produce hate offenders are so many and varied. In many respects, this latter approach is really about finding out what works and what doesn't.

A number of probation areas have recently developed and piloted specific programmes of intervention for RMOs in an attempt to find out what works in practice. In reviewing this programme development, Dixon (2002) suggests that many probation areas have drawn on the 'From Murmur to Murder Manual' (Kay and Gast, 1999), which emphasises the need for effective interventions to holistically address issues of offender denial and minimisation, enhance pro-social values, examine the basis of the offender's racism, raise awareness of the victim's perspective and help the offender develop new skills to reduce reoffending.

Dixon describes in further detail the Diversity Awareness Programme (DAP) piloted in the London Probation Area. The ultimate purpose of the Diversity Awareness Programme is to assist practitioners in challenging the prejudicial assumptions that inform hate offending with the aim of reducing reoffending. According to Dixon (2002: 212):

Crucially, the DAP seeks to expose the targeted nature of the offending by focusing on issues of race, cultural identity and the need to develop skills to manage anger and aggression on a single programme. It is thus informed by the research which suggests that cultures of violence and cultures of racism both need to be challenged. The programme works to help offenders develop a positive non-racist identity – it challenges the factors that inform racial violence and seeks to highlight their receptivity to some of the myths circulated in their communities.

In considering his experience of piloting the DAP, Court (2003: 56) states that:

I have been encouraged by the response of offenders participating in the programme, both in custody as well as in the community. The programme consists of seven modules that assess and explore socialization processes from childhood, moving onto the development of racial identity, attitudes, beliefs and values. The purpose is to encourage the offender to consider how prejudicial attitudes have contributed towards their offending and how to develop the thinking skills and practice strategies to avoid offending in the future.

Dixon and Court (2003) further explain that the use of 'race diaries' as part of the programme has been a particularly effective way of engaging with hate offenders. Here, offenders are encouraged to record, consider and positively manage their thoughts and behaviour in relation to any interactions with members of minority groups. In describing the race diary as a 'powerful tool in prompting behavioural change', Court (2003: 56 and 57) further suggests that the programme enables participants to identify and disclose their racial prejudices and encourages them to take greater responsibility for the impact of these prejudices upon their behaviour both within the offence and in their lives generally. Court also suggests that when offenders have reached this stage of recognition, they are often more prepared to learn and develop the skills and strategies to manage their behaviour in a less offensive and more pro-social manner.

While these are encouraging signs this remains a developing area of intervention work and, given that the interventions involved are not universally used across all probation areas, it is difficult to draw firm and generalisable conclusions as to what might universally work. Nevertheless, this ongoing activity within the probation arena is clearly cause for a certain degree of optimism.

However, it is not just probation that is looking at innovative approaches to hate offenders. Gerstenfeld (2004) suggests that potential success in rehabilitating hate offenders might be found in restorative justice through victim-offender mediation. This approach, which has grown in popularity in recent times, seeks to actively involve the offender, the victim and the wider community in the justice process by bringing the victim and the offender together with the aim of achieving reparation and reconciliation. Under mediated and controlled circumstances the victim has the opportunity to explain to the offender the impact that the offence had on them and to discuss related issues and to ask questions of the offender. In response, the offender has the opportunity to explain their actions and to apologise for what they have done.

According to Shenk (2001) victim–offender mediation is ideal for responding to hate crimes for three reasons. Firstly, because hate offenders often 'dehumanise' the objects of their stereotypes, coming face to face with their victim allows the offender to understand the harm they have caused and to view their target as an individual, as a human as opposed to a 'faceless' representative of a hated group. Such an experience can play an important role in deconstructing an offender's stereotypes. Second, both parties are afforded the opportunity for emotional release, an important factor in overcoming the effects of crime; and third, the experience may serve to encourage reporting of hate crimes by victims and curtail future offending by the perpetrator.

We might also reasonably add a fourth and fifth benefit to this list. First, such an approach places the victim at the centre of the delivery of justice (a situation hitherto largely avoided by the justice system) and signifies empowerment of the victim; and second, the use of victim–offender mediation does not necessarily mean that other more punitive approaches cannot be used as well (Gerstenfeld, 2004).

Community sentences: limitations, problems and solutions

Despite these recent and ongoing developments there are, however, a number of problems associated with the community punishment/rehabilitation approach, both generally and specifically. The first and most obvious problem is that we still have remarkably little idea about what really works when responding to hate offenders. This is a product of a number of factors, most notably the relative novelty of this type of offending (or at least of our interest in it) and the complexity of prejudice as a human emotion and as a motivational factor in criminal behaviour

(Allport, 1954). As we have seen, hate offending can be underpinned by one or more of a wide range of factors and thus developing effective interventions can never be a straightforward task. Of course the only way to overcome this issue is for research into hate to continue, for interventions to be based on the findings of such research, for those interventions to be tried and tested by practitioners in the field. We have already noted in this chapter that this is already occurring, but we should be prepared for a long journey. This is not a problem that can be solved overnight.

In addition we are faced with a number of more specific problems. The first is that the probation service is at present largely dependent upon the courts to provide them with their clients before they can work with them. The attrition rate for racially motivated offending within the criminal justice system is very high. Home Office figures (1996a) suggest that in only 2 per cent of notifiable offences is an offender caught and convicted, and research suggests that this figure is even less for racially motivated crimes (Bowling, 1999; Lemos, 2000). Therefore relatively few hate offenders ever reach court for their offence, which means that the probation service will simply not have the opportunity to work with the vast majority of offenders.

Plea-bargaining offers a further obstacle. Because the hate element of a crime is difficult to prove evidentially, research has demonstrated extensive plea-bargaining in cases whereby the 'racist' element of a crime is dropped before the case reaches court in order to secure a conviction of a lesser offence (Burney and Rose, 2002). Because of this, those offenders sentenced to probation but with the hate element of their offence not officially recognised are unlikely to be subject to any specific 'hate'-related interventions. In this sense then, even where offenders don't slip through the net, the hate element does, unless of course the offender displays some form of hatred during the course of their supervision. Put simply, the high rate of attrition ensures that most hate offenders are never identified and officially labelled as such in which case it is quite irrelevant how good any interventions might be.

It is of concern that the probation service and youth offending teams continue to rely on the courts to identify their racist offenders. Many racist offenders remain hidden from view and their underlying prejudices are therefore not addressed. The danger here is that the risk assessments carried out by probation officers may subsequently be inaccurate. Indeed, despite some positive progress, Court (2003: 58) concludes his evaluation of recent probation work in this field by stating that:

... until the probation service and the youth offending teams develop the skills and confidence to explore racial hostility, in particular where the victim rather than the court alone have identified it, assessments of harm to the public can only be partial at best, and at worst dangerously misleading.

Such a proposition may well have merit. There might be a role for probation in identifying hate. The foundations are there because the probation service has adopted ACPO's definition of hate crime, whereby the hate element of an offence can be identified by anyone. If adequate screening for offenders can be implemented as part of their initial interview and assessment by probation officers, as is the case in parts of the London probation area, then perhaps the need to rely so heavily on the courts for identifying offenders can be lessened and more effective interventions can be made where they are necessary. This situation might be eased by, for example, closer liaison with court officials, improved assessment of offenders and through the training of probation staff to confidently identify racist attitudes in offenders (Court, 2003).

A resulting problem of failing to properly identify racist or hate offenders is that they will remain a tiny fraction of the probation service's caseload and may not be seen as a priority. In a bureaucratic world the logical follow on is that if hate offenders are so small in their number then where is the urgency or need to devote finite resources to developing interventions for them? In reality the likelihood is that there are many more offenders under the supervision of the probation service who have racist or hateful tendencies, but who have just not been officially recognised.

It is telling that in her study of racist offenders and responses to them, Sibbitt (1997) found that very few of the probation officers she studied had experience of dealing with racist offenders and, where racist attitudes were expressed, that few knew what to do about them. This was again reflected in research by Lemos (2000). The offender's racist tendencies either remained hidden from view or remained unchallenged, which shows that without training, probation workers appear ill equipped to deal with hate.

As a related issue, Sibbitt suggests that part of the problem for the probation service has been that as an organisation it has traditionally viewed offenders as needy and disadvantaged individuals in need of help and guidance. Sibbitt argues that racist offenders, like sex offenders and child abusers, do not neatly 'fit' this traditional image of the offender and therefore pose something of a unique but rare challenge to the cultural orientation of probation officers. Perhaps selecting 'specialist' probation officers to deal specifically with racist offenders might offer a solution here.

Despite its apparent benefits, we should not assume that the restorative justice approach will prove to be some kind of panacea for hate offending. There is an ongoing scholarly debate surrounding the practical efficacy of victim–offender mediation with its true value at present uncertain, particularly for hate offences where its success remains unproven (Gerstenfeld, 2004). Furthermore, this approach is entirely dependent on the offender being caught and convicted, the victim wishing to meet them and cooperation being established between the two parties. There may also be the possibility that the offender's hatred of the victim's group may be so strong as to render the process useless. As such, to the extent that it can be done at all, the cases suitable for mediation need to be chosen carefully.

Whatever approach we take, being able to explain to the offender *why* their actions were wrong is a key element. Sibbitt (1997) argues that when dealing with racist offenders (and therefore by analogy hate offenders) agencies need to look beyond the offender and recognise both the relationship between the individual and the wider 'perpetrator community' from which he or she is drawn, and the function that the hatred serves for the individual offender. Attempts to combat hatred need to extend beyond the individual offender and also consider the social situation in which the hatred was fostered and shaped and the purpose it serves.

Once the importance of these two factors is recognised, Sibbitt argues, it will become easier to engage the offender in a constructive manner. She describes four responses that professionals might adopt in dealing with an offender's expressions of hatred. Firstly, the professional may not respond at all, in which case the problem remains unchallenged. Second, the professional may respond with 'moral opprobrium', where the inappropriateness of the offender's views are explained and further sanctions threatened. Third, the professional may attempt to deconstruct and challenge the logic of the offender's arguments by pointing out the irrationality of their thinking, although Sibbitt cautions against making the offender feel intellectually inferior and appearing insensitive to what may be genuine underlying concerns on the offender's part. Finally, Sibbitt advocates the challenging of hatred in the context of a holistic approach in which individual perpetrators, potential perpetrators and the perpetrator community should be targeted.

With regard to individual perpetrators, Sibbitt suggests that the most appropriate intervention for the perpetrator will be dependent upon a number of issues including their criminal history both specifically in racist activity and anti-social behaviour more generally, the wishes of the victim, the risk posed to the public, the effectiveness or otherwise of previous attempts at intervention and the perpetrator's personal circumstances. To this end Sibbitt highlights the importance of multi-agency information sharing so that a comprehensive account of relevant information and related issues is kept and can be used to determine which agency is best suited to working with the offender, be it the police, the probation service, housing officers or youth, community or social workers.

In addition to the provisions for racially and religiously aggravated offending, the Crime and Disorder Act 1998 includes a legal requirement for local agencies and groups to work together to find solutions to local crime problems. Lemos (2000) suggests that multi-agency forums typically have three areas of concern when dealing with hate crime. First, they are responsible for developing and implementing a coherent strategy for preventing and dealing with hate crime, including the publication of targets and progress made towards those targets. Second, they are required to cooperate on policy and practice and, third, they may cooperate in dealing with individual cases of hate crime. The emphasis is therefore on the forming of alliances with any group or individuals who are in a position to contribute information and intelligence and who can assist in the development of strategies to combat hate crime in a community.

Such strategies might include, for example, the development of information-sharing protocols to effectively identify the nature of the local hate crime problem and to allocate appropriate resources where they are most needed. They might also include the creation of 'hate crime panels' to develop, implement and oversee anti-hate initiatives with offenders and the wider community, or the development of informal or civil sanctions, for example through tenancy agreements, that might prove more effective in certain cases than the traditional criminal justice approach (see ACPO, 2000, for further examples of multi-agency partnerships and strategies). However, the existence of a legal requirement to tackle hate crime holistically is not a guarantee of success, and neither is the mere existence of a multi-agency forum.

With regard to working with potential perpetrators, which Sibbitt defines as those who have not yet offended (or more to the point, have not yet been caught) but who are at risk of offending, the role of local community diversionary projects and schemes is advocated, particularly aimed at (disillusioned and often bored) youths. Agencies such as the police and probation service may play a part here by helping to identify where such schemes would be most beneficial and who might be best placed to run them. Sibbitt points to the apparent success of an established youth project in London that engaged youths on a housing estate and challenged their specific prejudices and general attitudes to criminality in a variety of ways using a variety of methods (for a detailed account see Sibbitt, 1997).

Finally, in respect of 'perpetrator communities', professionals may play a part by challenging inappropriate language or behaviour whenever it occurs in the course of their work by, for example, using one of the four strategies suggested for individual offenders, described above. Furthermore, Sibbitt outlines the positive benefits of community projects where members of a community are required to work together to achieve a goal that is of mutual concern so that it becomes necessary to view each other in terms wider than just 'race' or 'religion' or 'sexuality' in order to achieve that common goal, such as, for example, a youth club, the acquisition of leisure facilities or through the formation of tenant associations on estates. Sibbitt points to the success of such schemes in various parts of inner London, Bristol and Leicester.

Despite this range of available options, and regardless of whether criminal justice agencies work individually or in partnership, there is a further issue that affects all interventions to hate crime. In England and Wales it is only possible to be convicted of a racially or religiously motivated or aggravated offence. Such a situation therefore at worst precludes, and at best hinders, other types of hate offending from being officially responded to by criminal justice agencies. For example, it is not possible to be convicted of a homophobically motivated offence in the same way as one could for a racially motivated offence, even though homophobia can be considered as an aggravating factor at sentencing. Such an offence is simply not on the statute books; it doesn't legally exist. Therefore the impetus and necessity for agencies such as the probation service to develop interventions for such offenders isn't there. Interventions therefore understandably focus largely on issues of racism and not on other forms of hatred.

It would require a change in the law to cover aspects of diversity other than just race and religion, but such a move would open up a myriad of moral and political dilemmas about exactly which prejudices to outlaw, an issue we touched upon in Chapters 1 and 2. The practical alternative would be for the probation service and others to develop the skills and confidence to identify and challenge all negative prejudice as and when it surfaces in offenders.

Preventing hatred?

Thus far in this chapter we have considered responses to and interventions with individuals who have already developed and expressed negative prejudice. But if we accept the assumption that when we are born we are free from prejudice it naturally follows that we must learn or acquire our beliefs as we grow up. Is it not reasonable to assume then that if we can learn or acquire negative prejudices, then we might also learn to be tolerant, given the right circumstances? With this in mind, preventing the development of negative prejudice rather than responding to it once it manifests itself and becomes physically expressed might hold more hope for success in addressing hate crimes. For this reason, educating and schooling individuals in a manner that will promote the value of diversity and reduce negative prejudice has become an important issue for consideration, particularly in the case of children before their prejudices fully develop.

The significance of educative approaches has long been recognised. Allport, writing back in 1954, stated that there were too many educational programmes (for both adults and children) for him to report in one volume, but broadly categorised them under six headings (informational, vicarious, community study-action, exhibits, festivals and pageants, small-group process and individual conference; see Allport for a full examination of these categories). At the time, Allport was only able to speculate on the effectiveness of these approaches, stating that 'desirable effects' were achieved in approximately two-thirds of the programmes, particularly in relation to those that adopted indirect approaches that focused not on *knowledge of* but on *acquaintance with* the subject in question.

More recently, Bigler (1999: 689) has highlighted the 'broad array of specific strategies for integrating multiracial and ethnic material into the curriculum in order to reduce racial bias in children'. Firstly there are those in which multicultural themes and concepts are attached to the standard educational curriculum. Second, there are those approaches that use multicultural materials to provide counter-stereotypical information about groups. Thirdly, there are those that involve significant changes to the structure and aims of the curriculum to incorporate a more specific focus on issues of diversity, and finally there are those that encourage children to recognise and confront racism (Bigler, 1999). Today, educative programmes exist, although much of the available literature relates to those ongoing in the American education system. Nevertheless, many of the principles remain universally applicable.

However, in their consideration of the role of education, the US-based advocacy group Partners Against Hate (PAH) suggest that curriculum change alone is not enough to effectively challenge prejudice. As such, they draw upon research in the field to make a number of recommendations of how to maximise the potential for proactively reducing prejudice in children. Their publications on the subject can be found at www.parnersagainsthate.org/educators/pag_2_ed.pdf but for our purposes we shall focus briefly on seven key points.

First, the organisation points to the importance of *curriculum reform*. Here it is held beneficial to restructure school curricula and teaching techniques to include the history, culture, experiences and learning styles of the school in order to promote an inclusive learning experience for all students. The underlying hypothesis here is that a classroom culture of inclusiveness that uses multiple teaching perspectives that are tailored to suit different learning styles will help to ensure that each student has an equal chance of academic success.

Second, improvements in students' interethnic attitudes can be achieved though the creation of *equitable schools and classrooms*. By creating a learning environment that is essentially democratic where each student is respected as a participating citizen, the aggravating issue of inequality that can heighten prejudice can be potentially avoided. PAH suggests that the creation of egalitarian classrooms will provide opportunities for both students and teachers to consider their prejudices, evaluate different perspectives or points of view, acquire information that can challenge the development of stereotypes, and also help them to view the undertaking of social action as their responsibility. Furthermore, PAH suggests that schools that avoid the segregation of students on the basis of ability have better interethnic relations among their students.

Third is the recognition of the importance of *teacher training and retraining*. PAH stresses that extensive and ongoing diversity training for teachers that addresses their own prejudices, enables them to detect and rectify prejudicial attitudes and practices in their classroom, and allows them to develop cultural awareness in relation to the groups they will teach is crucial.

The fourth point to be expressed relates to the *desegregation of schools*. While in the UK this has never been official policy the principle remains the same: that students who attend desegregated schools (or in the UK context, schools with a diverse population) are more likely to experience diverse environments later in life.

Fifth, the educative strategy of *cooperative learning* is advocated. PAH suggests that traditional teaching methods, based on competition and individualisation, are often poor at developing intergroup rapport. Instead, cooperative learning encourages students to work in small groups where they are rewarded for their ability to work interdependently towards a common learning goal. Such an approach, which requires cooperation, the support of authorities, equal status among group members and an interaction that is intimate, individualised, non-stereotypical and interdependent has, according to PAH, consistently shown positive results in terms of improving student achievement, conflict resolution and intergroup relations.

The sixth and seventh approaches are *conflict resolution* and *peer mediation* respectively. Mirroring Sibbitt's suggestion for promoting community cohesion, PAH suggests that conflict resolution programmes can play an important role in enhancing intergroup relations by utilising communication skills and creative thinking to achieve mutually agreed solutions to problems. These programmes can teach students conflict resolution skills that they can employ to overcome any tensions or problems that may exist between themselves and others. Similarly, peer mediation ultimately seeks the same goal of resolving conflicts, teaching students to mediate between conflicting peers, but places less emphasis on prejudice awareness than the conflict resolution method.

In light of these recommendations, PAH lists what they describe as a number of promising programmes across America that are based on these guiding principles. Although there is not the space here to examine these, the overriding aims of the programmes are held to be the promotion of understanding, civility and respect, and to help students overcome diversity-related conflicts in imaginative and progressive ways.

In the UK, work with school children in this field has traditionally been less sophisticated than that described above, often involving short, one-off 'talks' by police school liaison officers or local community groups. One such example is cited by Lemos (2000) who describes a race-based diversity project in Milton Keynes jointly run by the police and the local racial equality council. During a one-hour training session the children were encouraged to explore stereotypes of ethnic groups, watch videos of people's experiences of racist harassment, explore and discuss issues that may be of concern to them and work together in a role-play exercise to devise strategies to combat racial harassment in their school.

Lemos also identifies further examples of school-based interventions in the London Borough of Newham. Here, schools can apply to the local race equality council (REC) for financial assistance for anti-hate campaigns to raise awareness of the problem of racial harassment. In addition, the REC in question also provides home and school liaison visitors who visit and offer support to those who have been victimised. The REC also runs a scheme to recruit and train youths to raise awareness of racial harassment among their peers (Lemos, 2000). Similar peer leadership programmes are also used in the United States.

But while preventing hate in children before it develops through educative approaches sounds ideal in principle, it remains a complex and uncertain process. In her review of educative approaches, Bigler (1999) paints a somewhat gloomy picture by stating that such approaches have been relatively ineffective mainly because they have been based upon theoretical and empirical models of attitude formation and change that are far too simplistic and narrow for a concept that is not fully understood. Again, we find that our lack of understanding in relation to prejudice hinders our attempts at influencing its development. She suggests that if educative measures are to be effective then an ongoing approach that is based upon numerous different theoretical foundations and that combines many of the existing techniques is required across all levels of schooling.

The problem here is that such an approach is simply not available in practice in any coherent or implementable format, and even if it was it would likely be complex and expensive to implement and with no guarantee of any tangible and lasting success. The overriding issue here, as Bigler suggests, is that stereotyping is pervasive among children and is highly resistant to change. As such, some interventions work some of the time with some children, and others are known to be counterproductive. There is simply no certainty over the outcomes of either existing or speculative educative approaches.

Two further issues compound this uncertainty. First, many of the preventative and educational measures described above are based on the assumption that knowledge of, and association with, the objects of our negative prejudice will somehow prevent that prejudice developing. But this is optimistic. Sullivan (1999: 4–5), for example, argues that:

It is one of the most foolish clichés of our time that prejudice is always rooted in ignorance, and can usually be overcome by familiarity with the objects of our loathing. The racism of many Southern whites under segregation was not appeased by familiarity with Southern blacks; the virulent loathing of Tutsis by many Hutus was not undermined by living next door to them for centuries. Theirs was a hatred that sprang, for whatever reasons, from experience.

To these examples we can also add the persecution of Jews in Nazi Germany. In this instance, familiarity failed to prevent the ultimate of hate crimes: the killing of over six million Jews in the Holocaust. There is surely no better example to illustrate the old cliché that familiarity can indeed breed contempt. Overcoming ignorance is not necessarily the key to success.

Second, Sibbitt's research on racist offenders (see Chapter 5) highlighted the influence exerted over youths by both their elders and their peer group in terms of their attitude formation and subsequent behaviour. Sibbitt's findings imply that should such individuals be educated at school in the ways described above, then they would likely encounter opposite views at home or with friends. The question then becomes one of who has the greatest influence over the youth, the school or their family and friends? In essence, no matter how positive the message, it has to be both heard and accepted before any difference can be made. This leads us to our final point for consideration in this chapter.

Public awareness campaigns

Of course, it is not just the formal education system that can provide an educative role. The emergence of anti-hate advocacy groups, and particularly the spreading of their message through the Internet, represents an important development in the fight against hate and bigotry. To this end, Gerstenfeld (2004) suggests that such groups concentrate their efforts on two key issues. Firstly they seek to educate both the public and law enforcement agencies and therefore raise awareness about the problem of hate and bigotry, and secondly, they are concerned with the lobbying of authorities to support, promote and take action in the name of their cause. We have already noted the significance of the lobbying activities of advocacy groups in Chapter 3, but their educative role represents another important function. In the UK too a number of advocacy organisations exist, both nationally and locally, that perform a similar function to their American counterparts. Readers are advised to see, for example, the websites of the Runnymede Trust, The Joseph Rowntree Foundation, RaceActionNet (www.raceactionnet.co.uk) and Stonewall, to name just a few.

One increasingly popular approach to combating hatred has come in the form of persuasive public awareness campaigns and mass media publicity, both by independent organisations and advocacy groups, and by government and law enforcement agencies. In a society where we are constantly and inescapably bombarded by advertising messages at every turn, such an approach has become popular presumably because of its ability to inform and 'educate' a large audience with relative ease.

For example, in the summer of 2004 the ADL launched their 'Anti-Semitism is Anti-Me' advertising campaign across New York City and a related 'Anti-Semitism is Anti-Everyone' campaign across the rest of the US. This high profile campaign, which featured a number of celebrities, was designed to raise public awareness about anti-Semitism and global terrorism. The campaign utilised every facet of the media, including poster advertising in towns, cities and university and college campuses, magazines, television and other media outlets across the whole of America.

In the UK, publicity campaigns by the police aimed at raising awareness about hate crime and their approach to hate crime have become increasingly popular, particularly since the publication of the Stephen Lawrence Inquiry report in 1999 (see Chapter 10). In London, the Metropolitan Police Service ran a number of high-profile publicity campaigns around that time to accompany the launch of the Community Safety Units. In addition to raising public awareness that hate crimes would not be tolerated by the organisation, the campaign, which focused primarily on the use of posters in highly visible and densely populated or visited areas, contributed significantly to a rise in both intelligence reports and reports of hate incidents (Lemos, 2000). In the case of the MPS the publicity campaign served to raise awareness of the problem, and in that respect can be deemed a success. The question remains, however, as to how effective public awareness campaigns are at reducing prejudice and combating hate more generally.

As with many of the other interventions discussed in this chapter, on the available evidence the answer appears to be that sometimes publicity has an effect and sometimes it doesn't. In reviewing the limited available literature, Winkel (1997) found that exposing people to material aimed at reducing prejudice caused a reduction in prejudicial attitudes in some people, but conversely an increase in others. In addition, the generalisability of these results is highly questionable and thus we are again unable to draw any firm conclusions about the utility of responding to hate using this method.

On the other hand, however, throughout this book I have made reference to media reports, particularly those relating to the British tabloid press, that have presented a negative picture of intergroup relations, most notably with regard to immigration and asylum. In this sense it would seem reasonable to suggest that such media accounts are damaging to social cohesion and serve to undo the messages of the positive publicity campaigns described above. For example, on 7 March 2005 following an article about an Islamic rap video made to recruit young British Muslims to al'Qaida's cause, the *Daily Star* newspaper announced that 99 per cent of voters in its readers' poll feared that Britain was becoming an Islamic state, although the actual number of votes was not stated (Wickham, 2005). Similarly, on 9 March 2005 the *Sun* newspaper announced on its front page a 'Sun war on Gypsy free-for-all' in which the newspaper launched a campaign against 'illegal gypsy camps across Britain' and invited readers to e-mail their experiences 'of gypsies or travellers being treated as if they are above the law' (Phillips, 2005: 5).

While I do not wish to engage in a discussion about the merits of the *Sun*'s campaign, the *Daily Star*'s poll or the issues that have led to them, my point is simply that publicity concerning negative aspects about diversity is probably more powerful, more frequent and more persuasive than positive publicity. This is perhaps because it appeals to our natural propensity that we discussed in Chapter 2 to view those that are different to ourselves as inferior and with suspicion, and as a threat to the interests of our own in-group. This is arguably reflected in the terminology used by the *Sun*'s campaign when it describes the government as putting the interests of gypsies ahead of those of 'hard-working people who pay their taxes and obey the law' (2005: 4). While the concerns periodically expressed by the media may or may not be legitimate, the point is that they do little to help the social cohesion of a multicultural and diverse society.

Concluding comments

In this chapter I have presented a brief overview of existing and ongoing efforts to combat hate crime and the prejudice that underpins it. But despite recent advances the obvious question still remains: *just how effective are these responses to hate?* Unfortunately, as we have implied throughout this chapter, this is a question that is impossible to answer with any great degree of certainty at the present time. As Gerstenfeld (2004: 193), speaking primarily of efforts to combat hate crimes in the US, suggests:

There is no shortage of individuals and organisations that wish to combat hate crimes, but there is almost a complete lack of assessment of their efforts. If we knew which endeavours work and which do not, these people could channel their energies and finances in much more useful ways. It will not necessarily be easy to determine what works, but, at this point, any addition to existing knowledge would be of great benefit.

The same can also be said for efforts here in the UK. It seems that the best we can suggest is that some techniques work better than others, depending on different circumstances and situations. The only thing we can say with any certainty is, ironically, that nothing is certain with regard to what works. The nature of the criminal justice system ensures that regardless of how effective criminal justice interventions may be the majority of hate offenders will never be subjected to them, and even when they are the success of existing interventions and preventative methods is uncertain largely because we still do not know very much about this 'new' concept called 'hate' that has become the operative word. Perhaps then the question should be, are we attempting the impossible by even trying to prevent hate and hate crimes? In the conclusion to this book I shall explore this question further.

Chapter 13

Conclusions

Throughout this book I have posed a number of questions. I have done so primarily because I am concerned that as a society we are attempting to respond to the threat posed by an apparently growing social problem, but in my opinion without a thorough consideration or understanding of exactly what it is we are trying to tackle. Having examined much of the available literature on hate crimes, I would now like to return to some of those questions to see if we are any clearer about what hate crime actually is, or any clearer about how we should respond to it.

What is hate?

The most obvious thing we have learned is that this simple four-letter word, 'hate', in fact masks a multitude of complexities. This is primarily because when we talk about *hate* in the context of *hate crime*, what we are really referring to is *prejudice*. Because of this, 'hate' in its contemporary meaning actually refers to variety of human emotions that are often far removed from real hatred. These other emotions range from prejudice, to bias, or anger, or hostility, through to unfriendliness or a mere aversion to others (Sullivan, 1999). The definitions of hate that we discussed in Chapter 1 for the most part refer to all of these emotions. The issue of how strong a prejudice or attitude must be before it officially becomes *hate* is for the most part of little importance when transforming ordinary crime into hate crime. For reporting and recording purposes the policing definition in this country is only interested in the presence of any prejudice at the time of the offence (ACPO, 2000, 2005), while legal definitions seek evidence of *hostility*.

The problem here is that if we are to respond to all these varieties of human emotion that we have conveniently labelled as 'hate', then we face a challenge of enormous proportions. The more we widen the search for prejudice in criminal behaviour, the more we will find it. But if on the other hand we choose to respond to a specific set of beliefs, attitudes or prejudices that we deem to be unacceptable, the task will become more manageable but we then have to ask serious moral questions about how it is that we can justify outlawing some prejudices and not others, and in doing so justify affording some groups greater protection than others.

Is hate normal?

If when we talk about hate, we actually mean prejudice, then the evidence presented in Chapter 2 poses something of a problem. In Chapter 2 I argued that prejudice is natural to, and definitive of, the human condition. As Sullivan (1999) points out, as human beings we associate, and therefore we disassociate; we have feelings of loyalty and disloyalty, a sense of belonging and unbelonging, and these are entirely natural. If everyone naturally has prejudices, then while we can respond to the *crime* element of hate crime, serious questions should be asked about whether we can and should respond to the *hate* element.

To illustrate the normality of 'hate', Andrew Sullivan (1999: 3) uses two examples that I think will resonate with many of us:

Of course by hate we mean something graver and darker than this lazy kind of prejudice. But the closer you look at this distinction, the fuzzier it gets. Much of the time we harbour little or no malice toward people of other backgrounds or ethnicities or ways of life. But then a car cuts you off at an intersection and you find yourself noticing immediately that the driver is a woman, or black, or old, or fat, or white, or male. Or you are walking down a city street at night and hear footsteps quickening behind you. You look around and see that it is a white woman and not a black man, and you are instantly relieved. These impulses are so spontaneous they are almost involuntary. But where did they come from?

This raises the question of whether or not hate is a self-conscious activity. If it is then that is one thing, but if as Sullivan points out it is primarily an unconscious activity then the matter becomes considerably murkier. Do humans deliberately and consciously hate, or is hate a normal and subconscious product of human differentiation? And how can we know for certain either way? However we look at it we are faced with the question that if prejudice is normal, then how can we ever hope to stop it being expressed in one form or another?

Have we complicated hate?

The definitions that we have adopted have also considerably complicated our understanding of hate. If we think back to Jacobs and Potter's (1998) model that we examined in Chapter 1, then hate crime would not be difficult to understand if we only applied the term to offenders who truly hate their victim and the group they represent, and where that hate is the sole or predominant cause of that offending behaviour. Chapter 6 examined more extreme examples of hatred that are perhaps easier to understand. They are certainly more clear-cut and more easily identifiable as 'hate' in lay terms. But this is often not the case for the majority of hate crimes. The strength of the offender's prejudice, and the causal relationship between that prejudice and the commission of the offence, do not have to be particularly strong for a crime to become a hate crime. In some cases a causal relationship may not be evident at all.

In Britain this is reflected in legislation that requires only a *demonstration* of hostility towards the victim of a particular group (where 'demonstrates' and 'hostility' are not defined and where the victim and offender may in fact be members of the same group), and a police definition that requires no evidential test at all for a hate crime to be recorded and investigated. In the post-Macpherson era a racist incident is *any* incident that is *perceived* to be racist by the victim or any other person. Similarly, the ACPO definition of hate crime requires only that the perpetrator's prejudice against an identifiable group of people is a factor in determining who is victimised.

In other words, any crime might be a hate crime because, as we have seen, everyone has prejudices, and everyone is a member of an identifiable group and is therefore potentially a victim. So if everyone is a potential victim and every crime is potentially a hate crime, then it simply becomes another term for crime. But if in response to this we start to make distinctions between who can and who cannot be a victim of hate crime, then we once again enter immediately into an immoral and illiberal venture concerning rights to particular and specific protection. In other words, hate is considerably more complicated as a result of our recent attempts to simplify it.

Hate is also complicated because it manifests and expresses itself in different ways in different people, and indeed serves a different purpose for different people to the extent that no two expressions of hate are ever identical. Yet despite its obvious complexity we still try to label each expression of hate as the same. The significance of understanding and appreciating different types of hate is emphasised by Sullivan (1999). If we think of the hatred felt by the Nazis towards the Jews, the Hutus towards the Tutsis, and South Africa's former Apartheid regime towards blacks, then for any decent thinking person these are hates that are wholly unacceptable. But it is reasonable to assume that, as a consequence of their treatment, Jews also feel hatred towards Nazis, Tutsis towards Hutus and South Africa's blacks towards the Apartheid regime. Yet this hate is far more acceptable and easier to understand. What else, Sullivan asks, are the victims of these extreme hates expected to feel towards their haters? So some forms of hate are more acceptable and understandable than others, and some haters are ascribed more blame than others.

The problem here, Sullivan suggests, is that if we regulate hate among some, then we are forced to regulate it against others, despite the fact that not all hates are equivalent. Similarly, in Chapter 11 I discussed how the meaning and purpose of new policies and responses to hate crime were being subverted. Where this happens, those whom such policies and legislation were designed to protect frequently find themselves on the receiving end of attempts to combat hatred. For example, FBI figures show that throughout the 1990s blacks were three times more likely to commit a hate crime than whites. Andrew Sullivan suggests that this is not just because of deliberate subversion, but also because those who have historically been the victims of hate may in fact develop a hate towards their tormentors that is more hateful than the prejudice they themselves were originally subjected to. It is just that now they become caught up in the new legal mechanisms designed to protect them in the first place.

Why treat hate differently?

All of the issues discussed above raise the question of why it is that we should treat hate crimes differently to other crimes. In Chapter 3 I examined the history and rise of hate crime as a contemporary social issue. In Chapter 7 I outlined legislative efforts to combat hate crime, and in Chapter 8 I presented the debate surrounding the existence of hate crime laws. The key justifications for treating hate crimes differently were presented in Chapter 4 when we discussed victimisation. The differential treatment of hate crimes is justified by the widely held belief that these crimes have a disproportionate impact on both the victim and the wider community, are socially divisive and are increasing in both incidence and violence. However, many of these assumptions are, as we have seen, based upon evidence that is far from conclusive and that is the subject of uncertainty, debate and a degree of confusion. Yet they form the basis for our differential approach to hate crime. Given that we know relatively little for certain about the phenomenon we have labelled 'hate crime', we should ask ourselves what exactly it is that we are responding to, and if these are really the best foundations upon which to base our response to it. My concern is that as a society we seem to be sailing full steam ahead in our attempts to combat hatred, but without really knowing for sure what hatred is. All of this raises the rather uncomfortable questions of whether we can actually stop hatred, and indeed whether we should even try to do so.

Can hatred be prevented?

Throughout this book, and particularly in these concluding comments, I have made reference to the thoughts of Andrew Sullivan. I was given a copy of his article entitled 'What's So Bad About Hate?' while I was researching in New York in late 2002. His critical approach to hate crime caused me to seriously consider points that hitherto I had not. At that time, while I was aware of the opposition to hate crime laws, I was content to accept the view that hate is bad and we should do everything we can to stop it, and my work with the police had been with that goal in mind. While I still believe this to be true, I have become more sceptical and critical of our seemingly unquestioning approach to this problem, and believe that many of the points that Sullivan and other critics make deserve to be taken seriously, particularly with regard to whether or not attempts to eradicate hate and prevent hate crimes are futile.

Consider these points made by Sullivan (1999: 15–16):

Hate crime law advocates cram an entire world of human motivations into an immutable, tiny box called hate, and hope to have solved a problem. But nothing has been solved, and some harm may even have been done. In an attempt to repudiate a past that treated people differently because of the colour of their skin, or their sex, or religion or sexual orientation, we may merely create a future that permanently treats people differently because of the colour of their skin, or their sex, or religion or sexual orientation. This notion of hate crime, and the concept of hate that lies behind it, takes a psychological mystery and turns it into a facile political artefact. Rather than compounding this error and extending it even further, we should seriously consider repealing the concept altogether.

To put it another way: violence can and should be stopped by the government. In a free society, hate can't and shouldn't be. The boundaries between hate and prejudice and between prejudice and opinion and between opinion and truth are so complicated and blurred that any attempt to construct legal and political firewalls is a doomed and illiberal venture ...in an increasingly diverse culture, it is crazy to expect that hate, in all its variety, can be eradicated. A free country will always mean a hateful country. This may not be fair, or perfect, or admirable, but it is reality, and while we need not endorse it, we should not delude ourselves into thinking that we can prevent it.

For Sullivan our best hope is to achieve toleration of hatred, that is coexistence despite its presence in society. The answer to hatred, he suggests, is not majority persecution of it, but minority indifference to it. While we can and should create a climate in which hate is disapproved of, he argues, hate is only foiled not when haters are punished, for that may entrench differences, but rather when the hated are immune to the bigot's beliefs. According to Sullivan, therefore, there is no solution to the problem of hatred, just transcendence of it. In this sense, hate can never be eradicated, it can merely be overcome.

I do not believe, however, that we should abandon the concept yet, nor give up on our attempts to make life better for those who are the genuine victims or potential victims of expressions of hate. Much has been achieved, and much more can be achieved. But I do believe that these are important points that Sullivan makes, and they illustrate a complexity that is often overlooked in our efforts to combat hate crime.

Gerstenfeld (2004) has similarly suggested that while we believe that a problem exists, we have asked very few questions about it, opted for simplistic solutions and simply reapplied them when they have failed. Breaking this cycle is crucial. Criminal justice professionals and others seeking to combat hate are required to 'think outside the box' and be imaginative and creative in their approach when dealing with the perpetrators of hate crime in order to address the range of associated risk factors. Some issues can be relatively easily overcome. Others cannot.

We also need to think a little more clearly about exactly what it is that we are trying to challenge: broad prejudice or narrow hatred? We should perhaps then take a step back and carefully consider exactly what it is that we are responding to in order to ensure that our efforts are appropriate, effective and above all built upon solid foundations, particularly in relation to the factors that cause the natural prejudice present in all of us to become the motivation for criminal behaviour. I hope that the issues raised in this book may serve as a starting point for debate and discussion about the best way to move forward. In a world where prejudice and hate are embedded in social structures and public discourse from neighbour disputes to international relations, this is a moral, political and above all a social issue that transcends the concerns of criminal justice.

Appendix

Racist incidents for all police force areas 1996/97 to 2002/03

Police force area	1996/97	1997/98	1998/99	1999/00	2000/01	2001/02	2002/03	Change % 2001/02 to 2002/03
Avon & Somerset	310	409	626	887	956	940	1,125	20
Bedfordshire	77	75	134	300	301	289	293	1
Cambridgeshire	141	147	205	519	691	736	878	19
Cheshire	92	78	158	421	399	405	184	-55
Cleveland	68	76	147	204	307	399	444	11
Cumbria	37	46	45	85	97	155	162	5
Derbyshire	208	174	208	383	504	678	678	0
Devon & Cornwall	82	90	116	538	776	874	781	-11
Dorset	67	86	145	185	212	69	260	277
Durham	24	37	75	178	247	275	224	-19
Essex	116	160	229	431	679	813	452	-44
Gloucestershire	34	32	83	258	389	432	380	-12
Greater Manchester	595	624	1,197	2,324	2,663	3,955	2,642	-33
Hampshire	178	219	271	654	845	888	864	-3
Hertfordshire	295	288	325	703	984	1,237	1312	6
Humberside	55	72	111	215	422	100	350	250
Kent	256	276	273	914	1,278	888	986	11
Lancashire	337	311	450	917	1,274	2,178	1,521	-30
Leicestershire	299	237	367	878	908	1,132	1,181	4

Lincolnshire	7	6	14	19	42	150	149	-1
London, City of	10	6	28	55	91	72	103	43
Merseyside	162	241	324	822	761	690	763	11
Metropolitan Police	5,621	5,862	11,050	23,346	20,628	16,711	15,453	-8
Norfolk	56	89	94	253	259	287	363	26
Northamptonshire	195	318	282	597	591	663	619	-7
Northumbria	488	444	623	1,159	1,626	1,747	1,552	-11
North Yorkshire	43	41	64	96	128	228	58	-75
Nottinghamshire	330	391	475	714	914	1,097	1,090	-1
South Yorkshire(')	169	213	293	557	698	698	201	-71
Staffordshire	225	214	220	202	500	1,138	466	-59
Suffolk	74	54	150	234	291	375	345	-8
Surrey	55	45	126	338	573	607	648	7
Sussex	260	298	399	934	1,526	1,120	1,106	-1
Thames Valley	233	279	486	999	1,088	1,470	1,445	-2
Warwickshire	66	107	111	150	175	314	310	-1
West Mercia	64	57	83	464	871	978	864	-12
West Midlands	725	632	988	1,548	3,321	4,058	3,009	-26
West Yorkshire	623	644	1,068	2,118	2,534	2,919	2,602	-11
Wiltshire	35	59	101	221	356	121	332	174
Dyfed-Powys	18	17	37	99	142	167	135	-19
Gwent	60	45	98	213	269	191	232	21
North Wales	4	12	36	80	248	301	369	23

References and further reading

Ackerman, N.W. and Jahoda, M. (1950) *Anti-Semitism and Emotional Disorder*. New York: Harper.

Ackroyd, P. (2000) *London: A Biography*. London: Vintage.

Adlam, R. and Villiers, P. (eds) (2002) *Police Leadership in the Twenty-First Century*. Winchester: Waterside Press.

Agnew, R. (1992) 'Foundation for a general strain theory of crime and delinquency'. *Criminology*, 30, 47.

Alba, R.D., Logan, J.R. and Bellair, P.E. (1994) 'Living with crime: the implications of racial/ethnic differences in suburban location'. *Social Forces*, 73(2), 395–434.

Albrecht, H.J. (1993) 'Ethnic minorities: crime and criminal justice in Europe', in F. Heidensohn and M. Farrell (eds), *Crime in Europe*. London: Routledge.

Alibhai-Brown, Y. (1999) 'Black people and the criminal justice system', *Violations of Rights in Britain, Series 3*, no. 26.

Allport, G.W. (1954) *The Nature of Prejudice*. Reading, MA: Addison-Wesley.

American Psychological Association (1998) Hate Crimes Today: An age-old foe in modern dress. Retrieved on 11 December 2003 from: www.apa.org/pubinfo/hate/.

Amir, M. (1971) *Patterns in Forcible Rape*. Chicago: University of Chicago Press.

Anti-Defamation League (2004) *Extremism*. Accessed on 15 August 2004 from: www.adl.org.

Archer, J. (ed.) (1994) *Male Violence*. London: Routledge.

Arnold, M. et al. (2003) *A Matter of Trust: Recommendations from the Pink Shield Project. A community-led initiative to identify and address crime and safety issues in Birmingham's lesbian, gay, bisexual and transgendered communities*. Birmingham: Birmingham Police Forum for the Gay Community.

Association of Chief Police Officers (1985) *Guiding Principles Concerning Racial Attacks*. London: ACPO.

Association of Chief Police Officers (1999) *ACPO Action Guide to Identifying and Combating Hate Crime–Second Draft*. London: ACPO.

Association of Chief Police Officers (2000) *ACPO Guide to Identifying And Combating Hate Crime*. London: ACPO.

Association of Chief Police Officers (2005) *Hate Crime: Delivering a Quality Service (Good Practice and Tactical Guidance)*. London: ACPO.

Association of London Authorities (1993) *Racial Abuse: An Everyday Experience for Some Londoners*. Submission by the Association of London Authorities to the House of Commons Home Affairs Committee Inquiry into Racially-Motivated Attacks and Harassment.

Banton, M. (1973) *Police Community Relations*. London: Collins.

Banton, M. (1983) *Racial and Ethnic Competition*. Cambridge: Cambridge University Press.

Baron, R.A. and Byrne, D. (1994) *Social Psychology: Understanding Human Interaction*. 7th edn. Boston: Allyn & Bacon.

Barton, A. and Evans, R. (1999) *Proactive Policing on Merseyside*, Police Research Series, Paper 105. London: Home Office.

Bates, V. (2000) *Speaking Out: Violence Against the Lesbian and Gay Community in Portsmouth*. Portsmouth: Portsmouth and Southeast Gay Men's Health Promotion Service.

Bauer, Y. (2002) *Rethinking the Holocaust*. New Haven, CT: Yale University Press.

Bayley, D.H. (2002) 'Policing hate: what can be done?' *Policing and Society*, 12(2), 83–91.

BBC News (1999) *Liverpool Anger at Straw Jibe*. Retrieved on 11 December 2003 from: http://news.bbc.co.uk/1/hi/uk_politics/324855.stm.

Belth, N.C. (1979) *A Promise to Keep: A Narrative of the American Encounter with Anti-Semitism*. New York: Times Books.

Berkowitz, L. (1993) *Aggresion: Its Causes, Consequences and Control*. New York: McGraw-Hill.

Berrill, K.T. (1990) 'Antigay violence and victimisation in the United States: an overview'. *Journal of Interpersonal Violence*, 5, 274–294.

Berrill, K.T. (1992) 'Organising against hate on campus: strategies for activists', in K.T. Berrill and G.M. Herek (eds), *Hate Crimes: Confronting Violence Against Lesbians and Gay Men*. London: Sage.

Betz, H.-G. (1999) 'Contemporary right-wing radicalism in Europe'. *Contemporary European History*, 8(2), 2 299–316.

Beynon, J. (1989) 'A school for men: An ethnographic case study of routine violence in schooling', in L. Barton and S. Walker (eds), *Politics and the Processes of Schooling*. Milton Keynes: Open University Press.

Bigler, R.S. (1999) 'The use of multi-curricula and materials to counter racism in Children'. *Journal of Social Issues*, 55(4), 687–705.

Billig, M. (2001) 'Humour and hatred: the racist jokes of the Ku Klux Klan', *Discourse And Society*, 12(3), 267–89.

Billig, M. (2002) 'Henri Tajfel's 'Cognitive Aspects of Prejudice' and the psychology of bigotry', *British Journal of Social Psychology*, 41, 171–88.

Bjorgo, T. (1993) 'Terrorist violence against immigrants and refugees in Scandinavia: patterns and motives', in T. Bjorgo and R. Witte (eds), *Racist Violence in Europe*. London: Macmillan.

Blackbourn, D. (2004) 'Homophobia', in N.R.J. Hall, N. Abdullah-Kahn, D. Blackbourn, R. Fletcher, and J. Grieve (eds), *Hate Crime*. Portsmouth: Institute of Criminal Justice Studies.

Blackstone, T., Bhikhu, P. and Sanders, P. (eds) (1998) *Race Relations In Britain: A Developing Agenda*. London: Routledge.

Bland, N. (1997) *Measuring Public Expectations of Policing: An Evaluation of Gap Analysis*, Police Research Series, Paper 24. London: Home Office.

Bland, N., Mundy, G., Russell, J. and Tuffin, R. (1999) *Career Progression of Ethnic Minority Police Officers*, Police Research Series, Paper 107. London: Home Office.

Blood and Honour/Combat 18 (2003) *Blood and Honour Field Manual*. Retrieved on 11 December 2003 from: www.skrewdriver.net/fmintro.html.

Blumenfield, W.J. (1992) *Homophobia: How We All Pay the Price*. Boston, MA: Beacon Press.

Bobo, L. (1983) 'Group conflict, prejudice and the paradox of contemporary racial attitudes', in P.A. Katz and D.A. Taylor (eds) *Eliminating Racism*. New York: Plenum.

Boeckmann, R.J. and Turpin-Petrosino, C. (2002) 'Understanding the harm of hate crime', *Journal of Social Issues*, 58(2), 207–25.

Boehnke, K., Hagan, J. and Merkens, H. (1998) 'Right-wing extremism among German adolescents: Risk factors and protective factors', *Applied Psychology: An International Review*, 47(1), 109–126.

Borkowski, M., Murch, M., and Walker, V. (1983) *Marital Violence: The Community Response*. London: Tavistock.

Bowling, B. (1993) 'Racial harassment and the process of victimisation: conceptual and methodological implications for the local crime survey', *British Journal of Criminology*, 33(2), 231–50.

Bowling, B. (1999) *Violent Racism: Victimisation, Policing and Social Context*. New York: Oxford University Press.

Bowling, B. and Phillips, C. (2003) *Racism, Crime and Criminal Justice*. Harlow: Longman.

Bradley, R. (1998) *Public Expectations and Perceptions of Policing*. Police Research Series, Paper 96. London: Home Office.

Brewer, M.B. (1999) 'The psychology of prejudice: ingroup love or outgroup hate?', *Journal of Social Issues*, 55(3), 429–444.

Bridgeman, C. and Hobbs, L. (1998) *Preventing Repeat Victimisation: The Police Officers' Guide* 2nd edn. London: Home Office.

Britton, N.J. (2000) 'Examining police/black relations: what's in a story?', *Ethnic and Racial Studies*, 23(4), 692–711.

Bronner, S.E. (1999) 'Making sense of hell: three meditations on the Holocaust', *Political Studies*, XLVII, 314–28.

Brown, C. (1984) *Black and White Britain: The Third PSI Survey*. London: Heinemann.

Brown, R. (1995) *Prejudice: Its Social Psychology*. Oxford: Blackwell.

Browning, C.R. (2001) *Ordinary Men: Reserve Police Battalion 101 and the Final Solution in Poland*. London: Penguin.

Brownmiller, S. (1975) *Against our Will–Men, Women and Rape*. London: Penguin.

Bryman, A. (1996) *Quantity and Quality in Social Research*. London: Routledge.

Buffum, P.C. (1982) 'Racial factors in prison homosexuality'. in A.M. Scacco (ed.) *Male Rape: A Casebook of Sexual Aggression*. New York: Ams Press.

Burke, M. (1993) *Coming Out of the Blue*. London: Cassell.

Burney, E. and Rose, G. (2002) *Racist Offences: How Is the Law Working?* Home Office Research Study 244. London: Home Office.

Byers, B., Crider, B.W. and Biggers, G.K. (1999) 'Bias crime motivation: a study of hate crime and offender neutralisation techniques used against the Amish', *Journal of Contemporary Criminal Justice*, 15(1), 78–96.

Byford, L. (1982) *Report into the Case of Peter Sutcliffe*. London: Home Office.

Calderbank, R. (2000) 'Abuse and disabled people: vulnerability or social Indifference?', *Disability and Society*, 15(3), 521–34.

Cambridge, P. (1999) 'The first hit: a case study of the physical abuse of people with learning disabilities and challenging behaviour in a residential service', *Disability and Society*, 14(3), 285–308.

Canter, D. and Hodge, S. (1998) 'Victims and perpetrators of male sexual assault,' *Journal of Interpersonal Violence*, 13(2), 222–39.

Cashmore, E. and McLaughlin, E. (eds) (1991) *Out of Order? Policing Black People*. London: Routledge.

Chahal, K. and Julienne, L. (2000) *'We Can't All Be White!': Racist Victimisation in the UK*. York: York Publishing Services.

Chaitin, J. (2002) 'Issues and interpersonal values among three generations in families of Holocaust survivors', *Journal of Social and Personal Relationships*, 19(3), 3, 379–402.

Chatterton, M.R., Langmead-Jones, P. and Radcliffe, J. (1997) *Using Quality of Service Surveys*. Police Research Series, Paper 23. London: Home Office.

Chenery, S., Holt, J. and Pease, K. (1997) 'Biting back II: reducing repeat victimisation in Huddersfield', Crime Detection and Prevention Series, Paper 82. London: Home Office.

Citizenship 21 (2001) *Profiles of Prejudice. The Nature of Prejudice in England: Indepth Analysis of Findings*. London: Stonewall.

Clendinnen, I. (1999) *Reading the Holocaust*. Cambridge: Cambridge University Press.

Commission For Racial Equality (1999a) *The Stephen Lawrence Inquiry: Implications for Racial Equality*. London: CRE.

Commission for Racial Equality (1999b) *Racial Attacks and Harassment*, CRE Factsheet. London: CRE.

Comstock, G.D. (1989) 'Victims of antigay/lesbian violence', *Journal of Interpersonal Violence*, 4, 101–6.

Cook, D. and Hudson, B. (eds) (1993) *Racism and Criminology*. London: Sage.

Council of Europe (1996) *The Management of Criminal Justice: Recommendation No. R(95) 12 and Report*. Strasbourg: Council of Europe Publishing.

Court, D. (2003) 'Direct work with racially motivated offenders', *Probation Journal*, 50, 1.

Craig, K.M. (2002) 'Examining hate-motivated aggression: a review of the social psychological literature on hate crimes as a distinct form of aggression', *Aggression and Violent Behaviour*, 7, 85–101.

Craig-Henderson, K. and Sloan, L.R. (2003) 'After the hate: helping psychologists help victims of racist hate crime', *Clinical Psychology: Science and Practice*, 10(4), 481–90.

Crandon, L. (1997) 'Intelligence driven', *Police Review*, 12 December.

Crawford, A. (1998) 'Delivering multi-agency partnerships in community safety', in A. Marlow, A. and J. Pitts, (eds), *Planning Safer Communities*. Lyme Regis: Russell House.

Cresswell, P., Howarth, G., Dolan, M. and Hedges, J. (1993) *Opportunities for Reducing the Administrative Burdens on the Police*. Police Research Series, Paper 3. London: Home Office.

Critchley, T.A. (1967) *A History of Police in England and Wales, 1900–1966*. London: Constable.

Crown Prosecution Service (2003) *Guidance on Prosecuting Cases of Racist and Religious Crime*. London: CPS.

Crown Prosecution Service (2004) *Annual Report 2003–2004*, London: CPS.

Cunningham, A., Jaffe, G., Baker, L., Dick, T., Malla, S., Mazaheri, N. and Poisson, S. (1998) *Theory-Derived Explanations of Male Violence Against Female Partners: Literature Update and Related Implications for Treatment and Evaluation*. London: London Family Court Clinic.

Davies, M., Croall, H. and Tyrer, J. (1998) *Criminal Justice* (2nd edn.) Harlow: Longman.

Dekeseredy, W.S. and Maclean, B.D. (1991) 'Exploring the gender, race and class dimensions of victimisation: a left realist critique of the Canadian urban victimization survey', *International Journal of Offender Therapy and Comparative Criminology*, 35(2), 143–61.

Dennis, N. (ed.) (1998) *Zero Tolerance: Policing a Free Society*, 2nd edn. London: LEA Health & Welfare Unit.

Denny, D. (1997) 'Anti-racism and the limits of equal opportunities policy in the criminal justice system', *Social Policy and Administration*, 31(5), 79–95.

Ditton, J., Bannister, J. and Farrall, S. (1999) *Attitudes to Crime, Victimisation and the Police in Scotland: A Comparison of White and Ethnic Minority Views*. Edinburgh: Scottish Office Central Research Unit.

Dixon, L. (2002) 'Tackling racist offending: a generalised or targeted approach?', *Probation Journal*, 49(3), 205–16.

Dixon, L. and Court, D. (2003) 'Developing good practice with racially motivated offenders', *Probation Journal*, 50, 2, June.

Dobash, R. and Dobash, R.E. (1980) *Violence Against Wives*. Shepton Mallet: Open Books.

Dobash, R.E. and Dobash, R. (1982) *Women, Violence and Social Change*. London: Routledge.

Dobash, R.E. and Dobash, R. (1984). 'The nature and antecedents of violent events', *British Journal of Criminology*, 24(3), 269–88.

Dobash, R.E. and Dobash, R. (1998) *Rethinking Violence Against Women*. London: Sage.

Dobash, E., Dobash R., Cavanagh, K. and Lewis, R. (2000) *Changing Violent Men*. London: Sage.

Docking, M., Kielinger, V. and Paterson, S. (2003) *Policing Racist Incidents in the Metropolitan Police Service*. Paper given to the Research and Development Conference, 3 June 2003.

Donnelly, D. and Kenyon, S. (1996) 'Honey we don't do men: gender stereotypes and the provision of services to sexually assaulted males', *Journal of Interpersonal Violence*, 11(3), 441–8.

Dowing, J.D.H. (1999) 'Hate speech' and 'First Amendment absolutism' Discourses in the US', *Discourse and Society*, 10(2), 175–89.

Downes, D. and Rock, P. (2003) *Understanding Deviance*, 4 edn. Oxford: Oxford University Press.

Dunbar, E. (1999) 'Defending the indefensible: a critique and analysis of psycholegal defence arguments of hate crime perpetrators', *Journal of Contemporary Criminal Justice*, 15(1), 64–77.

Eatwell, R. (2000) 'The rebirth of the "Extreme Right" in Western Europe?', *Parliamentary Affairs*, 53, 407–25.

Edwards, S. (1989) *Policing 'Domestic' Violence*. London: Sage.

Erlich, H.J. (1992) 'The ecology of antigay violence', in K.T. Berrill and G.M. Herek (eds), *Hate Crimes: Confronting Violence Against Lesbians and Gay Men*. London: Sage.

Farrell, G. (1992) 'Multiple victimisation: its extent and significance', *International Review of Victimology*, 2(2), 85–102.

Federal Bureau of Investigation (2002) *Hate Crime Statistics 2001*. Washington, DC: US Department of Justice.

Federal Bureau of Investigation (2003) *Hate Crime Statistics 2002*. Washington, DC: US Department of Justice.

FFLAG (n.d.) *Families and Friends of Lesbians and Gays. A Guide for Families and Friends of Lesbian and Gays*. Retrieved on 11 December 2003 from: www.fflag.org.uk/guide.htm.

Fitzgerald, M. and Hale, C. (1996) *Ethnic Minorities, Victimisation and Racial Harassment*. Home Office Research Study No. 154. London: HMSO.

Franklin, K. (1998) 'Unassuming motivations: contextualising the narratives of antigay assailants', in G.M. Herek (ed.), *Stigma and Sexual Orientation: Understanding Prejudice Against Lesbians, Gay Men and Bisexuals*, Psychological Perspectives on Lesbian and Gay Issues 4. London: Sage.

Frost, M. (1999) *Clinical Issues in Domestic Violence*. Nursing Times Monograph, No 12. London: EMAP Healthcare.

GALOP (2001) Annual Report. London, GALOP.

Garofalo, J. (1991) 'Racially motivated crime in New York City', in M.J. Lynch and E.B. Patterson (eds), *Race and Criminal Justice*. Albany, NY: Harrow & Heston.

Garofalo, J. and Martin, S.E. (1993) *Bias-Motivated Crimes: Their Characteristics and the Law Enforcement Response*. Carbondale, IL: Southern Illinois University, Press.

Gaylin, W. (2003) *Hatred: The Psychological Descent into Violence*. New York: Public Affairs.

Geberth, V.J. (1996) *Practical Homicide Investigation. Tactics, Procedures and Forensic Techniques*, 3rd edn. Kansas City: CRC Publishing.

Genn, H. (1988) 'Multiple victimisation', in M. Maguire and J. Ponting (eds), *Victims of Crime: A New Deal?* Milton Keynes: Open University Press.

Gerstenfeld, P.B. (2004) *Hate Crimes: Causes, Controls and Controversies*. Thousand Oaks, CA: Sage.

Gilling, D. (1997) *Crime Prevention: Theory, Policy and Politics*. London: UCL Press.

Glaser, J., Dixit, J. and Green, D.P. (2002) 'Studying hate crime with the Internet: what makes racists advocate racial violence?', *Journal of Social Issues*, 58(1), 177–93.

Goldhagen, D.J. (1996) *Hitler's Willing Executioners: Ordinary Germans and the Holocaust*. London: Little, Brown.

Goleman, D. (1990) 'Studies discover clues to the roots of homophobia', *New York Times*, 10 July.

Graef, R. (1989) *Talking Blues*. London: Collins Harvill.

Grattage, K. (2003) 'Queue-jumping migrants are nicking homes', *Daily Star*, 6 October.

Graumann, C.F. (1998) 'Verbal discrimination: a neglected chapter in the social psychology of aggression', *Journal for the Theory of Social Behavior*, 28(1), 41–61.

Graycar, R. and Morgan, J. (1990) *The Hidden Gender of Law*. Sydney: Federation Press.

Green, D.P., McFalls, L.H. and Smith, J.K. (2003) 'Hate crime: an emergent research agenda', in Perry, B. (ed.), *Hate and Bias Crime: A Reader*. New York: Routledge.

Green, D.P., Strolovitch, D.Z., Wong, J.S. and Bailey, R.W. (2001) 'Measuring gay populations and antigay hate crime', *Social Science Quarterly*, 82(2), 281–96.

Gregory, J. and Lees, S. (1999) *Policing Sexual Assault*. London: Routledge.

Grieve, J. (2004) 'The investigation of hate crimes: art, science or philosophy?', in N.R.J. Hall, N. Abdullah-Kahn, D. Blackbourn, R. Fletcher and J. Grieve, (eds), *Hate Crime*. Portsmouth: Institute of Criminal Justice Studies.

Grieve, J. and French, J. (2000) 'Does institutional racism exist in the Metropolitan Police?', in D. Green (ed.), *Institutional Racism and the Police*. London: Institute for the Study of Civil Society.

Grimshaw, R. and Jefferson, T. (1987) *Interpreting Policework*. London. Allen & Unwin.

Groth and Burgess A.W. (1980) 'Male rape: offenders and victims', *American Journal of Psychiatry*, July, 137 (7).

Hall, N.R.J. (2000). 'Meeting the needs of ethnic minority victims in London? An assessment of a Metropolitan Police Service Community Safety Unit'. Unpublished MSc Thesis, University of Portsmouth.

Hall, N.R.J. (2002a) 'Policing racist hate crime in London: policy, practice and experience after the Stephen Lawrence Inquiry'. Unpublished research report presented to the Metropolitan Police Service.

Hall, N.R.J. (2002b) 'Blind prejudice: the impact of hate crime', *Police Review*, 18 October.

Hall, N.R.J. (2004) *A Tale of Two Cities: The Social Construction of Hate Crime in London and New York City*. Paper presented to the British Society of Criminology Conference, Summer.

Hall, N.R.J. (forthcoming) 'Policing hate crime in London and New York City: policy, practice and experience'. Unpublished PhD thesis. Institute of Criminal Justice Studies, University of Portsmouth.

Hardaway, Y. (1999) 'Addressing racial tension and other diversity issues through adult education: theories in practice', *International Journal of Lifelong Education*, 18(4), 295–306.

Harrison, J. and Cunneen, M. (2000) *An Independent Police Complaints Commission*. London: Liberty.

Harry, J. (1992) 'Conceptualising anti-gay violence', in G.M. Herek and K.T. Berrill (eds), *Hate Crimes: Confronting Violence Against Lesbians and Gay Men*. London: Sage.

Heitmeyer, W. (1993) 'Hostility and violence towards foreigners in Germany', in T. Bjorgo and R. Witte (eds), *Racist Violence in Europe*. London: Macmillan.

Her Majesty's Inspectorate of Constabulary (1997a) *Policing with Intelligence, Criminal Intelligence – A Thematic Inspection of Good Practice*. London: Home Office.

Her Majesty's Inspectorate of Constabulary (1997b) *Winning The Race: Policing Plural Communities*. London: Home Office.

Her Majesty's Inspectorate of Constabulary (1999) *Winning The Race: Revisited*. London: Home Office.

Her Majesty's Inspectorate of Constabulary (2000) *Policing London: Winning Consent*. London: Home Office.

Herek, G.M. (1992) 'Psychological heterosexism and antigay violence: the social psychology of bigotry and bashing', in K.T. Berrill and G.M. Herek (eds), *Hate Crimes: Confronting Violence Against Lesbians and Gay Men*. London: Sage.

Herek, G.M., Cogan, J.C. and Gillis, J.R. (2002) 'Victim experiences in hate crimes based on sexual orientation', *Journal of Social Issues*, 58(2), 319–339.

Hester, M., Kelly, L. and Radford, J. (1997) *Women, Violence and Male Power*. Buckingham: Open University Press.

Herek, G.M., Gillis, R.J. and Cogan, J.C. (1997) 'Hate crime victimisation among lesbian, gay and bisexual adults: prevalence, psychological correlates and methodological issues', *Journal of Interpersonal Violence*, 12(2), 195–215.

Hill, M.E. and Augoustinos, M. (2001) 'Stereotype change and prejudice reduction: short- and long-term evaluation of a cross-cultural awareness programme', *Journal of Community and Applied Social Psychology*, 11, 243–62.

Hillman, R.J. (1990) 'Sexual assault of men: a series', *Genitourinary Medicine*, 66, 247–250.

Hintjens, H.M. (1999), 'Explaining the 1994 Genocide in Rwanda', *Journal of Modern African Studies*, 37(2), 241–86.

Hirschfield, A. and Bowers, K. (1998) 'Monitoring, measuring and mapping community safety', in A. Marlow and J. Pitts (eds), *Planning Safer Communities*. Lyme Regis: Russell House.

Hirsh, D. (2001) 'The trial of Andrei Sawoniuk: Holocaust testimony under crossexamination', *Social and Legal Studies*, 10(4), 529–45.

Hirschi, T. (1969) *The Causes of Delinquency*. Berkeley, CA: University of California Press.

Hitler, A. (1992) *Mein Kampf*. London: Pimlico.

Hofstadter, D. (1980) *Godel, Escher, Bach. An Eternal Golden Braid*. London: Penguin.

Holdaway, S. (1996) *The Racialisation of British Policing*. Basingstoke: Macmillan.

Home Office (1989) *The Response to Racial Attacks and Harassment: Guidance for the Statutory Agencies. Report of the Inter-Departmental Racial Attacks Group*. London: HMSO.

Home Office (1996a) *Action for Justice*. London: HMSO.

Home Office (1996b) *The Victim's Charter: A Statement of Service Standards for Victims of Crime*. London: Home Office Communications Directorate.

Home Office (1998) *Speaking Up for Justice*. London: HMSO.

Home Office (2001) *Statistics on Race and the Criminal Justice System: A Home Office publication under Section 95 of the Criminal Justice Act 1991*. London: Home Office.

Home Office (2002) *Statistics on Race and the Criminal Justice System: A Home Office publication under Section 95 of the Criminal Justice Act 1991*. London: Home Office.

Home Office (2003) *Statistics on Race and the Criminal Justice System: A Home Office publication under Section 95 of the Criminal Justice Act 1991*. London: Home Office.

Home Office (2004) *Statistics on Race and the Criminal Justice System: A Home Office publication under Section 95 of the Criminal Justice Act 1991*. London: Home Office.

Home Office (n.d.) *Government Policy Around Domestic Violence*. Retrieved on 5 December from: www.homeoffice.gov.uk/crimpol/crimreduc/domviolence/domviol98.html.

Hope, T. (1998) 'Community safety, crime and disorder', in A. Marlow and J. Pitts (eds), *Planning Safer Communities*. Lyme Regis: Russell House.

Horowitz, D.L. (2001) *The Deadly Ethnic Riot*. Berkeley, CA: University of

California Press.

Hough, M. and Tilley, N. (1998) *Getting the Grease to the Squeak*, Crime Detection and Prevention Series, Paper 85. London: Home Office.

Hovland, C. and Sears, R.R. (1940) 'Minor studies in aggression VI: correlation of lynchings with economic indicators', *Journal of Psychology*, 9, 301–10.

Huber, T. (2001) 'Holocaust compensation payments and the global search for justice for victims of Nazi persecution', *Australian Journal of Politics and History*, 48(1), 85–101.

Hudson, B. (1993) 'Racism and criminology: concepts and controversies', in D. Cook and B. Hudson (eds), *Racism and Criminology*. London: Sage.

Hudson, B. (1998) 'Restorative justice: the challenge of sexual and racial violence', *Journal of Law and Society*, 25(2), 237–56.

Human Rights Watch (1997) *Racist Violence in the United Kingdom*. London: Human Rights Watch/Helsinki.

Iganski, P. (1999a) 'Legislating against hate: outlawing racism and antisemitism in Britain', *Critical Social Policy*, 19(1), 129–41.

Iganski, P. (1999b) 'Why make hate a crime?', *Critical Social Policy*, 19(3), 386–95.

Imperial Klans of America (2003) *Doctrinal Statement of Beliefs*. Retrieved on 11 December 2003 from: www.k-k-k.com/doctrinalstatements.htm.

Irving, B. and Dunnigham, C. (1993) *Human Factors in the Quality Control of CID Investigations*, Research Study No. 21. London: Home Office.

Israel, M. (1999) 'Hate speech and the First Amendment', *Journal of Contemporary Criminal Justice*, 15(1), 97–110.

Jacobs, J.B. and Potter, K. (1998) *Hate Crimes: Criminal Law and Identity Politics*. New York: Oxford University Press.

Jacobson, H. (2004) 'Did you hear the one about the vicar, the rabbi and the imam? Well, you won't now ...', *Independent Arts and Books Review*, 10 December.

Jefferson, P.N. and Pryor, F.L. (1999) 'On the geography of hate', *Economics Letters*, 65, 389–95.

Jeffery, C.R. (1971) *Crime Prevention Through Environmental Design*. Beverley Hills, CA: Sage.

Jenkins, G., Asif, Z. and Bennett, G. (2000) *Listening Is Not Enough: An Analysis of Calls to Elder Abuse Response–Action on Elder Abuse's National Helpline*. London: Action on Elder Abuse.

Jenkins, P. and Davidson, B. (2001) *Stopping Domestic Violence: How a Community Can Prevent Spousal Abuse*. London: Plenum Publishers.

Johnson, N. (ed.) (1985) 'Marital violence', *Sociological Review*, Monograph No. 1. Keele: University of Keele Press.

Johnson, S. (1997) 'Without prejudice', *Police Review*, 31 January 28–9.

Jones, A. (2002) 'The politics of genocide', *International Studies Association*, 129–39.

Jones, S. (2000) *Understanding Violent Crime*. Buckingham: Open University Press.

Jones, T., Maclean, B.D. and Young, J. (1986) *The Islington Crime Survey: Crime,*

Victimisation and Policing in Inner City. London: Aldershot, Gower.

Jukes, A. (1993) *Why Men Hate Women*. London: Free Association Books.

Jupp, V. (1998) *Methods of Criminological Research*. London: Routledge.

Karpman, B. (1951) 'The sexual psycopath', *Journal of Criminal Law and Criminology*, 42, 184–98.

Kaufman, A., Divasto, P., Jackson, R., Voorhees, D. and Christy, J. (1980) 'Male rape victims: non-institutionalised assault', *American Journal of Psychiatry*, 137(2), 221–3.

Kay, J. and Gast, L. (1999) *From Murmur to Murder: Working with Racially Motivated Offenders*. West Midlands: West Midlands Probation Training Consortium.

Khan, U. (1998) 'Putting the community into community safety', in A. Marlow and J. Pitts (eds), *Planning Safer Communities*. Lyme Regis: Russell House.

Kimmel, M. (1994) 'Masculinity as Homophobia', in H. Brod and M. Kaufman (eds), *Theorising Masculinities*. London: Sage.

Laming, H. (2003) *The Victoria Climbie Inquiry*. London: HMSO.

Landau, S. (1981) 'Juveniles and the police', *British Journal of Criminology*, 21(1), 27–46.

Lea, J. and Young, J. (1984) *What Is to Be Done About Law and Order?* Harmondsworth: Penguin.

Lee, K.S. (2002) 'Building intergroup relations after September 11', *Analyses of Social Issues and Public Policy*, 2(1), 131–41.

Lees, S. (1997) *Ruling Passions: Sexual Violences Reputation and the Law*. Buckingham: Open University Press.

Leets, L., Giles, H. and Noels, K. (1999) 'Attributing harm to racist speech', *Journal of Multilingual and Multicultural Development*, 20(3), 209–15.

Lehne (1976) 'Homophobia among men', in R. Brannon and D.S. David (eds), *The Forty-Nine Percent Majority: The Male Sex Role*. London: Addison-Wesley.

Leigh, A., Mundy, G. and Tuffin, R. (1999) *Best Value Policing: Making Preparations*, Police Research Series, Paper 116. London: Home Office.

Leigh, A., Read, T. and Tilley, N. (1998) *Brit Pop II: Problem-Oriented Policing in Practice*, Police Research Series, Paper 93. London: Home Office.

Leishman, F., Loveday, B. and Savage, S.P. (eds), (1996) *Core Issues in Policing*. New York: Longman.

Lemos, G. (2000) *Racial Harassment: Action on the Ground*. London: Lemos & Crane.

Levin, B. (2002) 'From slavery to hate crime laws: the emergence of race and status-based protection in American criminal law', *Journal of Social Issues*, 58(2), 227–45.

Levin, B. (1999) 'Hate crimes: worse by definition', *Journal of Contemporary Criminal Justice*, 15(1), 6–21.

Levin, J. and McDevitt, J. (1993) *Hate Crimes: The Rising Tide of Bigotry and Bloodshed*. New York: Plenum Press.

Levin, J. and McDevitt, J. (2002) *Hate Crimes Revisited: America's War on Those Who Are Different*. Boulder, CO: Westview Press.

Liddle, A.M. and Gelsthorpe, L.R. (1994) *Crime Prevention and Inter-Agency Co-operation*, Crime Prevention Unit Series, Paper 53. London: Home Office.

Lieberman, M. (1999) *Enforcing Hate Crime Laws: Defusing Intergroup Tensions and Advancing Police–Community Relations*. Washington, DC: Anti-Defamation League.

Logan, J.R. and Stults, B.J. (1999) 'Racial differences in exposure to crime: the city and suburbs of Cleveland in 1990', *Criminology*, 37(2), 251–76.

McDevitt, J., Balboni, J. and Bennett, S. (2000) *Improving the Quality and Accuracy of Bias Crime Statistics*. Washington, DC: US Bureau of Justice.

McDevitt, J., Levin, J. and Bennett, S. (2002) 'Hate crime offenders: an expanded typology', *Journal of Social Issues*, 58(2), 303–17.

McDevitt, J., Balboni, J., Garcia, L. and Gu, J. (2001) 'Consequences for victims: a comparison of bias- and non-bias-motivated assaults', *American Behavioral Scientist*, 45: 647–713.

McDevitt, J., Balboni, J., Garcia, L. and Gu, J. (2001) 'Consequences for victims: a comparison of bias- and non-bias-motivated assaults', in P. Gerstenfeld and D.R. Grant (eds) (2004) *Crimes of Hate: Selected Readings*. Thousand Oaks, CA: Sage.

McLaughlin, E. (1999) 'The search for truth and justice', *Criminal Justice Matters*, 35: 13–15.

McLaughlin, E. (2002) 'Rocks and hard places: The politics of hate crimes', *Theoretical Criminology*, 6(4), 493–8.

MacLean, B.D. (1993) 'Left realism, local crime surveys and policing of racial minorities: a further analysis of data from the first sweep of the Islington Crime Survey', *Crime, Law and Social Change*, 19(1), 5–86.

McLoughlin, K. (1997) 'Building trust', *Police Review*, 9 May, 20–21.

Macpherson, W. (1999) *The Stephen Lawrence Inquiry*, Cm 4262. London: Stationery Office.

Marlow, A. (2000) 'Policing in the pillory: Macpherson and its aftermath', in A. Marlow and B. Loveday (eds), *After Macpherson: Policing after the Stephen Lawrence Inquiry*. Lyme Regis: Russell House.

Marlow, A. and Loveday, B. (eds) (2000) *After Macpherson: Policing after the Stephen Lawrence Inquiry*. Lyme Regis: Russell House.

Matza, D. (1964) *Delinquency and Drift*. New York: John Wiley.

Mawby, R. (1998) ''Victims' perceptions of police services in East and West Europe', in V. Ruggiero, N. South and I. Taylor (eds) *The New European Criminology: Crime and Social Order in Europe*. London: Routledge.

Maynard, W. and Read, T. (1997) *Policing Racially Motivated Incidents*, Crime Detection and Prevention Series, Paper 84. London: Home Office.

Merton, R. (1949) *Social Theory and Social Structure*. New York: Free Press.

Messerschmidt, J. (1993) *Masculinities and Crime: Critique and Reconceptualization of Theory*. Maryland: Rowman & Littlefield.

Metropolitan Police Service (1994) 'Cracking crime the high tech way', *The Job*, 10 June.

Metropolitan Police Service (1998a) *Delivering Information for Action. Strategies for Information and Communications Systems in the Metropolitan Police Service*. London: MPS.

Metropolitan Police Service (1998b) *Submission to Part Two of the Inquiry into Matters Arising from the Death of Stephen Lawrence*. London: Metropolitan Police Service.

Metropolitan Police Service (1999a) *Protect and Respect: The Met's diversity strategy*. London: Metropolitan Police Service.

Metropolitan Police Service (1999b) *A Police Service for All the People: A Report of the MPS Ethnic Minority (Recruitment and Advancement) Working Group*. London: Metropolitan Police Service.

Metropolitan Police Service (1999c) *CSU Reference Material: Racial Incident Guidance Manual*. London: Metropolitan Police Service.

Metropolitan Police Service (1999d) *Action Guide to Race/Hate Crime: Consultation Draft*. London: Metropolitan Police Service.

Metropolitan Police Service (1999e) *Minimum Investigative Standards for Community Safety Units: Special Notice 7/99*. London: Metropolitan Police Service.

Metropolitan Police Service (1999f) *Racial and Violent Crime Task Force: Action Plan Update* (26 May 1999). London: Metropolitan Police Service.

Metropolitan Police Service (1999g) *Report of the Commissioner of Police of the Metropolis 1998/99*. London: Home Office.

Metropolitan Police Service (1999h) *Racial Incidents and Understanding the Diverse Community We Serve: A Trainers' Resource Pack*. London: Metropolitan Police Service Training Design and Research Unit.

Metropolitan Police Service (2000a) *Third Party Reporting*. London: Metropolitan Police Service.

Metropolitan Police Service (2000b) *The Investigation of Racist, Domestic Violence and Homophobic Incidents. A Guide to Minimum Standards*. London: MPS.

Metropolitan Police Service (2000c) *Tackling Hate Together: Community Safety Units–Protecting Our Communities*. London, Metropolitan Police Service.

Metropolitan Police Service (2001a) *Protect and Respect: Everyone Benefits*. London: Metropolitan Police Service.

Metropolitan Police Service (2001b) *Athena Spectrum. A Menu of Tactical Options for Combating Hate Crime*. London: Metropolitan Police Service.

Metropolitan Police Service (2002a) *Guide to the Management and Prevention of Critical Incidents*. London: Metropolitan Police Service.

Metropolitan Police Service (2002b) *The Damilola Taylor Murder Investigation Review*. London: Metropolitan Police Service.

Mezey, G.C. and King, M.B. (1989) 'The effects of sexual assault on men: a survey of 22 victims', *Psychological Medicine*, 19, 205–9.

Mezey, G.C. and King, M.B. (1993) *Male Victims of Sexual Assault*. Oxford: Oxford University Press.

Midgely, N. (1998) 'It could never happen here could it?', *The Pink Paper*, 30 October, 10.

Miller, A.R. (2003) 'Civil rights and hate crimes legislation: two important asymmetries', *Journal of Social Philosophy*, 34(3) 437–43.

Mirlees-Black, C., Mayhew, P. and Percy, A. (1996) *The 1996 British Crime Survey*, Home Office Statistical Bulletin, Issue 19/96. London: Home Office.

Mooney, J. (1993) *The North London Domestic Violence Survey*. London: Middlesex University, Centre for Criminology.

Morley, R. and Mullender, A. (1994) *Preventing Domestic Violence to Women*. Police Research Group, Paper No. 48. London: HMSO.

Morran, D. and Wilson, M. (1997) *Men Who Are Violent to Women: Group Work Practice Manual*. Lyme Regis: Russell House.

Morris, A. (1999) 'Race relations and racism in a racially diverse inner-city neighbourhood: a case study of Hillbrow, Johannesburg', *Journal of Southern African Studies*, 25(4), 667–94.

Morton, J. (1993) *Bent Coppers: A Survey of Police Corruption*. London: Warner Books.

Mullender, A. (1996) *Domestic Violence, Social Work and Probation Response*. London: Routledge.

Mundy, G. (1999) *Tenure: Policy and Practice*, Police Research Series, Paper 106. London: Home Office.

Munyard, T. (1988) 'Homophobia at work and how to manage it', *Personnel Management*, June, 50.

Naffine, N. (1990) *Law and the Sexes: Explorations in Feminist Jurisprudence*. Sydney: Allen & Unwin.

National Center For Policy Analysis (2001) *The Disparate Effect of Hate Crime Laws*. Retrieved on 11 December 2003 from: www.ncpa.org/pi/crime/cri1297f.html.

NCIS (2000) *The National Intelligence Model*. London: National Criminal Intelligence Service.

NCIS (2002) *Annual Report: A Year in the Fight Against Serious and Organised Crime*. London: NCIS.

National Probation Service (2004) *About Us: Our Aims*. Retrieved 2 February 2005 from: www.probation.homeoffice.gov.uk.

New York City Police Department (2000) *Patrol Guide: Bias Motivated Incidents*, Procedure No. 207-10. New York: NYPD.

New York City Police Department (2001) *Hate Crime Task Force 2000 Year End Report*. New York: NYPD.

New York City Police Department (2002) *Hate Crime Task Force 2001 Year End Report*. New York: NYPD.

Newman, O. (1972) *Defensible Space: Crime Prevention Through Urban Design*. New York: Macmillan.

Neyroud, P. and Beckley, A. (2001) *Policing, Ethics and Human Rights*. Cullompton: Willan.

Nolan, J.J. and Akiyama, Y. (1999) 'An analysis of factors that affect law enforcement participation in hate crime reporting', *Journal of Contemporary Criminal Justice*, 15(1), 111–27.

Norris, F.H. and Kaniasty, K. (1992) 'A longitudinal study of the effects of various crime prevention strategies on criminal victimisation, fear of crime and psychological distress', *American Journal of Community Psychology*, 20(5), 625–48.

O'Byrne, M. (1998) 'Policing in an uncertain world', in A. Marlow and J. Pitts (eds), *Planning Safer Communities*. Lyme Regis: Russell House.

Osborn, D.R., Ellingsworth, D. and Hope, T. (1996) 'Are repeatedly victimised households different?', *Journal of Quantitative Criminology*, 12(2), 223–45.

Osborn, S. (1998) 'Evaluating community safety initiatives', in A. Marlow and J. Pitts (eds), *Planning Safer Communities*. Lyme Regis: Russell House.

Pahl, J. (1978) *A Refuge for Battered Women: A Study of the Role of a Women's Centre*. London: HMSO.

Partners Against Hate (2004) *Program Activity Guide: Helping Youth Resist Bias and Hate*, 2 edn. Washington: DC: PAH.

Perry, B. (2001) *In the Name of Hate: Understanding Hate Crimes*. New York: Routledge.

Perry, D. (2002) 'Racially motivated offenders: the way forward', *Probation Journal*, 49(4), 305–10.

Perry, B. (ed.) (2003) *Hate and Bias Crime: A Reader*. New York: Routledge.

Petrosino, C. (1999) 'Connecting the past to the future: hate crime in America', *Journal of Contemporary Criminal Justice*, 5(1), 22–47.

Pettigrew, T.F. (1969) 'The ultimate attribution error: Extending Allport's cognitive analysis of prejudice', *Personality and Social Psychology Bulletin*, 5, 461–76.

Philadelphia Police Department (1999) *Reporting and Investigation: Bias Incidents. Directive 73/139*. Philadelphia: PPD.

Philadelphia Police Department (2003) *Conflict Prevention Resolution Unit: Mission Statement, Unit Profile and Policy Statement*. Philadelphia: PPD.

Phillips, M. (2005) 'Stamp on the camps: Sun campaign to stop flood of gypsies', *Sun*, 9 March, 4–5.

Plotnikoff, J. And Woolfson, R. (1998) *Policing Domestic Violence: Effective Organisational Structures*. Home Office Police Research Series, Paper 100. London: Home Office.

Prutzel-Thomas, M. (2000) 'German criminal justice and right wing extremists: is German criminal justice "blind in the right eye"?', *Debatte*, 8(2), 209–25.

Public Forum (1998) *Homophobia: Analysis of a 'Permissable' Prejudice*. Retrieved on 11 December 2003 from: www.cyberpsych.org/homophobia/.

Public Law (1990) *Hate Crime Statistics Act of 1990*, 104 Stat. 140. London: HMSO.

Radford, J. and Stanko, B. (1991), 'Violence against women and children: the contradictions of crime control under patriarchy', in K. Stenson and D. Cowell (eds), *The Politics of Crime Control*. London: Sage.

Read, T. and Oldfield, D. (1995) *Local Crime Analysis. Crime Detection and Prevention Series*: Police Research, Paper 65. London: Home Office.

Reiner, R. (1992) *The Politics of the Police*, 2nd edn. Hemel Hempstead: Harvester Wheatsheaf.

Renton, D. (2003) 'Examining the success of the British National Party, 1999–2003', *Race and Class*, 45(2), 75–85.

Rideau, M. and Sinclair, B. (1982) 'Prison: the sexual jungle', in A.M. Scacco (ed.), *Male Rape: A Casebook of Sexual Aggression*. New York: Ams Press.

Riley, D. and Mayhew, P. (1980) *Crime Prevention Publicity: An Assessment*. London: HMSO.

Rock, P. (1986) *Helping Victims of Crime*. Oxford: Clarendon.

Roxburgh, A. (2002) *Preachers of Hate: The Rise of the Far Right*. London: Gibson Square Books.

Runnymede Trust (2000) *Report of the Commission on the Future of Multi-Ethnic Britain*. London: Profile Books.

Russell, Lord (2002) *Scourge of the Swastika: A Short History of Nazi War Crimes*. London: Greenhill Books.

Sampson, A. (1991) *Lessons from a Victim Support Crime Prevention Project*. Crime Prevention Unit, Paper 25. London: Home Office.

Sampson, A. and Phillips, C. (1992) *Multiple Victimisation: Racial Attacks on an East London Estate*, Police Research Group Crime Prevention Unit Series, Paper 36. London: Home Office.

Sampson, R.J. (1995) 'The Community', in J.Q. Wilson and J. Petersilia (eds), *Crime*. Oakland, CA: ICS Press.

Sandhu, B. (2002) 'After Oldham and September 11th–capacity building for stronger communities?', *Local Economy*, 17(2), 90–5.

Sardar, Z. and Davies, M.W. (2002) *Why Do People Hate America?* Cambridge: Icon Books.

Scacco, A.M. (1982) *Male Rape: A Casebook of Sexual Aggression*. New York: Ams Press.

Scarman, L. (1981) *The Brixton Disorders: 10–12 April 1981: Report of an Inquiry: Presented to Parliament by The Secretary of State for the Home Department, November*. London: HMSO.

Sears, J.T. and Williams, W.L. (1997) *Overcoming Heterosexism and Homophobia: Strategies that Work*. New York: Columbia University Press.

Seibel, W. (2002) 'The strength of perpetrators: the Holocaust in Western Europe, 1940–1944', *Governance*, 15(2), 211–240.

Sheffield, C. (1995) 'Hate violence', in P. Rothenberg (ed.), *Race, Class and Gender in the United States*. New York: St. Martin's Press.

Shenk, A.H. (2001) 'Victim-offender mediation: the road to repairing hate crime injustice', *Ohio State Journal on Dispute Resolution*, 17, 185–217.

Sherman, L.W. and Berk, R.A. (1984) 'The specific deterrent effects of arrest for domestic assault', *American Sociology Review*, 49, 261–72.

Sibbitt, R. (1997) *The Perpetrators of Racial Harassment and Racial Violence*. Home Office Research Study No. 176. London: Home Office.

Sims, J. (1993) 'What is intelligence?', in A. Shulsky and J. Sims (eds), *What Is Intelligence? Working Group on Intelligence Reform*. Washington: Consortium for the Study of Intelligence, Georgetown University.

Smart, C. (1976) *Women, Crime and Criminology: A Feminist Critique*. London: Routledge & Kegan Paul.

Smith, D.J. (1997) 'Ethnic origins, crime and criminal justice', in M. Maguire *et al.* (eds), *The Oxford Handbook of Criminology*, 2nd edn. New York: Oxford University Press.

Smith, L. (1989) *Domestic Violence*. London: HMSO.

Snibbe, J.R. and Snibbe, H.M. (1973) *The Urban Policeman In Transition: A Psychological and Sociological Review*. Springfield, IL: Charles C. Thomas.

Solomos, J. and Back, L. (1996) *Racism and Society*. London: Macmillan.
Soule, S.A. and Van Dyke, N. (1999) 'Black church arson in the United States, 1989–1996', *Ethnic and Racial Studies*, 22(4), 724–742.
Southern Poverty Law Centre (2004) *The Intelligence Project'*, 35(1).
Stanko, E. (1990) *Everyday Violence*. London: Virago.
Stenson, K. and Cowell, D. (eds), (1991) *The Politics of Crime Control*. London: Sage.
Stermac, L., Sheridan, P.M., Davidson, A. and Dunn, S. (1996) 'Sexual Assault of Adult Males', *Journal of Interpersonal Violence*, 11(1), 52–64.
Stewart, H. (2003) 'Gays need psychiatric help, says bishop', *The Guardian*, 8 November, 7.
Stockdale, J. and Gresham, P. (1995) *The Presentation of Police Evidence in Court*, Police Research Group, Paper 15. London: Home Office.
Stockdale, J.E., Whitehead, C.M.E. and Gresham, P.J. (1999) *Applying Economic Evaluation to Policing Activity*, Police Research Series, Paper 103. London: Home Office.
Stonewall (2003) *Profiles of Prejudice*. London: Citizenship 21.
Stonewall (2004) *Understanding Prejudice: Attitudes Towards Minorities*. London: Citizenship 21.
Streissguth, T. (2003) *Hate Crimes*. New York: Facts on File.
Sullivan, A. (1999) 'What's so bad about hate? The illogic and illiberalism behind hate crime laws', *New York Times Magazine*, 26 September.
Summerskill, B. (2002) 'How smears brought top gay cop to brink of ruin', *Observer*, 24 March.
Sykes G. and Matza, D. (1957) 'Techniques of Neutralisation', *American Sociological Review*, 22, 664–70.
Tajfel, H. (1982) 'Social psychology and intergroup relations', *Annual Review of Psychology*, 33, 1–30.
Tilley, N. (1995) *Thinking about Crime Prevention Performance Indicators*. Crime Detection and Prevention Series, Paper 57. London: Home Office.
Torres, S. (1999) 'Hate crimes against African Americans: the extent of the problem', *Journal of Contemporary Criminal Justice*, 15(1), 48–63.
Travis, G., Egger, S. and O'Toole, B. (1995) 'The international crime surveys: some methodological concerns', *Current Issues in Criminal Justice*, 6(3), 346–61.
Turpin-Petrosino, C. (2002) 'Hateful sirens ... who hears their song? An examination of student attitudes toward hate groups and affiliation potential', *Journal of Social Issues*, 58(2), 281–301.
United States Department of Justice (1997) *Hate Crime Data Collection Guidelines*. Washington, DC: United States Department of Justice.
United States Department of Justice (1999) *Hate Crime Training: Core Curriculum for Patrol Officers, Detectives and Command Officers*. Washington, DC: United States Department of Justice.
Upson, R. (2000). 'Gay officers have little confidence in Federation', *Police Review*, 26 May, 11.
Uribe, V. (1992) *Homophobia–What It Is and Who It Hurts*. Los Angeles: Friends of Project 10.

Victim Support (1995) *The Rights of Victims of Crime*. London: Victim Support.

Virdee, S. (1994) *Racial Violence and Harassment*. London: Policy Studies Institute.

Waddington, P.A.J. (1999) *Policing Citizens*. London: UCL Press.

Walklate, S. (2001) *Gender, Crime and Criminal Justice*. Cullompton: Willan Publishing.

Waller, J. (2002) *Becoming Evil: How Ordinary People Commit Genocide and Mass Killing*. New York: Oxford University Press.

Webber, F. (2001) 'The Human Rights Act: a weapon against racism?', *Race and Class*, 43(2), 77–94.

Weiss, J. (1993) 'Ethnoviolence's impact upon and response of victims and the community', in Kelly, R. (ed.), *Bias Crime*. Chicago: Office of International Criminal Justice.

West, D.J. and DeVilliers, B. (1993) *Male Prostitution*. London: Duckworth.

White, R.K. (1977) 'Misperception in the Arab–Israeli Conflict', *Journal of Social Issues*, 33, 190–221.

Whitfield, J. (2004) *Unhappy Dialogue: The Metropolitan Police and Black Londoners in Post-war Britain*. Cullompton: Willan.

Wickham, J. (2005) 'The most sinister DVD in Britain', *Daily Star*, 7 March, p 7.

Williams, K.S. (1994) *Textbook on Criminology*, 2 edn. London: Blackstone Press.

Willis, C.F. (1983) *The Use, Effectiveness and Impact of Police Stop and Search Powers*, Home Office Research and Planning Unit, Paper No. 15. London: Home Office.

Winkel, F.W. (1997) 'Hate crimes and antiracism campaigning: testing the psychological approach of portraying stereotypical information processing', *Issues in Criminological and Legal Psychology*, 29, 14–19.

Wittebrood, K. and Nieuwbeerta, P. (2000) 'Criminal victimisation during one's life course: the effects of previous victimisation and patterns of routine activities', *Journal of Research in Crime and Delinquency*, 37(1), 91–122.

Wolfe, L. and Copeland, L. (1994) 'Violence against women as bias-motivated hate crime: defining the issues in the USA', in M. Davies (ed.), *Women and Violence*. London: Zed Books.

Wright, A. (2002) *Policing: An Introduction to Concepts and Practice*. Cullompton: Willan.

Yanay, N. (2002) 'Understanding collective hatred', *Analyses of Social Issues and Public Policy*, 53–60.

Young, M. (1990) *An Inside Job: Policing and Police Culture in Britain*. Oxford: Clarendon Press.

Younge, G. (2000) 'Race after Macpherson: a year of reckoning', *Guardian*, 21 February.

Zaslove, A. (2004) 'The dark side of European politics: unmasking the radical right', *European Integration*, 26(1), 1, 61–81.

Zedner, L. (1994) 'Victims', in M. Maguire et al. (eds), *The Oxford Handbook of Criminology*, 2nd edn. New York: Oxford University Press.

Index